Chefs sharing at....

TRAVELER'S INDEX

COASTING & COOKING

BOOK FOUR

Cover Restaurant: Lord Bennett's Restaurant and Lounge
                    Bandon-by-the-Sea, Oregon

Cover art: Barbara Williams

Layout, art and production: Barbara Williams
            All restaurant sketches by Barbara Williams, except for
            Garden Path Cafe, Rubio's, 1/2 of Captain Whidbey Inn,
            Kyllo's and Bay Cafe

Proofreading: Serena Lesley

Recipe reading and checking: Susan Ambrosius and Linda Rohrs

Assembling Assistance: Donna Gleason

Typesetting: Sue's Secretarial Service
              Sue Christle, Port Townsend, WA

Published and Distributed by
Graphic Arts
908 Oak Street
Port Townsend, Washington 98368
(360) 385-7037

International Standard Book Number: 0-9609950-2-1

Published in the United States of America

Printed by Oregon Lithoprint, McMinnville, Oregon
First Printing: May 1997

About the book.....

Here is Book 4 ... will this be my Swan Song? As the saying goes "It ain't over till the fat lady sings!" and the truth is that I usually put on almost 20 pounds each time I work on a book, then need to work hard to take it off again, usually losing only 10 or 11 pounds -- **not 20!** So many great restaurants, so little time, and so much eating to do!

The decision to do book 4 took a lot of thought. Those of you who have book 2 know about my head-on car accident in England in 1991 and the following 7 surgeries. Since English courts are so different, I now have a pretty good grasp of their way of handling cases such as mine. Earlier this year the settlement was made, and I am able to now go on with my life.

Also in Book 2 I stated "Doing a book is like having a baby. As the new mother is wheeled out of the delivery room following the baby's arrival, often you hear 'Never again!' But in time, the pain is forgotten. So here I am again ... doing book number 2." So it is in creating a book. Now I say "Here I am again ... doing book number 4!!"

MAY 1, 1996

Sitting in the Chestnut Cottage having fajitas, two things hit me. First, it was "May Day". My accident in 1991 occurred on May 1. Also as I loaded my fajita with all of the trimmings, the decision to do book 4 was made. The Chestnut Cottage is one of my favorite places, and they were on the cover of book 3. After lunch, it happened that Diane and Ken were there (the owners of the Chestnut Cottage). We talked and they were excited to hear that there would be book 4.

MONTH OF MAY

What do I always say to someone who's coming by ferry to visit? Check the ferry schedule because occasionally low tide stops a ferry or two between Whidbey Island and Port Townsend.

My alarm was set for 5:45 a.m., and after a bowl of fresh strawberries and cream I put my suitcase in the car and headed for the Port Townsend ferry. Had I checked the ferry schedule? No. After a 2 hour wait in the ferry line with a constant drizzly rain, I was finally on my way. Almost as the ferry landed on Whidbey Island, the sun broke through and the rest of the day was glorious. My destination was the San Juan Islands with reservations to stay overnight at the Orcas Hotel. This is a beautifully restored, small Victorian inn overlooking the ferry landing. At the front of the second floor are two guest rooms, "Port Harbor View Room" and "Starboard Harbor View Room". I had the Port room. This makes me think of what I recently learned about the British word "Posh". The word is related to boats. When someone wealthy wished to have the same best side of the boat on the trip out to India and the trip returning. Therefore, P port, O out, S starboard, H home.

In the morning I awoke in my room at the Orcas Hotel to the wonderful aromas wafting from the kitchen. Although there are rumors of ghosts here, I had no encounters. It was again a bright sunny day!

The next two days traveling on the islands were enjoyable. For those of you not familiar with the island ferries, the best way is to travel to the most westward islands and then island-hop returning eastward.

The ferry is much more reasonable, because you are charged each time you board as you head westward, and not charged traveling to the east.

MID-JUNE

Several years ago, Judith Weinstock who was then at the Streamliner Diner mentioned that she was interested in buying the old

Kingston Hotel, and that if I did book 4, to come and see her. Yes, she had indeed moved to the Kingston Hotel. Judith's husband, David, was just putting some finishing touches on the new garden. My lunch was served in the garden while I sat and drew their picture.

END OF JUNE

Away from home, but I won't mention where ... because the restaurant visited that day did a great job, the meal was tasty, but it seems that some restaurants lately are more interested in creating an "artful" plate, but don't include enough food to satisfy, so you leave still hungry.

JULY

Trips this month were to destinations close by ... Silverdale, Bremerton, Poulsbo, Bainbridge Island, Chimacum and Port Townsend.

EARLY AUGUST

A little farther afield ... starting with breakfast at the Oak Table in Sequim. The gardens are magnificent here, and I had taken 2 Polaroid close-ups of the flowers and had the prints pressed against my ribs. A couple saw me standing there, came up and asked, "Are you in pain? Is there something we could do to help?" I replied "No, thank you, I am just speeding the print image on my Polaroids."

MID-AUGUST

Traveling now on the Oregon coast: I hate to admit it, but as much as I love the Washington coast, there is no more beautiful scenic coast than in Oregon. In fact, just a month ago my dear friend from Texas, Ann Galloway, made arrangements to arrive in Seattle just as the books are ready for distribution. She will travel with me as I deliver Book 4 from Brookings to Astoria. Ann has never been on the Oregon coast. It will be good having company and sharing her joy in seeing all of this for the first time!

SEPTEMBER

About 2 1/2 years ago I invited interested people [to my home] who were concerned about living arrangements for developmentally disabled adults to discuss the time after the parents die or are no longer able to care for their son. My idea was to form a nonprofit board, buy a home and hire a full-time live-in manager under the direction of the board. The reason I said "son" is that I have a son who will need this, and it seemed better to start with a project that would be easier and had a good chance of success.

This did happen, and in March of 1996 four DD men moved into a refurbished home. I will not go into the reasons, but due to problems involved by the end of August, 1996 a doctor had me on medication and I was very close to a breakdown. The solution for me was to resign as president, walk away from the organization, and bring my son back to live with me again.

No work was done on the book this month, obviously.

OCTOBER 1

Every 18 months I am tour leader for groups of Washingtonians. Destination: interesting places in the British Isles. My plan with these groups is to stay 3 or 4 nights at one hotel, seeing places in more depth than most tour companies do. We have trips out, but allow time for individuals to see whatever interest them. This was my third group. We spent 3 nights in Chester, with one of the days using our own coach sight-seeing in northern Wales. Then on to Edinburgh, Scotland 4 nights, with side trips. I chose the little town of Iffley located on the outskirts of Oxford for our last stop. Only a 5 minute bus ride into Oxford and a good springboard for day trips through the Cotswolds. We stayed in an old mansion that had been converted into a beautiful hotel. From the second floor the roof tops of Oxford could be seen. The Thames river was only blocks away.

MID-OCTOBER

The first three books have all been with restaurants in Washington painted for the covers. Knowing that I would decide on an Oregon restaurant for this book, the decision was made for me when I first was seated upstairs at the Lord Bennett's Restaurant in Bandon. I thought to myself, okay, this is it ... if the meal is noteworthy. It most definitely was. The plate was a work of art, but it was also hearty, and I took several pictures of the salad. (Just wish I could put a picture in color of my lunch here.)

After leaving Lord Bennett's, I stopped next door at an old home with a yard full of driftwood and much more. A little gift shop is in front of Hazel Colgrove's home. We visited for over an hour. For years she has been chosen as Queen of the Cranberry Festival. Apparently there will be no more food fairs put on here by the VFW, after putting on fairs for 20 years.

The picture of Hazel shows her gargantuan carrots she raises in her yard, the longest is 16" in length. (The Guinness Book of Records lists 18" as the longest.) Her yard was previously a chicken yard, and Hazel adds fish scraps to this. Plants love it and grow nonstop!

END OF OCTOBER

Returned home October 29, with 2 days to get ready for the annual dinner my son and I hold each Halloween for from 20 to 40 of our local adult developmentally disabled people ... always fun? Everyone is in costume, games are played and then dinner for all.

NOVEMBER

I am always amused at some of the signs along the highways. A small country restaurant with a gas pump had this sign: "Eat here and get gas." Another: "Wine tasting - children welcome". ???

Arriving in Winchester Bay, I made the decision to stay overnight because a new restaurant "Cafe Francais" looked interesting. Where to stay for the night? Spotting the "Salmon Harbor Belle", a sternwheeler riverboat that has been made into a bed and breakfast, I drove over to investigate. It is 97' long with a 24' beam. What a treat! In the morning, "Dutch Babies" were served for breakfast. Sharon Porter, the owner was so charming. I wish I could have stayed longer. I highly recommend staying here!!! Sherry served the following for breakfast and she is sharing her recipe.

```
TENDER DUTCH BABY
3 large eggs
6 T. all-purpose flour
1 T. sugar
6 T. milk
3 T. butter or margarine
In a blender or food processor, whirl eggs,
flour, sugar and milk until smooth. This can
be made ahead, covered and chilled overnight.
Stir before baking.
Put butter or margarine into a 10 to 12 inch
fry pan that can go into the oven. Set pan in
a 425° oven on a rack placed slightly above
center. Let butter melt. Tilt pan to coat bot-
tom and sides.
Quickly pour in batter. Bake until pancake
puffs at edges (it may also puff irregularly in
center) and is golden brown, about 15 min-
utes.
Working quickly cut into 6 wedges using a
wide spatula. The wedges may deflate some
after cutting.
Sprinkle with powdered sugar and squeeze
lemon juice to taste. Makes 6 servings.

Provided by: Sherry Porter, Salmon Harbor Belle
```

Winds can occasionally be very strong on the coast. The morning after my stay on the Salmon Harbor Belle, I drove down the coast a ways. When I tried to open the door of my car, the wind was so strong that I had to park at a different angle to be able to get out of the car. (Read my comments about the wind in the write-up for Kyllo's.)

MID-NOVEMBER

Two nights before my planned trip to the Oregon coast again, Port Townsend had sev-eral inches of snow. The local tire store was swamped with people getting studded tires in-stalled. No time for me. Weather predictions were for temperatures in the 20's and 30's. Rising early, I heard that instead there were predictions for warmer weather for the next 2 or 3 days, so I tossed my suitcase in the car and was off for Oregon. Some drizzle, but mostly okay and soon becoming crispy, but clear.

Mixed weather the next 4 days, but usually a spectacular sunset each evening. About mid-night I pulled into the parking area at the Riverhouse, having just signed in at a nearby motel for the night. Sure enough, Steven was there working. The recent flooding had wreaked havoc everywhere. Remodeling, new floors, and more should be completed soon.

FIRST WEEK OF DECEMBER

With weather predictions of 46° to 48° high and 34° to 36° low, it seemed like a good time to go traveling again. Very funny! The alarm rang at 2 a.m., suitcase in the car at 2:30 and the car is "on the road again".

Snow and hail just 15 miles from home. Roads very slippery, and even with 4-wheel drive, the car slipped some. Never going more than 25 miles an hour, it began to look like this timing wasn't very good. Next came the fog, and this seemed to go back and forth, first rain, then fog and so on. By Portland, with the sun up, going was much better. On the Oregon coast 8 miles south of Newport, I pulled in for a lunch at Yuzen Japanese Cuisine res-taurant.

After my lunch there and discovering that this place should be in my book, I showed Book 3 to the owner Takaya Hanamoto. When he saw the picture of me in my "About the book ..." section, he smiled and said, "Do you know what this says?! He was looking at the Japa-

10

nese kimono in the picture. (It is what I frequently wore while I worked at home and it had Japanese characters down the front of it.) When I said "No, but I always wondered. Would you tell me?" He replied that it was the name "Shibata Construction Company." Since I'm in the business of constructing books ... eating, traveling, sketching, talking to restaurateurs, writing and then assembling everything for the printer ... maybe this could be construction work?

SECOND WEEK OF DECEMBER

Traveled to Mount Vernon to check on the progress of the soon-to-be Calico Cupboard. Workmen were everywhere. It seemed that there wasn't any possibility of this being ready by the middle of December for the scheduled opening, but the following Saturday, cars were everywhere and the tables were full, with a waiting line. In the same building this day the bookshop next door had several authors with their new books, giving autographs to customers. What a busy, busy place!!

LAST HALF OF DECEMBER

No Christmas shopping, no preparations had been done until now, so no more bookwork for these last two weeks.

1997 MID-JANUARY

The first half of this month was spent working in my studio, writing and sketching. Then in mid-January the work in Seattle began. Pulling into a parking place near the Space Needle, I watched as the small van in front of me first went forward two spaces, paused, then backed up, paused, then repeated this over and over. Later, upon returning to my car, I wondered if he was trying to avoid putting money in the meter? There were two small children in the car with him, and one was asleep now. So I

walked over and said "I have 25 minutes left on the meter if you want my space." It turned out that the children were cranky and tired, but the motion of the car kept them happy. When he stopped, the fussing would begin again!

A problem I have had since my '91 auto accident is the fear of driving in big cities. Getting to the Space Needle was workable, but I put my car in a parking lot near Pike Place and taxis were my way of getting around.

The second trip to Seattle, just as I got out of the car to start my day's adventuring, the keys in my hand pulled the thread from the two top buttons on my shirt. What to do? A lady was just putting out her wares for the day in a booth at Pike Place Market ... there I spied a cotton loose gray jacket with some handpainting on it. Solved! The jacket covered the button loss for the day ... and I had a new jacket.

JANUARY

A workslump sent me into a tailspin ... could the book possibly be ready for distribution in June? After periods of no production, I visited my friends at Port Townsend Travel and asked them to make plane reservations for me to fly to England April 28th. This date allowed enough time for the printing company to shoot all of the negatives and have a "blue line" copy when I returned.

Wow! Like a super vitamin shot ... Now that I had an unchangeable deadline, it was "full speed ahead".

FEBRUARY AND MARCH

Trips to Seattle, Tacoma and Olympia ended the traveling. Now 14 to 18 hour days of writing and completing the sketches were needed.

FIRST WEEK OF APRIL

Serena Lesley arrived from Portland to proofread all that was ready. She has done this for the last three books. She is a writer and is familiar with restaurants and the terminology … a great help!

Although we were deep in work, we took time out to drive to Poulsbo for dinner at Molly Ward's Garden for dinner.

Sam and Lynn Ward are the owners. I had been curious since the previous visit here … who is Molly?

It was their labrador. She died, was buried in the yard, and a rose bush planted above. The rose is now a beautiful large flowering plant … what better remembrance could there be?

This celebration dinner was for "almost" finishing the pages and the proofing. One more packet will be sent to Serena by Fast Mail before the book is ready.

A SPECIAL THANKS TO:

1. Sue Christle for putting all of the recipes on computer, as well as this write-up, the many changes or additions, plus much more!

2. Susan Ambrosius and Linda Rohrs who arrived last winter in time to stay in my home with my son during my absences. Then reading aloud the recipes from each restaurant and checking for errors or omissions. I said they were "my angels .. arriving in my time of greatest need".

3. Donna Gleason, my daughter, for many hours spent doing whatever was needed (in between her care of my two precious grandsons).

4. Gene, my son. His mom has been unable to spend as much time as usual doing things with him. He goes to work at Skookum 5 days a week, spends 2 afternoons a week cleaning the Port Townsend Athletic Club, does his rug latching, and is now working in his garden readying the ground for spring planting.

5. Mitchie, our cat who has not had my lap very much and has missed a lot of petting and neck scratching lately.

6. Kara Blake, who moved here from Ohio in March and is staying in my lower floor apartment for a while. The last 10 days of deadlines were hectic, and she generously stepped in to help with jobs large and small.

7. Lastly, all of you who have made this 4th book possible and for the many friendly letters I have received over the years from so many of you.

Barbara Williams

Webster's Dictionary defines "coast" as "shore ... along the shore". It then defines "shore" as "land at or near the edge of a body of water". So (loosely) in the title of this book "Coasting" is used as I traveled roads beside the Pacific Ocean in Washington and Oregon. ... also along the Strait of Juan de Fuca, the Hood Canal and the Columbia River.

Be adventurous ... try new restaurants as you travel. Lots of chefs doing creative, good jobs. Don't settle for a greasy hamburger from one of the fast food places. . —————— .

I try to have something for everyone in my books ... even those looking for errors.

ENJOY!

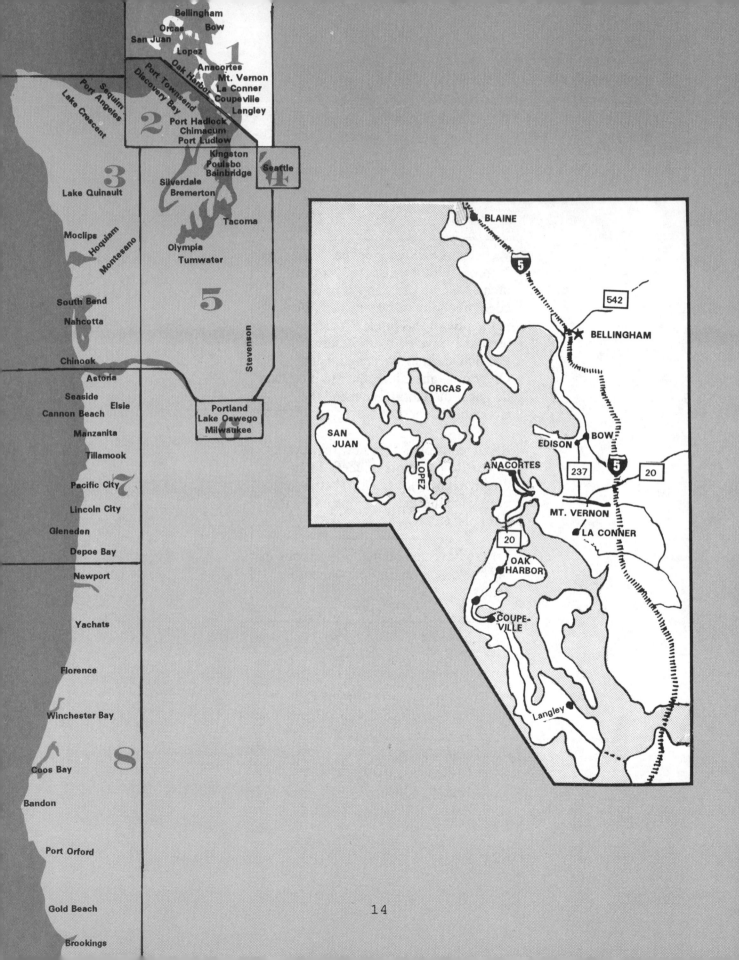

Bellingham
Orcas   Bow
San Juan
Lopez
Anacortes
Oak Harbor   Mt. Vernon
Port Townsend   La Conner
Discovery Bay   Coupeville
Langley

1

Sequim
Port Angeles
Lake Crescent

2
Port Hadlock
Chimacum
Port Ludlow

Kingston
Poulsbo
Bainbridge   Seattle
4

3
Lake Quinault

Silverdale
Bremerton

Moclips
Hoquiam
Montesano
Tacoma

Olympia
Tumwater

South Bend

5

Nahcotta

Chinook   Stevenson

Astoria
Seaside
Cannon Beach   Elsie
Manzanita
Tillamook

Portland
Lake Oswego
Milwaukee

Pacific City   7

Lincoln City

Gleneden

Depoe Bay

Newport

Yachats

Florence

Winchester Bay

8

Coos Bay

Bandon

Port Orford

Gold Beach

Brookings

BLAINE

I-5

542

BELLINGHAM

ORCAS

SAN
JUAN

LOPEZ

EDISON   BOW

ANACORTES

237   I-5   20

20

MT. VERNON

LA CONNER

OAK
HARBOR

COUPE-
VILLE

Langley

14

SECTION 1 WASHINGTON

BELLINGHAM: Bagelry, Colophon

BOW: Chuckanut Manor

ANACORTES: Calico Cupboard, Gere-a-Deli, Salmon Run

SAN JUAN ISLANDS:

　　LOPEZ: Bay Cafe, Gail's

　　ORCAS: Cafe Olga, Orcas Hotel

　　SAN JUAN: Friday Harbor, Garden Path, Roche Harbor Boatel
　　　　　　　and Resort, Springtree Cafe

MOUNT VERNON: Calico Cupboard

LA CONNER: Calico Cupboard

OAK HARBOR: Kasteel Franssen

COUPEVILLE: Captain Whidbey Inn

LANGLEY: Inn at Langley

NAVY BEAN AND CASHEW SALAD

SALAD
1 cup broccoli pieces
1 cup cauliflower pieces
1 cup cooked navy beans
1/2 cup cashew bits

DRESSING
1/4 cup olive oil
1 T. lemon juice
1/4 cup cider vinegar
1 1/2 t. salt
1/2 t. mustard powder
1/2 t. paprika
pepper
1 1/2 t. basil, oregano or
   tarragon

Steam broccoli and cauliflower pieces until just cooked (not mushy). They will have a bright color. Combine with cooked beans.
Combine dressing ingredients and whir in the blender. Pour dressing over vegetable and bean mixture and refrigerate for 1 hour. Toss in the cashews.

My mom said "Look for the recipe with spots and spills – well used and a definite favorite!"

OATMEAL FRUIT BARS
8 oz. dried prunes
1/4 cup hot water
3 T. arrowroot
3 T. water

4 cups old-fashioned oats
1 cup wheat flour
1/2 cup white flour
1 cup sugar
1 cup brown sugar
3/4 cup applesauce

1 lb. Sun Maid sun-ripened
   dried mixed fruit
1 1/2 cup orange juice
2 T. lemon juice

Preheat oven to 350⁰
Purée prunes in food processor with hot water. Blend arrowroot with the water and add to mixture in processor and blend. Set aside 1/2 of this mixture.

Stir together oats, flours, sugars and applesauce and add to 1/2 of the prune mixture. Sprinkle 1/2 this mixture into a greased 9 x 13 pan to cover the bottom. Set the other 1/2 aside.

Chop dried fruit mix in the food processor with the remaining prune mixture. Place mixture in a saucepan with the orange and lemon juice, heat just until all liquid is absorbed. Spread this mixture over the crust. Sprinkle remaining oatmeal mix on top. Before baking, sprinkle a small amount of oatmeal over the top.
Bake for 40 minutes.

Open every day and well patronized every day... young and old are drawn here. I am in Bellingham several times a year... always stop here to eat, or at least to pick up a supply of their top quality bagels for my return to my home in Port Townsend.

The Ryans are ex-New Yorkers and are experts in making bagels the old-fashioned way. Ken said "When it comes to food, flavor is everything."

12 different types of bagels made daily, with a variety of cream cheese spreads to enhance them. The spreads also are available "to go" in the Deli section. Made fresh daily are soups, deli sandwiches, muffins and lately a larger selection of desserts.

After eating one of their Oatmeal Fruit Bars, I asked Ken if this recipe could be shared for Coasting and Cooking Book 4. (You will find it here on the page left of this one.) Moist, healthy, delicious!

Boar's Head premium cold cuts are served, delicious omelettes and espressos. Gelato made on the premises.

Thought it would be fun to show the inside looking out (sketch above), and the outside looking in. (sketch left.)

Breakfast & lunch every day
Closed Thanksgiving and Christmas Days

17

CURRIED TURKEY AND APPLE SOUP

2 cups water
3/4 cups pearl rice
1 1/2 cups chicken stock or
   consommé

1 small red onion, minced
1 med. carrot, peeled and
   chopped
1 t. salt
2 t. cinnamon
1 t. black pepper
2 t. thyme
1/4 t. Tabasco sauce
3 T. curry
2 Granny Smith apples, cored,
   peeled and chopped
1 lb. cubed turkey, cooked
dry chow mein noodles

Place water, pearl rice and chicken stock in a soup pot and cook rice until fluffy, about 20 minutes.
Add the onion, carrot, salt, cinnamon, pepper, thyme, Tabasco sauce, curry, apples and turkey. Bring to a slow boil and reduce heat. Simmer for 30 minutes. Thin with water as needed.
Garnish with dry chow mein noodles.

Yield: 4 to 6 servings

cows, cows every where. Holsteins on T-shirts, mugs, ceramics, aprons, more.

PEANUT BUTTER FANTASIES

3/4 cup butter
3/4 cup brown sugar
1 egg
1/2 t. vanilla
1/2 cup wheat flour
1/2 t. baking powder
1/4 t. baking soda
1/4 t. salt

1/2 cup butter
2 cups crunchy peanut butter
1/2 t. vanilla
1 cup powdered sugar

1 1/2 cups semi-sweet chocolate chips
1/4 cup butterscotch chips

toasted coconut

Preheat oven to 325⁰
Cream together butter, brown sugar, egg and vanilla.
Add dry ingredients and mix.
Dip fingers in water and press mixture into a greased and floured 9 x 13 inch pan.
Bake for 15 minutes, or until crust is light-medium brown.

Cream the butter, peanut butter, vanilla and powdered sugar together and spread on top of crust.
Sprinkle chips on top of peanut butter mixture and place back in oven for 1 to 2 minutes to melt the chips.
Garnish with toasted coconut.
Chill before cutting.

The Colophon Cafe and Deli is located in the heart of historic Fairhaven District, south Bellingham. The cafe is legendary for its award-winning food, and casual, but intellectual ambiance. On 2 floors: a Deli upstairs and a more intimate dining area downstairs.   They share this 100 year old Pythias building with Village Books. Sidewalk seating is popular in the summer.

My bowl of African Peanut soup was served on a wooden board with a cut-out for the bowl, and included slices of French bread.

The Greek word Colophon means "summit, finishing touch, the last word." The finishing touch here is the decadent desserts made in their own bakery. Complement one with an espresso drink, fine wines or beer.

Listen to this: chocolate chunk cake, carrot cake, natural fruit pies in unbleached flour crusts (lots of flavors), cheesecake with real cream cheese. Homemade Mega-muffins served warm.

Breakfast, lunch & dinner every day
Closed Thanksgiving and Christmas days

19

SEARED HALIBUT with HERBS, SESAME SEEDS and PEPPER IN A LOBSTER BROTH

1 oz. olive oil
6 to 8 oz. halibut
1 T. herbs, (parsley, thyme and basil)
1 T. sesame seeds
1 T. coarse black pepper
4 oz. lobster broth

LOBSTER BROTH

Lobster base to taste
1 qt. water
1/2 cup celery, carrots and onions, firmly diced
salt and pepper to taste
2 oz. olive oil

Mix herbs and sesame seeds in a bowl.

Heat oil in skillet, cook halibut for 2 minutes on each side, sprinkle with herb mix. Place in 300° oven to keep warm.

Lobster Broth: In a saucepan heat oil. Add vegetables and sauté for 2 minutes. Add water and bring to a boil. Add lobster base and salt and pepper to taste.

In a glass bowl, place halibut in the center, ladle broth over halibut. Garnish with a fresh thyme sprig.

BROCCOLI SALAD

4 cups raw broccoli, chopped in 1/2" pieces
1 med. onion, diced (optional)
1 cup raisins
1 cup mushrooms, sliced
6 slices bacon, cooked, then crumbled

DRESSING

1 whole egg
1 egg yolk
1/2 cup sugar
1/2 T. cornstarch
1/4 cup white vinegar
2 T. butter
1/2 cup mayonnaise
1 t. dry mustard

Dressing: Whisk together egg and egg yolk, sugar, dry mustard and cornstarch.
In a saucepan bring vinegar to a boil. Whisk in egg mixture, cook for 1 minute or until thickened.
Remove from heat, add butter, then add mayonnaise.
Let dressing chill for 1 hour.
Add dressing to broccoli, onions, mushrooms, raisins and bacon.

As you can see from this sketch, the windows open the view across Samish Bay, with the San Juan islands in the distance. Breathtaking sunsets at many times of the year.

To reach Chuckanut Manor if you are in Bellingham, head south from the Fairhaven District, along Chuckanut Drive.

Sundays there is a Champagne Brunch offered, with Eggs Benedict, Crepes, Breakfast burritos, Samish Bay oysters, Omelettes, a pasta bar, plus potatoes, bacon, sausage, salads, fresh fruits and pastries and desserts.

A real winner, too, is the Seafood Smorgasbord on Friday nights. Poached salmon, fresh snapper, clams, mussels, prawns, scallops, Dungeness crab. Beyond seafood offerings, there are also roast beef and baked ham. Pasta, a variety of salads and no, I wouldn't forget to mention their clam chowder. Now if you can't find enough choices to please you, something's wrong. Bon Appetit.

Lunch and dinner Tuesday - Saturday   Brunch & dinner Sunday
Closed Christmas Eve, Christmas Day, New Years Day & July 4th

WILD RICE HARVEST SALAD

RICE
8 cups water
2 t. salt
2 cups wild rice
2 T. canola oil

SALAD
2 cups cooked chicken, cubed
1/2 cup celery, sliced
1 cup broccoli florets
1 cup red pepper, chopped
8 green onions, chopped

DRESSING
1 cup toasted almonds
1 cup mayonnaise
1 cup plain yogurt
2 T. lemon juice
4 t. sugar
1 1/2 t. celery salt
1/2 t. pepper
2 medium apples, chopped

Wash rice thoroughly. Combine water, rice and salt in heavy saucepan. Bring to a boil, reduce heat, cover and simmer for 35 to 40 minutes or until kernels puff slightly open. Drain excess liquid and fluff rice with fork. Let cool. Toss with oil to prevent kernels from sticking together.

Combine salad ingredients with rice and mix well.

In a separate bowl, combine dressing ingredients and mix well. Combine with salad and let chill to blend flavors.

Yield: 12 to 16 servings.

Salad keeps in refrigerator 2 to 3 days.

BUTTER SHORTBREAD
2 lbs. butter
3 1/2 cup pastry flour
1 t. baking powder
2 cups powdered sugar
3 1/2 cups bread flour
1 t. salt.

Preheat oven to 350⁰
Gradually stir dry ingredients into butter and sugar. Mix well. Cover and chill for 1 hour.
Roll out dough to 1/4" thick. Cut into rounds (with rickrack edge) or into 3" squares. Prick with a fork and sprinkle lightly with sugar.
Bake for approximately 20 minutes or until edges are lightly brown.

2 Variations for Shortbread. For either of these, mix added ingredients and follow above directions.

LEMON POPPY SEED
add: 1/4 cup poppy seeds
      2 T. fresh lemon peel

BUTTER PECAN
      substitute packed brown sugar for powdered
add: 1 cup chopped pecans

22

Calico Cupboard offers a very big assortment on their menus of items with "heart healthy" logos. But on this visit I closed my eyes to this and ordered the smoked salmon scramble.... with tomatoes, red onion, chives and cream cheese... served with fresh fruit. I also chose a homemade bagel.

I couldn't help smiling when I overheard a lady ready to be seated tell the waitress "Please, may I have a table in front of the dessert display case, so that can look at all of them while I eat!"

The bakers arrive early each day to begin preparing the huge assortment that is always available — using freshly milled, organically grown whole grains, unbleached flours, honey and other natural ingredients. No preservative or additives.

For those on restricted diets, have specific food allergies, or want to request (for example) soy cheese, etc., ask the waitress.

Linda Freed has now been in business for 15 years (starting in La Conner) with each year finding expanded offerings. For examples: 3 types of cinnamon rolls – regular, raspberry or hearty grain. Rocky Road bars, Fudgy wudgie Brownies, Apple Dumplings, Fruit Crisps or Cobblers, muffins, scones, Danish pastries, and much much more.

Breakfast & lunch every day
Closed Thanksgiving and Christmas days   ♿

GERE-A-DELI'S BLACK BEAN SOUP

I cup black beans
I large onion
I large garlic clove, minced
1/2 cup carrots, diced
1/4 t. pepper
7 cups chicken, beef or
  vegetable stock
1/4 cup celery, diced
3/4 t. cumin
1/4 t. salt

Soak beans overnight - drain off water next day.
Add broth to drained beans, bring to a boil, reduce heat to low. Add garlic, onion, celery and carrots. Cook 2 hours.
Season with cumin, pepper and salt.

Serve with a dollop of non-fat yogurt, salsa and fresh minced cilantro to garnish.

GERE-A-DELI MANGO CHUTNEY PENNE SALAD

6 chicken breasts, skinned
  and baked or poached
2 cups mayonnaise
2 cups mango chutney, preferably a commercial brand
  with large pieces of mango
2 T. mild curry powder
2 to 3 T. honey
3 cups bite-size broccoli
  flowerets, blanched
I large red bell pepper,
  julienned
6 cups cooked penne pasta,
  cooled

Cut chicken into strips and turn into a large bowl. In a separate bowl, blend together mayonnaise, chutney, curry powder and honey, mixing well. Add chicken with broccoli, red pepper and pasta. Gently combine all ingredients.
Cover and chill 2 to 24 hours before serving.

Gere-a-Deli is a community gathering spot, and has been since their opening in 1981. Sixteen years later - still going strong. They've been voted best lunch, best sandwich, best soup and best catering in 1997 for Anacortes. I saw groups and couples relaxed and enjoying their meals, desserts and/or coffee. The day I visited this winter, new chairs were just being delivered. Very nice!

Laurie Gere told me that over 750,000 Gere-a-Deli Supremos and over 150,000 Beef-a-Rooms have been consumed over the years. The Supremo has

turkey, ham, roast beef, Cheddar and Swiss cheese, onions, lettuce, sprouts and tomatoes on either a 12" or 16" French roll.

Several years ago, they began the "Heart Smart Choices" program, sponsored by 2 area hospitals and others. The menu boasts 15 red hearts beside menu items signifying Heart Smart choices. This includes salads, sandwiches and seasonal fruits.... delicious and good for you.

Laurie stated "We're not just another place to eat. People feel comfortable here.... we're about community and feeling at home.

Breakfast Monday - Saturday   Lunch until 5:00 PM

25

GREEK MARINADE FOR BROILED FISH

6 T. olive oil
3 T. garlic, finely minced
2 1/2 t. fresh thyme, chopped
1/4 cup fresh basil, chopped
3 T. oregano, use full leaves
   off stem
zest of 1 lemon
4 T. fresh lemon juice
1/3 cup Ouzo or another
   anise flavor liqueur
salt
fresh ground pepper

4 to 6 fish fillets
lemon wedges to decorate
   the serving plates

Simmer olive oil, garlic, oregano, thyme and basil for 2 to 3 minutes. Remove and put into a bowl. Add lemon zest, juice, Ouzo, salt and pepper.
Let cool completely.
Coat fish evenly. Let this marinate at least 3 hours in the refrigerator.
Broil or grill approximately 4 minutes on each side.
Place lemon wedges on plates and serve.

TUNA STEAKS WITH CRACKED PEPPERCORNS

1/3 cup butter, softened
3 T. fresh lemon juice
2 T. lemon zest
salt
4 T. olive oil
4 T. fresh cracked black
   pepper
3 T. fresh cracked pink
   peppercorns

4 tuna steaks 1 1/2" thick
   (about 8 oz. each)

Note: You may use halibut in
   place of the tuna.

In a small bowl put butter, lemon juice, zest and salt. Whisk and put aside.
Pour olive oil on 1 plate. Put pepper on another plate.
Dip tuna in oil, then press peppercorns on both sides.
Sprinkle a little salt on each steak.
Cook on hot grill or in a hot pan on the stove with a little added olive oil.

Put the lemon butter over top of each steak.
Serve.

Inside the beautiful Majestic Hotel you will find the newly named Salmon Run Bistro. Owner/chef Billy Ray was voted the best chef and bartender in Anacortes for 1997. The lower sketch shows the entrance to the Pub/bar.... a showplace! It is very much like the old pubs in England. Casual food such as fish and chips, scampi, soups, appetizers and salads can be ordered in the pub.

Billy Ray has a good background and has brought many new ideas. To show some of these, here are samplings of what's new. The menu at Thanksgiving included curried butternut soup with frizzled leeks and a cranberry-pecan cornbread with pecans and cardamom. The green beans had toasted hazelnuts and lemon. Gruyère was added to the whipped potatoes. So many special touches!

Take time while you are here to see the outstanding remodeling that was completed on the hotel... or better yet, stay awhile. Hard to believe that in the late 1900's this was originally a meat market.

Lunch & dinner Monday - Saturday
Brunch & dinner Sunday

SMOKED SALMON SCALLOPED POTATOES

12 oz. chopped smoked
  salmon
2 cups Swiss cheese, grated
1/2 cup parsley, roughly
  chopped
1 yellow onion, sliced
1 1/2 t. salt
1/2 t. Tabasco
3 cups heavy cream
3 - 4 lbs. new potatoes,
  sliced

Preheat oven to 350°.

In a bowl mix the salmon, cheese and parsley. In another bowl mix the cream, salt and Tabasco. Using a buttered 9 x 13 inch baking pan, place 1/3 of the onion in the pan followed by a single layer of potatoes. Next, place the salmon-cheese mixture. Repeat layering until all ingredients are used.

Pour cream mixture evenly over layered ingredients.

Bake for 45 minutes covered with aluminum foil. Remove foil and bake an addition 30 minutes or until potatoes are tender when tested with a sharp knife.

LOPEZ RED CHILE AND GARLIC MUSSELS

2 lbs. mussels in shells,
  washed and bearded
1/2 cup white wine
1 cup crushed tomatoes
4 garlic cloves, minced
2 T. Asian chile sauce
  (found in Asian Markets,
  Sriacha)

fresh cilantro
lime wedges

Mix wine, tomatoes, garlic and chile sauce together in a 2 quart saucepan with mussels. Cover and bring to a boil over high heat. Steam mussels until just open, about 3 minutes. Place mussels on serving dish and pour remaining liquid over mussels.

Yield: 4 servings as an appetizer, 2 servings as an entrée.

This old 1920's building has been a Post Office, a general store and is currently the Bay Cafe, a very popular spot. It recently changed hands, but the new crew is carrying on with the same great food. The specialties are ethnic offerings from south west USA, south-east Asia and the Middle east. The day I visited the menu included Moroccan barbecued breast of chicken with a mango papaya salsa and saffron rice cakes. Currently salsas are popular and are quite inventive.

An Indonesian Chile-coconut sauce enhanced the grilled pork tenderloin on another dinner choice. It was served with a sweet potato pumpkin mash with bacon and onions. (a thoughtful note on the menu advised that this wasn't suitable for those with a nut allergy).

If you love seafood, what do you think of this astonishing dinner? Seafood tapas: black tiger prawns with the mango papaya salsa... chile, shrimp, corn cakes with a chipotle aioli.... sea scallops in a peanut coconut curry. All of this on one dinner!

Dinner every day March - November
Dinner Friday, Saturday & Sunday December - February

SHITAKE MUSHROOM SOUP

4 oz. dried Shitake mushrooms
6 cups warm water for soaking
   and stock + extra as needed
1/4 cup peanut oil
2 T. sesame oil
2 cups onions, chopped
2 T. garlic, minced
2 T. ginger, chopped
2 cups celery, chopped
2 T. fresh minced lemon grass
1/2 cup soy sauce
2 cups dry rice wine
1/3 cup corn starch mixed with 1
   cup cold water
dried red pepper flakes to taste
1 cup green onions, thinly sliced

Soak Shitake mushrooms in water for 1 hour. With scissors cut mushrooms into thin strips and return to water/stock.

In stock pot, heat oils and add onions and sauté for five minutes. Add garlic and ginger and sauté for five minutes. Add celery and lemon grass and sauté mixture for five minutes, stirring as needed. Add mushrooms, water, soy sauce and rice wine. Cover and simmer on low for one hour. Add cornstarch mixture while stirring, then the red pepper and season to taste adjusting soy sauce and red peppers. If the soup is too thick, add some water and cook a little longer.

Garnish with green onions.

SESAME-GINGER NOODLE SALAD

1/4 cup peanut oil
1/8 cup sesame oil
1 cup onions, chopped
1/8 cup garlic, minced
1/8 cup fresh ginger, minced
2 cups orange juice
1/4 cup soy sauce
1 lb. fresh steamed Chinese
   noodles

1 cup plain rice wine vinegar
1/2 cup roasted sesame seeds
1 cup celery, finely chopped
1/4 cup pickled red ginger strips
1/2 cup green onions, thinly sliced

In wok, heat the oils on high and add onions, garlic and ginger. Cook until well browned, stirring frequently.
Add orange juice and soy sauce and bring to a boil. Add noodles and lower temperature to medium-low and cook noodles for about 5 minutes until the liquid is absorbed. You will have to stir this carefully to keep from sticking and breaking.
Transfer noodle mixture to a large bowl and cool completely, uncovered, in the refrigerator. (Skip this step if you wish to serve this dish hot.)
To noodles add remaining ingredients and stir gently, separating noodle strands and incorporating all ingredients.

Enjoy!!

Located in Lopez Town, Gail's is very popular with both the "locals" and the tourists. Now in the 17th year, the Wine Spectator Magazine gave Gail's an Award of Excellence for the past two years. I'm going to quote from owner Gail Pollack's letter to me. "I continue to cook in a jazzy global vein... lots of fresh seafood and organic produce from my garden.... I continue to work on my own cook book. We are proud to offer local artists an outlet for their works and have also included live jazz music for dinner during the summer whenever possible."

Gail also told me that catering has become a very large part of her business, and that she loves the planning and the implementing of special events for customers. Some of the jobs have been as far away as Bellingham to the north and Seattle to the south! Still using their own organic garden of herbs.

Lunch & dinner every day June - September   Lunch only − off season
Closed Thanksgiving and Christmas Day

SWEET POTATO SOUP WITH JALAPEÑO LIME CREAM

4 lbs. sweet potatoes
2 1/4 cups onions, diced
2 quarts homemade chicken
  broth
2 small jalapeños
salt to taste
LIME CREAM
1 cup sour cream
1 t. lime zest
3 T. lime juice

Cook all soup ingredients in a pot on the stove until potatoes are soft. Purée in food processor.

Mix sour cream, lime zest and juice together. Garnish soup.

POLENTA CHILE RELLENO PIE

1 cup uncooked polenta
3 cups water, mildly salted
1/4 cup red wine
2 t. chili powder
green roasted Anaheim chiles
  (may be 32 oz. can)
Cheddar cheese, shredded
4 eggs
1 cup half-&-half
pinch red pepper flakes
salt and pepper to taste

Bring water to a boil, add polenta, wine and chili powder. Cook until soft, about 5 minutes.

Preheat oven to 375°.
Spread polenta into the bottom of a 9 x 9 inch pan.

Stuff chiles with 1 T. (+ or -) Cheddar cheese. Place stuffed chiles on top of polenta layer.

Mix eggs, half-&-half, red pepper flakes, salt and pepper and cover stuffed chiles.
Bake until set, about 30 to 40 minutes.

Marcy Lund joined with a group of artists and craftsmen (known as the Orcas Island Artworks) in 1980, and they renovated an historical building from the '30s. It was a strawberry packing plant. The cafe occupies about ⅓ of the floor space with a gallery surrounding it, and a bookstore is upstairs. Marcy's goal was and is to provide high quality food country-style food, a serene and friendly place to gather, reflect on the beauty of Orcas Island and enjoy the qualities of a small but vital community.

All of the food is made at the Cafe...it's home cooking that features a variety of ethnic traditions. During the summer growing season, she buys fruit and vegetables from local farmers. People come from all over the island (and further) for the famous pies and cinnamon rolls. I had a bowl of this great Sweet Potato Soup and was happy that she shared the recipe! I hope to try the recipe myself this next weekend. A little hard to find: it's in Olga, east of Moran State Park.

ORCAS FERRY LANDING

(Is it my imagination? Orcas Island looks like the shape of a limp bow-tie pasta to me.)

Lunch and dinner until 6:00 PM March thru October
Dinner until 5:00 PM November thru December
Closed Thanksgiving, Christmas, January and February

LENTIL SOUP

1 1/2 cups lentils
9 cups water
3 cloves garlic, crushed
1 large carrot, cut small
1 medium onion, finely diced
1/4 bunch celery, finely diced
1/2 t. black pepper, ground
1/4 T. basil
1/4 T. oregano
1/4 T. thyme
2 bay leaves, whole
1/4 bunch parsley, finely
  chopped
1 28 oz. can tomatoes, diced in
  juice, (or puréed tomatoes)
1 t. salt (or to taste)

Rinse lentils. Place all ingredients in a heavy kettle and bring to a boil. Lower heat and simmer for at least an hour. Add more water if necessary.

Note: This soup (as with all legume soups) is best made a day or two before serving.
For variety add cooked white or wild rice. If you don't care about this soup being a vegetarian offering, add knockwurst, kielbasa or ham.

Yield: 10 to 12 cups.

LUSCIOUS LOW-FAT LEMON POPPYSEED BREAD

3 1/4 cups all-purpose flour
1 egg
4 egg whites
1 1/2 cup skim (or nonfat)
  milk
2 1/4 cups sugar
1/2 t. salt
1 1/2 t. baking powder
1/2 cup canola oil
1/2 cup applesauce (or plain
  lowfat yogurt)

2 T. poppy seeds
1 t. vanilla extract
4 T. grated lemon zest
1 t. fresh lemon juice

Preheat oven to 350⁰.
Grease and flour or line with parchment, three 5 x 9 inch loaf pans.
Place flour, egg, egg whites, milk, sugar, salt, baking powder, canola oil and applesauce or yogurt in a large mixing bowl and mix until smooth.
Add poppy seeds, vanilla extract, lemon zest and juice and mix.

Glaze: Whisk ingredients until smooth. Drizzle mixture over the loaves while still warm and in the pan.

Note: Makes three rich, moist, heavy loaves (about 7 thick slices per loaf). These do not keep well unless wrapped air tight after cooling. Do not slice until ready to use.

GLAZE

1/3 cup powdered sugar
2 t. fresh lemon juice
1/2 t. skim (or nonfat) milk
2 t. grated lemon zest

I could feel the history of the Orcas Hotel on my stay overnight..... walking down the hall that patrons had traveled for many years. The rooms are very nicely appointed.

It was during the winter, and the dining room was closed, but in the pub there was an array of sticky buns, muffins and breads... as well as other breakfast items.

My previous visit was in the spring when their garden was in full bloom and many colorful hollyhocks highlighting and bordering the yard.

I had dinner on that visit... fresh seafood caught from the channel waters nearby.

Both the Pub and the Dining room have windows facing the water..... ferries are in view and are just across the road.

When weather permits, a large deck is the place for dining.

Come and stay a few days.

Breakfast, lunch & dinner every day

DUNGENESS CRAB BISQUE

1 medium carrot, peeled and rough cut
1 stalk celery, rough cut 1" pieces
1 red bell pepper, cored, seeded and
    rough cut
1 green bell pepper, cored seeded and
    rough cut
1 yellow onion, rough cut
1 clove garlic, puréed
1 oz. brandy
2 T. Spanish paprika
1/4 cup Old Bay seasoning
1/4 t. ground black pepper

dash of cayenne pepper
1 T. fresh parsley, minced
1/2 T. chives, fresh, cut 1/8"
1 t. fresh tarragon, coarsely chopped 1/8 to 1/4"
    pieces
1/3 cup all-purpose flour
3 T. butter
1 T. crab base
12 oz. milk
18 oz. heavy cream
4 oz. fresh Dungeness crab meat

Place vegetables in food processor with the garlic and process to a fine mince. Transfer ingredients into a large heavy-gauge sauce pot. Heat ingredients over medium heat, with the fresh herbs, until al dente in texture.

Meanwhile, melt butter in sauce pot over medium heat. Whisk in the flour to create a roux, let roux cook for 4 to 5 minutes, stirring frequently to prevent scorching. Reserve. Add and de-glaze vegetables with brandy. Add the remaining spices and crab base, let mixture cook for an additional 3 to 4 minutes. Add and whisk in the milk and heavy cream. Heat the bisque soup to an internal temperature of 160°, stir frequently.

Add and whisk in the roux. Let the bisque cook over low heat until an internal temperature of 180° is achieved (approx. 30 to 40 minutes). Stir frequently to prevent scorching the bottom of the pot. Bisque should be thick in consistency.

Cool in ice bath. Transfer, label and store refrigerated until needed.

CEDAR PLANK ROASTED KING SALMON

2 fresh king salmon sides (skin-on,
    pin bones removed) steak cut 4
    oz. ea. no more than 1 1/2" thick
1 1/2 t. dry rub seasoning
1 lemon - 1/8th squeeze
1 T. butter, melted
1 lemon wedge, 1/6"
vegetables, rough cut

DRY RUB SEASONING

2 t. lemon pepper
1 t. granulated garlic
1 t. dry whole tarragon
1 t. dry whole basil
1 T. paprika
1 T. kosher salt
2 t. brown sugar

Dry Rub Seasoning: Place all ingredients into a food processor and process until well blended. Transfer into small air tight container and store at room temperature until used.

Preheat oven to 425°

Place salmon skin side down on sheet pan. Sprinkle evenly over all sides (except skin side) with 1 1/2 t. seasoning. Press seasonings into the salmon flesh.

Refrigerate salmon steaks uncovered at least 2 hours before using.

Place salmon pieces, skin side down, between 3 and 9 o'clock of a pre-heated, oiled cedar plank. Squeeze lemon over top of salmon. Place rough cut vegetables between 10 and 2 o'clock on plank beside salmon.

Place plank in oven and bake for approx 10 to 12 minutes, or until 130° internal temp.

Remove plank from oven. Liberally baste top of salmon and vegetables with melted butter.

Garnish with lemon and serve.

The Roche Harbor Resort is listed on the National Historic Register, and the restaurant was once the home of a well-known limestone executive. Many guests have visited here, including Theodore Roosevelt, who loved the Northwest.

The view from the restaurant couldn't be better! There can be many dozen boats in the harbor, coming and going... and at sunset - magnificent! The new chef has a good reputation. He's adding new touches, but continuing to feature salt-water fare of the Pacific Northwest .... oysters, salmon, clams and shrimp. Of course the steaks continue as good as ever.

The recipe (opposite) talks about the cedar plank cooking method. It imparts its own sweet flavor to seafood, poultry and meat. After the meat is cooked, the plank makes a dramatic platter for serving. They have had so many requests that now the cedar planks may be purchased in the gift shop here at Roche Harbor.

Breakfast, lunch & dinner every day April - October

HUNGARIAN GOULASH SOUP

1 lb. lean ground beef
2 cups celery, chopped
2 cups carrots, chopped
2 cups onion, chopped
3 quarts beef broth
1/4 cup lemon juice
1 T. brown sugar
1 t. hot paprika
3 T. sweet paprika
1 16 oz. can tomato sauce
2 tomatoes, chopped
1 t. sweet basil (dry)
salt and pepper to taste
2 cups cooked noodles

In a frying pan cook and crumble ground beef. Add salt and pepper. Drain off fat. Place cooked ground beef on several layers of paper towels.

In a large soup pot place celery, carrots, onion and beef broth, bring to a boil, lower heat and simmer for 30 minutes. Add ground beef and remaining ingredients. Simmer for 30 minutes longer.

Place 1/4 cup noodles in bottom of bowl. Add soup and serve.

Yield: 6 to 8 servings.

COUSCOUS WALNUT SALAD

1 10 oz. box of couscous
  cooked according to package directions
1 T. cooking oil
2 cups walnuts chopped
1 cup Greek olives, pitted and
  chopped
1 cup Feta, crumbled
2 cups parsley, chopped

Dressing:
6 oz. frozen concentrated
  orange juice
2 T. apple vinegar
3 cloves garlic
1/2 cup canola oil

As soon as the 5 minute wait is up on the couscous, remove immediately from the pan into a large bowl. Sprinkle oil into couscous and toss with a fork until fluffy. Set aside to cool slightly.

Add walnuts, olives, Feta and parsley.

Place ingredients for dressing in a blender and mix thoroughly. Chill and serve.

After ordering Couscous salad and coffee "to go" (it was closing time), I sat and talked to owner Marilyn Gresseth for almost an hour! (Husband John did this sketch.) They moved here about 3 years ago, and opened first in a small location in rear of this building.

Many locals say that this place has "the feel of Old San Juan."

There's usually "from scratch" soup every day and served with home-made bread. Also good salads... in a display case so you can see what you're getting. Belgian waffles with fresh fruit are offered in the summer. Then enjoy (weather permitting) the outside seating area — with a view of the water. Located close to the car-holding parking for the ferry.

Marilyn was formerly an accountant (a good background for most occupations). She said "We serve lunch, dinner and treats. Not vegetarian, but careful about whole and fresh ingredients. No MSG."

Open 10:30 - 4:30 Monday - Saturday   Closed Sundays

ISLAND SMOKED HALIBUT PATÉ WITH APPLES AND OLIVE OIL CROSTINI

PATÉ
1/2 lb. smoked halibut
1/2 lb. raw halibut
2 oz. unsalted butter, softened
2 oz. cream cheese, softened
2 scallions, chopped
fresh juice of one small lemon
1 T. white pepper, or to taste
sea salt to taste
1/2 cup white wine

CROSTINI
one baguette
olive oil
fresh ground black pepper

Paté: Combine raw halibut and white wine in small saucepan set over medium-high heat. Poach until fish is cooked throughout and drain off poaching liquid. Reserve for later use or discard. In food processor, combine the chopped scallions, smoked halibut and poached halibut. Process until well combined, about 30 seconds. Transfer halibut mixture to a medium sized bowl and add all other ingredients, one by one, combining each one thoroughly before adding the next. Mix well until paté is smooth and creamy.

Crostini: Heat oven to 350°. Slice baguette into rounds about 1/8" thick. With pastry brush, dab baguette slices on both sides with olive oil. Arrange on baking sheets and sprinkle with pepper. Bake until crisp, about 6 minutes.

To serve: Spread paté onto crostinis with small knife. Arrange on an attractive serving platter and garnish with slices of crisp Granny Smith or other delicious eating apple, although the tartness of Granny Smiths goes wonderfully with this paté. If you like, sprinkle fresh chopped parsley over the platter for additional color. If possible, enjoy this wonderful appetizer with Lopez Island Apple-Pear wine!

PAN ROASTED SHOAL BAY MUSSELS WITH GARLIC BLACK BEAN SAUCE

2 oz. fermented black beans
1 cup dry sherry
4 scallions, chopped, reserve half for garnish
3 T. peanut or corn oil
1 T. fresh ginger, chopped
1/2 T. fresh garlic, chopped
1 T. red chili pepper flakes (optional)
2 T. fish sauce
2 T. soy sauce
1 T. white sesame seeds, untoasted
2 lbs. fresh mussels, debearded and scrubbed

In a small bowl, soak black beans in sherry. Set aside. Over medium flame, heat one T. of oil in small sauce pan. Add ginger, garlic, half of the scallions and the red chili flakes, if using. Sauté aromatics, never allowing ingredients to brown, if they start to brown pull pan off heat and adjust temperature. While aromatics are cooking, strain black beans, reserving the sherry. Add black beans to aromatic mixture and continue to cook for one minute longer. Add liquids (fish sauce, soy sauce and reserved sherry), raise heat to high and bring mixture just to a boil. Remove sauce from heat.

In a large sauté pan, heat remaining oil until slightly smoking. Add mussels and sauté until they begin to open. Add sauce and continue to cook until mussels open fully. Transfer to serving bowl or platter, garnish with remaining scallions and sesame seeds, and serve.

Chef: Laurie Paul

Friday Harbor House sits atop a prominent bluff with guest rooms capturing views of the marina. In the time it took to do the sketch, I watched a seaplane land, a ferry arrive and depart, many small boats. There can be playful seals, porpoise, otter or bald eagles. In the distance can be seen the dramatic San Juan channel with Mt. Constitution on Orcas Island. In the restaurant the huge windows open to all of this grandeur!

The suites and some of the rooms enjoy this panoramic scenery. Jacuzzi tubs, fireplaces add to the ambiance.

There's a garden for the exclusive use of the chef - salad ingredients, herbs and more. Also local farms and the nearby waters assure an abundant fresh source for the chef's creations... ultimate flavors and freshness. On the menu are Westcott Bay oysters, giant scallops, Ellensburg lamb, and many other seafood and fish items.

Preferred seating is for hotel guests, but others may make reservations.

Advance reservations recommended.

Dinner every day in Summer
Dinner Thursday - Monday in Winter

FRESH MANGO SALSA

3 large ripe mangos, peeled, seeded and
   small diced
1 red bell pepper, roasted, peeled and
   seeded, minced
2 T. ginger, chopped
2 t. shallot, minced
3 T. cilantro, chopped
2 T. mint, chopped
1 T. candied ginger, **thin** sliced

2 oz. Mirin
1 oz. rum (darker the better)
1 T. lemon zest, chopped
1/2 oz. fresh lemon juice
1/2 oz. fresh orange juice
1 T. brown sugar
a few grates fresh nutmeg
2 t. curry powder

Combine all ingredients and allow to sit at room temperature for about two hours.
At the Springtree, Mango Salsa is used with grilled fish and poultry. We've even used it in
a quesadilla with Dungeness crab, bay shrimp and jack cheese.

SWEET BELL PEPPER BUTTER

2 large red bell peppers, roasted, peeled,
   seeded and puréed
3 heads garlic, roasted, peeled and
   puréed
2 oz. fresh basil, puréed
3 T. fresh parsley, chopped
1/2 t. fresh nutmeg, ground
2 T. Worcestershire
2 T. lemon juice
4 oz. Asiago cheese, grated
1/2 lb. unsalted butter softened
salt and pepper to taste

Combine all ingredients in a mixer and
beat until smooth.

This is an excellent all around compound
butter. It can be used with grilled fish,
meats and poultry. It can be whisked into
reduced cream for a tasty pasta sauce.
Best of all ... used as a topping with baked
oysters.
At the Springtree we place 1 T. on top of
each Westcott Bay oyster and sprinkle
with Asiago. They are then baked at 400°
for about 7 minutes. The roasted garlic
and cheese hold the butter together for a
nice even coating.

Chef-owner James Boyle told me that the dragon hanging in this sketch means "Dragon that brings good fortune". It must be true, since good fortune seems to shine here... the food is great, the setting simple with no tablecloths to spill food on. Sit back (as I did) and enjoy a beautiful meal. In the summer months seating is popular on the outside deck.

Earlier this day, a couple were curious, stopped and visited. The husband asked if I could suggest a good place for lunch. After I mentioned the Springtree, he said "I have never done this before, but my wife and I would like to have you join us for lunch."

The 3 of us, each ordering different lunches, all agreed that the lunches were winners.

James strives to create unique meals, with a large wall-mounted blackboard listing the good selections. James began cooking professionally at age 12 in Missouri... hard to believe!

Later he attended the New England Culinary Institute in 1984. He's always creating new tastes.

Lunch & dinner every day Summer
Lunch & Dinner Tuesday - Saturday Winter, Spring & Fall

CALICO BREAD PUDDING

4 slices white or French bread,
  preferably homemade
4 slices whole wheat bread
1/4 cup soft butter
2/3 cup brown sugar
1 T. cinnamon
3/4 cup raisins
3/4 cup apple, finely chopped
2 1/2 cups half & half
2 1/2 cups milk
6 slightly beaten eggs
1 T. vanilla
2/3 cup granulated sugar

Preheat oven to 350⁰.
Toast bread and spread with butter. Top with brown sugar and cinnamon. Trim off crusts, cut into bite-sized pieces. Layer bread cubes, raisins and apples, alternating layers, in a glass 2 quart baking dish.
Combine eggs, granulated sugar and vanilla.
Scald milk and half & half. Add to egg mixture. Pour over bread in baking dish. Bake for approximately 1 hour or until soft in middle.

CREAM of FRESH CARROT SOUP

5 T. butter
2 medium onions, chopped or
  finely sliced
2 cloves garlic, minced
2 1/4 lbs. carrots, scrubbed and
  thinly sliced (use processor)
2 cups water
3 cups chicken broth
1 cup brown rice, raw
2 t. dried basil
1 t. dill weed
1/4 cup fresh parsley
1 1/2 t. salt (or to taste)
3 cups milk or half-&-half
1 T. tamari
1/2 t. white pepper

Cook onion and garlic in large pot until soft. Add remaining ingredients, except milk (or half & half). Bring to boil, then reduce heat and cook on low until rice is cooked.
Remove from heat and purée in blender.
Place back on stove, heating until it reaches boiling.
Reduce heat, add milk and serve.

During the winter of '96, I heard rumors of a third Calico Cupboard — this one in Mt. Vernon. No signs, so it took awhile, but I saw men unloading chairs and asked. This was it. Peeked in — it was a beehive of activity! Open in 2 weeks? Hard to believe, but true! My son and I returned to find a fire crackling in this lovely old fireplace, antique settee, old tables, lots of flowers, paintings, baskets, and a long row of display cases full of breads, muffins, cookies, bars, pies and more!

So while people waited for a table, there was time to study this presentation and decide on a dessert after lunch. How did so many know about the opening so quickly? This is Linda Freed's third restaurant/bakery.

They are all so good, and located in different towns, that you will be able to visit more than one if you are on vacation or on business. Very popular with the locals, especially for lunch … or breakfast. Very good breakfast and lunch selections on the menu. ♥ smart items.

Breakfast & lunch every day
Breakfast, lunch & dinner Thursday - Saturday
Closed Thanksgiving and Christmas days

BLACK BEAN ENCHILADAS

FILLING
2 med. carrots, diced
2 sm. red peppers, diced
2 med. onions, chopped
2 t. chili powder
1/2 t. cayenne pepper
1 t. (each) oregano, basil
   and salt
1/2 t. (each) coriander
   and cumin
4 1/2 cups black beans

ENCHILADA SAUCE
2 cups canned chopped
   chiles
5 cups tomatillos, drained
3/4 cup cilantro
2 1/4 cups whipping
   cream
3 eggs
1 t. salt

Blue corn tortillas or
   white corn tortillas
1 cup canola oil
4 cups pepper Jack
   cheese, grated

Preheat oven to 350^0. In a small amount of oil, sauté carrots, red pepper, onions, chili powder, cayenne pepper, oregano, basil, salt, coriander and cumin until onions begin to brown. Add black beans, stir in until well mixed. Remove from heat and set aside.
In a blender, combine sauce ingredients and blend until smooth. Set aside.
Brush oil on tortillas and warm in oven until softened. Place 1/2 cup filling on tortillas, sprinkle with cheese and roll up against the grain. Place seam side down in baking pan and cover with sauce. Bake until sauce starts to bubble, approximately 10 to 12 minutes. Garnish with cheese. Serve with salsa and sour cream.
Yield: 24 enchiladas, 10 to 12 servings.

PEANUT BUTTER VEGETABLES

16 cups chicken or vegetable
   broth
1 whole tomato, diced
1/4 cup vegetable oil
1 medium onion, chopped
1 T. garlic, minced
1 1/3 cups peanut butter
salt, to taste
1 t. red pepper flakes
1 t. black pepper
dried parsley
2 large potatoes, diced
2 large carrots, chopped
4 stalks celery, diced
1 large zucchini, diced
1 large green pepper, diced
2 cups broccoli

Sauté garlic in 1/4 cup vegetable oil until red in color. Add onions and cook until tender. Add broth and diced tomatoes and bring to a boil.
Stir in peanut butter and spices until peanut butter dissolves in broth.
Add diced potatoes and chopped carrots to pot.
When potatoes and carrots are about half cooked add the celery, green peppers and zucchini. Cook just until tender.
In a separate pan parboil broccoli florets. Add to soup just before serving. If not serving soup until next day, add broccoli when you re-heat.

Over 15 years of preparing great food made "from scratch" with fresh and unprocessed ingredients whenever possible. Bakery products are made right there from freshly milled, organically grown whole grain and unbleached flour, honey and other natural ingredients. No preservatives or additives are used. As in the other 2 locations, "heart healthy" low-cholesterol breakfasts and lunches are available.

Soups, salads and sandwiches are made daily using lots of fiber-rich beans and grains, light mayo, canola oil and low-fat cheese.

Now, after saying all of this, I'm going to talk about some of their decadent desserts. Pies are sold by the piece or by the whole pie.....chocolate silk pie, peanut butter pie, English trifle, pecan fudge & more! The bread list, more than a dozen, has Onion dill, pumpkin harvest, sundried tomato, sourdough, spinach, olive rosemary plus others. The Calico Cupboard is located at the foot of South First Street. Just follow your nose... at baking time the aroma will draw you in.

Breakfast & lunch every day
Closed Thanksgiving and Christmas days

MEDITERRANEAN-STYLE STUFFED CHICKEN

6 large plump chicken
  breasts

1 1/2 cups marinated
  artichoke hearts, diced
1 cup roasted red peppers,
  diced
1/2 cup black olives, sliced
8 oz. Feta cheese,
  crumbled
2 T. capers
1 cup soft fresh bread
  crumbs

Preheat oven to 375⁰.

In a large bowl mix together all stuffing ingredients and set aside.

With a long sharp knife, slice a pocket into each chicken breast leaving an opening of about 1 1/2 inches. Stuff each breast and brown with olive oil on top of the stove.

Bake for 30 to 40 minutes or until chicken is thoroughly cooked.

Serve with orzo and Greek salad.

KASTEEL FRANSSEN'S STUFFED BAKED APPLE IN A PASTRY CRUST

PASTRY
4 1/2 cups flour
1 1/2 cup soft butter
2 eggs
3 T. milk
2 T. superfine sugar
1 t. salt
FILLING
1 cup raisins
1 cup brandy
1 cup sugar
6 Red Delicious apples

1 egg yolk
2 T. milk

Preheat oven to 400⁰.

Pastry: In a food processor mix flour, sugar and salt. Add butter, process to a sandy mixture. Add eggs and milk to make a smooth ball. Chill at least 1 hour.

Filling: Combine brandy, sugar and raisins and soak (the longer the better). Core and peel the apples and bake for approximately 15 minutes, until the apple is barely cooked. Remove apples and cool. Where the core was removed, stuff the apples with the brandy-soaked raisins.

Reduce oven heat to 375⁰.

Roll out pastry 3/8 inch thick and cut into 6 x 6 inch squares. Place apples in the middle of each square. Brush the edge of each square with a little water. Fold the points of each square to the top of the apple pinching together each seam, totally enclosing the apple. Beat egg yolk and milk together. Glaze the apple with egg yolk mixture. Bake 25 to 30 minutes.

Serve warm with a scoop of vanilla ice cream.

If you're planning a special dinner, why not just register first at the Auld Holland Inn. No worry about driving if you decide to have that extra glass of wine with your dinner. Just a walk across the grounds to Kasteel Franssen.... since 1984 this restaurant has been providing Whidbey Island with the finest of classic French and Dutch cuisine. In 1991 Chef Scott Fraser took over and has been pleasing diners.

Kasteel Franssen was designed after the castles in Holland. The decor is antiques, museum prints, old world chandeliers and lace tablecloths. There's a cozy lounge and piano bar.

The menu features game: elk, venison and ostrich – (they're the first restaurant in Washington to put ostrich on the regular menu.)

Desserts are made here, and include white chocolate cheese cake, chocolate Grand Marniere mousse cake, and fresh strawberry tulip dessert. Flash! Just heard that Kasteel Franssen won "People's Choice" in recent "Taste of Elegance" in Seattle.

Dinner every day   **Reservations accepted**

CHILLED CUCUMBER-LEMON SOUP

5 English cucumbers, peeled
    and quartered
1/2 cup chopped mint
1/4 cup chopped scallions
    (about 2 scallions)
1/2 cup fresh lemon juice
2 t. lemon zest
1 t. sugar
2 cups cracked ice
salt and black pepper to taste

In food processor, combine cucumbers, mint, scallions, lemon juice, lemon zest and sugar. Process until smooth. Add ice and blend until smooth. Correct seasonings to taste.
Serve in chilled bowl.

Yield: about 1 quart.

OLIE BOLEN

These are Dutch Christmas doughnut holes, the grated apples keep them tender and they freeze very well.

3 eggs, beaten
3 cups milk
3/4 cup sugar
6 cups flour
6 t. baking powder
2 t. salt
1 1/2 t. cinnamon
1/4 t. ground cloves
1 1/2 cups currants
3 cups grated apple (about 3
    apples)
3 T. melted butter
oil for frying (at 375^0)

Combine eggs, milk and sugar in a mixing bowl. Combine dry ingredients (flour, baking powder, salt and spices) in a separate bowl. Add wet ingredients to dry; mix. Fold in currants, apples and butter.
Using a #70 scoop (or using a teaspoon), form balls and fry until brown on both sides. Turn balls onto paper towels to drain; dust in a cinnamon sugar mixture.
Serve or cool, bag and freeze for later use. Microwave when needed.

Yield: about 120 balls.

SMOKED SALMON AND ONION CHEESECAKE

3 1/2 8 oz. pkgs. cream
    cheese, at room
    temperature
4 large eggs
1/3 cup heavy cream
3 T. butter
1/3 cup fine bread crumbs
1/2 cup - plus 3 T. freshly
    grated Parmesan cheese
1/2 cup chopped onion
1/2 cup red pepper, diced
1/3 lb. Nova Scotia Salmon
    (or any smoked salmon)
1/2 cup Blue cheese
2 T. fresh tarragon,
    chopped

Preheat oven to 300^0.
Place cream cheese, eggs, and cream in electric mixer bowl and beat until thoroughly blended and quite smooth. Butter inside of metal cheesecake pan 10" wide x 3" deep. Sprinkle inside with bread crumbs and 1/4 cup Parmesan. Shake until coated and shake out excess crumbs.
Sauté onion and red pepper in 3 T. butter. Cut salmon into small pieces and fold in blue cheese, 3 T. Parmesan, sautéed onion, pepper and tarragon into basic cheesecake mixture. Add salt and pepper to taste. Pour batter into prepared pan and shake gently to level mixture. Set pan into slightly larger pan and pour boiling water into larger pan to a depth of 2". **Do not** let the edges on the pans touch. Bake 1 hour and 40 minutes, turn off heat and let cake sit in oven 1 hour longer. Lift cakepan out of water bath and place it on a rack to cool at least 2 hours more before unmolding.

Since 1907 the Captain Whidbey Inn has offered lodging, food and drink from the wooded shores of Penn Cove. The fare is classic country inn with a Northwest flavor. Famous mussels are from almost outside the inn's doors. The abundant fresh seafoods, fresh herbs and vegetables from their own extensive gardens all contribute to their reputation — a fine dining experience.

The registered guests have first say for meal reservations; however if you call in the morning, dinner that evening is possible. For lunch, it is "First come, first served." On the menu are ♥ smart choices, but not all are.

Based at the Inn, proprietor/Captain John Colby Stone's classic 52-foot ketch, the Cutty Sark, is available for trips for anyone... sailing the waters of Penn Cove and beyond. You could help trim the sails, take a turn at the helm, or just relax and enjoy.

From May to Sept. weekends at noon and 3 p.m. Or other times: sunset, moonlight, and more.

Reservations a "must"

Lunch & dinner every day Summer
Lunch Saturday & Sunday remainder of year
Dinner Friday - Sunday remainder of year

MUSSELS IN CORN CHOWDER

2 lbs. fresh mussels, cleaned and debearded
2 oz. melted butter (4 T.)
1 cup dry white wine
3 cups chicken stock
2 oz. flour
2 red bell peppers, diced into 1/4" cubes,
   ribs removed

1 bunch flat leaf parsley, finely chopped
12 oz. heavy cream
sea salt, ground black pepper to taste
1 lb. corn off the cob (fresh preferred, but
   frozen okay)
1 oz. peanut oil

Need: Wok with lid and base ring, heavy sauce pan, cutting board, knife, serving bowls, stock pot and food mill.
Clean mussels. Bring stock to a boil, reduce to simmer, add white wine.
In large heavy pot, melt butter over medium heat, add flour and stir until roux begins to color. Temper roux with one cup of stock/wine liquid. Whip until very thick, add remaining stock/wine liquid. Bring to a gentle simmer and reduce heat. Simmer until volume is reduce by 1/3.
Add 1/2 of the corn and return to a simmer for 5 minutes. Remove from heat. Pass this mixture through medium-screened food mill. (Do not use food processor. Chops too much of the corn.) Return milled sauce to original pan, add cream and season with salt and pepper. Keep HOT.
Assemble all ingredients near the stove, have warmed serving dishes ready.
Add peanut oil to a dry wok, place over heat and bring wok to temperature. Just as oil begin to smoke, add mussels and red pepper. Stir to coat all pieces with peanut oil. Cover wok.
Once mussels begin to open, add corn chowder, stir to coat, and cover. As most mussels begin to open, add remaining fresh corn and stir again. Check seasoning, adjust if necessary, stir again.
Place mussels and chowder in bowls, dust with chopped parsley and serve immediately. Do not cook mussels until all are opened or you will overcook the rest. <u>Simply do not eat unopened mussels.</u> Serve with warm crusty bread/rolls. Enjoy.

PAN ASIAN GINGER AND GARLIC SOUP

1/2 cup peanut oil
1/2 cup garlic
1 T. crushed red chiles

4 large eggs
1/2 gallon chicken stock
3 oz. ginger

1 cup sugar snap peas
1 large bunch Vietnamese
   coriander

Need: Heavy soup pot, fine strainer, ladle, whip, mixing bowl, omelet pan - oven proof, straight-sided sauté pan, stock pot, stainless steel bowl or insert.
Place stock in stock pot and bring to a boil. Wash, then slice unpeeled ginger as thin as possible. Add ginger to stock and reduce volume by 1/3 to 1/2, depending on the richness of the stock; the heat you will taste comes from the ginger.
Chop by hand the garlic to uniform pieces, not too fine. Place in sauté pan and cover with peanut oil. Place on medium heat, fry until golden color, stirring to keep from sticking. Remove from heat and add chiles. Reserve mixture in a stainless or glass container.
Whip eggs in bowl, allow to settle in refrigerator. Clean sugar snaps. Chop coriander.
Once stock is reduced, heat soup pot on high heat for 10 minutes. Preheat oven to 350°
Heat soup bowls and prepare wok station very quickly.
Heat omelet pan, add small amount of peanut oil, (no garlic at this time). When hot, pour in eggs, stirring slowly to create some ridges. Drizzle in garlic/oil/chile mixture over top of omelet, then place pan in oven for 8 to 10 minutes. Remove from heat, remove from pan in one piece, and slice into thin strips on cross/diagonal.
Add sugar snaps to hot soup pot, stir quickly to allow simple scorch marks to appear. Stir in stock, carefully as liquid will come to high boil. After adding all stock over sugar snaps, and snaps are brilliant green, ladle soup in bowls immediately, distributing peas evenly.
Add five pieces of omelet, garnish with coriander, serve and enjoy!

Built into a bluff overlooking Saratoga Passage, the Inn at Langley's guest rooms all have a 180° waterfront view. From their private porches the guests can watch the sun rise above the Cascade Mountains on the mainland. The sun sets over the Passage to the west. Each room has a jacuzzi tub facing both the fireplace and the sea. (Sketch is from the window over the tub.)↗

The heart of the Inn is its country kitchen overlooking the formal herb garden where they grow many of the herbs used in cooking. On Friday and Saturday nights innkeeper/chef Stephan Nogal prepares a 5-course dinner with products from Whidbey Island's rich bounty. This is complemented by selections from the extensive wine collection. To give you a feel for what is offered in chef Nogal's 5-course meal, here is a sample dinner.

Start with mussels in saffron cream over spinach, followed by Italian plum tomato-basil soup. For the entrée either roast leg of lamb or marinated, grilled spot prawns are the choices. The green salad has Miso vinaigrette.

The dessert is sour cream blueberry cake.

Although the dinners are foremost for the registered guests, call. Often reservations for dinner are possible. You can see why this would be worthwhile

Dinner every day, Summer
Dinner Wednesday - Sunday, Winter

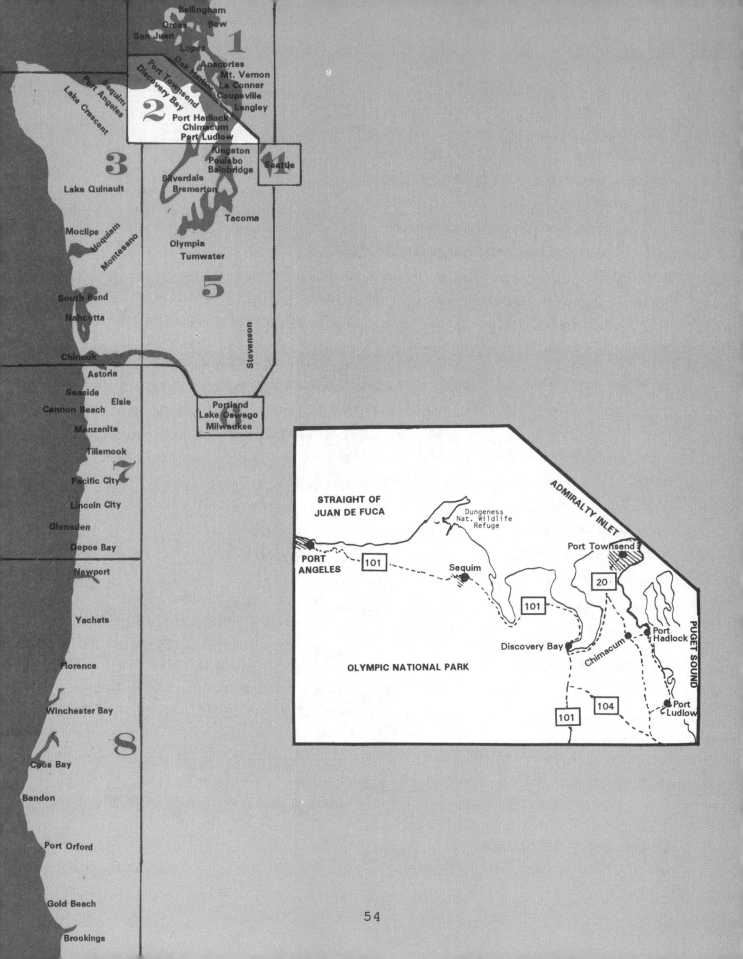

Bellingham
Bow
Orcas
San Juan
Lopez
Oak Harbor
Anacortes
Mt. Vernon
La Conner
Coupeville
Langley

1

Port Townsend
Discovery Bay
Sequim
Port Angeles
Lake Crescent

2

Port Hadlock
Chimacum
Port Ludlow

Kingston
Poulsbo
Bainbridge

Seattle

4

Silverdale
Bremerton

3

Lake Quinault

Moclips
Hoquiam
Montesano

South Bend

Nahcotta

Tacoma

Olympia
Tumwater

5

Chinook

Astoria

Seaside
Elsie
Cannon Beach

Manzanita

Tillamook

Stevenson

Portland
Lake Oswego
Milwaukee

Pacific City

7

Lincoln City

Gleneden

Depoe Bay

Newport

Yachats

Florence

Winchester Bay

8

Coos Bay

Bandon

Port Orford

Gold Beach

Brookings

STRAIGHT OF
JUAN DE FUCA

ADMIRALTY INLET

Dungeness
Nat. Wildlife
Refuge

Port Townsend

PORT
ANGELES

101

Sequim

20

101

Discovery Bay

Chimacum

Port
Hadlock

PUGET SOUND

OLYMPIC NATIONAL PARK

104

101

Port
Ludlow

SECTION 2 WASHINGTON

PORT LUDLOW: Inn at Ludlow Bay

CHIMACUM: Chimacum Cafe

PORT HADLOCK: Ajax Cafe, Delmonico's on South Bay

PORT TOWNSEND: Bayview, Belmont, Bread and Roses, Fountain Cafe, Landfall, Lanza's Ristorante, Lonny's at the Boat Haven, Plaza Fountain, Public House, Silverwater Cafe

DISCOVERY BAY: Original Oyster House

SEQUIM: Oak Table Cafe

PORT ANGELES: Bonny's Bakery and Cafe, Bushwhacker, Cafe Garden, C'est si Bon, Chestnut Cottage, First St. Haven, Toga's International Cuisine

CHIOGGA BEET AND BLOOD ORANGE SALAD WITH CITRUS SOY VINAIGRETTE

6 large Red Chiogga beets
6 large Gold Chiogga beets
6 blood oranges
1/4 of red onion, julliened

VINAIGRETTE

juice of 1 lime
juice of 1 orange
juice of 1 lemon
1/4 cup rice wine vinegar
1/8 cup soy sauce
1/4 cup sesame oil
1/4 cup canola oil
1 t. ginger, chopped
1 t. garlic, chopped
1 t. cilantro, chopped

GARNISHES

Bibb lettuce leaves
carrot curls
pomegranate seeds
chopped chives

Blanch Chiogga beets until tender and chill in ice bath.

With a paring knife, peel and wedge blood oranges, removing all membrane. Mix ingredients for vinaigrette and let infuse for at least 2 hours.

In a small mixing bowl, toss beets, blood orange wedges and red onions with vinaigrette. Place Bibb lettuce leaves on center of plate and top with salad. Top salad with carrot curls. Sprinkle perimeter of salad with pomegranate seeds, chopped chives and drizzle with blood orange juice.

COCONUT LIME SEAFOOD CHOWDER WITH A CHILI OIL

18 oz. coconut milk
18 oz. fish stock
2 stalks, lemongrass, sliced
1 medium shallot, chopped
2 cloves garlic, chopped
1/4 cup cilantro, chopped
2 inches ginger root, chopped
juice of 2 large limes
2 kiefer leaves
3 large Shitake mushrooms,
    sliced
1/4 cup corn starch
1/4 cup water
6 mediterranean mussels
12 Manila clams
12 sea scallops
12 shrimp, size 16-20
12 oz. of your favorite fish,
    cubed

GARNISHES

cilantro sprigs
sesame seeds
chili oil

Combine first 10 ingredients in a shallow saucepan and bring to a boil. Once mixture is at a boil, reduce temperature and simmer for 15 minutes. Mix corn starch and water together and slowly add to the simmering mixture, whisking constantly. Allow contents to simmer for another 5 minutes. Pour broth mixture through a fine strainer and return to pan. Bring broth back to a simmer and add fresh seafood. Cook until seafood is just done and shellfish have opened. Be sure not to overcook.

To serve, portion seafood amongst 6 bowls and ladle broth over. Garnish with the cilantro sprigs, sesame seeds and chili oil.

Yield: 6 servings

I need a chapter to describe it all! The Inn at Ludlow Bay is poised on the eastern shores of the Olympic Peninsula, with over a half mile of shoreline and beach surrounding the Inn. Guest rooms each have a fireplace and oversized Jacuzzi soaking tub. 27 hole world-class Port Ludlow Golf Course is nearby.

Paul and Pam Schell stated the goal here "is to provide leisure and business travelers alike a quiet and elegant home away from home... it's the serenity that sets the Inn and the Northwest apart from anywhere else."

I was impressed by the very personal care and attention of the staff. Chef Joseph Merkling was able to come talk to me after our dinner. What an incredible job he is doing! He is always working out new creative dishes: one is his sweet potato, parsnip and Gruyere Ravioli. I asked and he agreed to share the Chioggia beet and blood orange salad.

He prepares dinner each evening using fresh ingredients from the region and from the culinary garden just outside the Inn's kitchen. In the dining room tables are spaced apart to allow private conversations.

Advance reservations requested.

Dinner every day, Summer   Call for Winter schedule

SPANISH RICE

1 bell pepper, diced
4 1/2 t. vegetable oil
2 cups rice, uncooked
2 cups tomatoes, diced
2 T. chili powder
2 T. cumin
1/4 t. leaf saffron,
    crumbled
salt to taste
1 1/2 cups chicken broth

Sauté rice and bell pepper in oil, stirring frequently. Add broth and other ingredients, bring to a boil. Cover and simmer for 20 minutes. (Add water if needed.)
Let stand until ready to use.
This dish may stand for 20 minutes before serving.

BEER AND CHEESE SOUP

1/4 cup butter or margarine
1/2 cup celery, thinly sliced
1/2 cup carrot, diced
1/4 cup onion, chopped
1/4 cup all-purpose flour
1/2 t. dry mustard
1/4 t. thyme leaves
4 cups chicken stock or
    canned chicken broth
1 1/2 cups sharp Cheddar
    cheese, shredded
2 T. Parmesan cheese, grated
1 can (12 oz.) beer
salt and pepper
pretzels

In a 3 quart pan, melt butter over medium heat. Add celery, carrot and onion and cook, stirring occasionally until onion is soft, about 10 minutes.
Stir in flour, mustard and thyme leaves and cook for 1 minute. Gradually add stock. Bring to a boil over medium-high heat, stirring often. Reduce heat, cover and simmer, stirring occasionally, until vegetables are tender, about 12 to 15 minutes.
Stir in Cheddar and Parmesan cheeses. When cheese is melted, add beer. Heat until steaming. Season to taste with salt and pepper.
Serve with pretzels.

Yield: 4 to 6 servings.

From their early morning opening and through the rest of the day, cars are lined up on 3 sides of the Chimacum Cafe. It's a family kind of place. The staff is friendly and keeps the coffee cups filled. The new owners, James Blake, Brian Horner and Debbie Lynes, are dedicated to keeping up the traditions - and the good food _has_ kept coming in the 3 years they've been at the helm.

Did you wonder why I sketched a row of Barbie dolls? The display wall in front of the counter is changed frequently. The locals share their hobbies, crafts, antiques, all different ideas.

The bakers arrive early to bake. You'll usually find at least 15 to 20 different pies displayed... also busy baking for the Bayview in Port Townsend.   You've heard "Practice makes perfect". They have made thousands of pies, and they are perfect.

Not many restaurants include soup _and_ salad _and_ ice cream - but they do!

Specials offered nightly and they are good!

Open since 1955.

Breakfast, lunch & dinner every day
Closed between Christmas and New Years Day

RASPBERRY HAZELNUT CHICKEN

4 - 5 to 6 oz. boneless,
    skinless chicken breasts
1 cup toasted hazelnuts,
    coarsely ground in food
    processor
1 cup bread crumbs
flour
2 eggs
1/2 cup milk
1/4 cup raspberry vinegar
1 medium shallot, minced
2 T. frozen raspberries
1/2 cup heavy cream
1/4 lb. unsalted butter, in
    pieces
fresh raspberries, if available
parsley, chopped

Prepare sauce: In non-aluminum saucepan put vinegar, shallot and frozen raspberries. Bring to a boil and reduce to about 2 T. Add heavy cream and continue to boil, reducing until quite thick. Remove from heat and whisk in the butter, returning to low heat if necessary.

Dip chicken into the flour, shake off excess. Beat eggs with milk and place floured chicken in mixture for 5 minutes. Remove and press into crumb mix. Place on paper towels and refrigerate until ready to cook.

Melt 4 T. butter in medium skillet. When hot, add chicken and brown on both sides making sure it is cooked through.

Place a small pool of sauce on plates, put chicken on sauce and drizzle more sauce over. Garnish with chopped parsley and fresh raspberries.

Serve with a green vegetable and rice.

Yield: 4 servings.

CHOCOLATE DECADENCE

30 oz. chocolate chips
2 oz. unsweetened chocolate
1/2 lb. unsalted butter
4 T. flour
4 T. sugar
4 T. water
10 eggs, separated
pinch of salt

Preheat oven to 400^0
Line pans with wax paper.
Melt chocolate chips, chocolate and butter over simmering water. Make a slurry from the flour, sugar and water and add to chocolate mixture.
Gradually beat in the egg yolks.

In a mixer with whip, beat egg whites with a pinch of salt until stiff, but not dry. Fold in chocolate mixture in two stages.

Bake for 22 minutes.

I am happy to report that the Ajax Cafe is now under the care of owners Tom and Linda Weiner, and doing beautifully!

This is a restaurant that truly can be "coasted" into... there's dock and moorage right in front and a boat launch too. So sail or kayak over.

For over 10 years Tom and Linda had a gourmet restaurant located on the coast of Maine, but are enjoying the casual atmosphere of the Ajax. The Ajax was voted "Best unknown restaurant in the NW" and "NW best kept secret," but the Weiners are making it known & no secret. I loved their raspberry hazelnut chicken, coated in nuts, sautéed till crisp, served with raspberry butter sauce and fresh raspberries.

Fresh local fish and shellfish.

Thoughtful desserts: one called "Chocolate Decadence".

On the menu: "prepared according to variety and the whim of the chef."

Dinner every day June - August
Dinner Tues. - Sun. September - May   Closed January

LAMB TOP SIRLOIN MEDALLIONS WITH PROSCIUTTO, MUSHROOM, GARLIC DEMIGLAZE AND TOMATO ROSEMARY RELISH

6 oz. lamb top sirloin
olive oil
salt and pepper to taste

TOMATO ROSEMARY RELISH

1 oz. olive oil
1 t. shallot, chopped
1 pinch rosemary, chopped
1/4 tomato, chopped
1/2 oz. balsamic vinegar
1 oz. white wine
1/2 oz. sugar
1 pinch, parsley, chopped
salt and black pepper to taste

PROSCIUTTO DEMIGLAZE

1 oz. olive oil
1 t. garlic
2 oz. mushrooms, sliced
1/8 oz. prosciutto, fine julienned
2 oz. white wine
3 oz. demiglaze
black pepper to taste
1 pinch fresh parsley, chopped
1 pinch fresh oregano, chopped

Cut lamb into 2 - 3 oz. medallions. Brush with olive oil and season with salt and pepper. Grill to desired doneness. (Roast rack of lamb, chops or leg of lamb may be substituted.)

Relish: Sauté shallot in olive oil, add rosemary and sauté 30 seconds. Add remaining ingredients and reduce for 1 minute more to concentrate flavors.

Demiglaze: Sauté mushrooms in olive oil for 30 seconds. Add garlic and prosciutto, sauté for 30 seconds more. Deglaze with wine. Add remaining ingredients and simmer to desired consistency.

Serve demiglaze on plate, lamb on demiglaze and tomato relish on top of the lamb.

FETTUCCINE CARBONARA

2 oz. whole butter
1 T. garlic
1 oz. onions, small julienned
2 oz. mushrooms, sliced
1 oz. prosciutto ham
3 oz. cooked Italian sausage
   (I like Insernios, mild)
6 oz. heavy cream
black pepper, to taste
pinch fresh parsley, chopped
pinch fresh oregano, chopped
5 oz. fresh fettuccine, cooked
3 oz. Romano cheese

Slowly melt butter and garlic on low heat, add onions, mushrooms, prosciutto and Italian sausage, sauté on low heat until onion becomes soft. Add cream, bring to a boil. Add pasta, cooking only long enough to heat pasta. Add herbs and cheese, simmer until sauce thickens. Top with grated Romano and chopped fresh parsley.

The Old Alcohol Plant is now Delmonico's on South Bay, and under the able hands of Rick Unrue. The dining room is a perfect spot to look out over the bay to Port Townsend in the distance... or on the deck during the summer months.

This was an alcohol plant from 1911 to 1913, with alcohol being made from sawdust, and shipped to San Francisco until big Eastern producers and San Francisco distillers got it stopped. The plant changed to making molasses, but the Sugar Trust bought controlling interest, then let the plant close. The buildings stood vacant most of the next 65 years, then 9 years and $3,000,000 were spent turning this into a hotel and resort.

Last fall a couple arrived from Sekiu, Washington for a "special occasion" weekend, checked in, then saw the sign on the restaurant door "Closed for a few days to paint." Very disappointed, they were in their room deciding what to do. The chef heard of their plight, knocked on their door and offered to fix them a special meal, and did so.... right in their room!! This is something that they will remember fondly for years. (However, please don't arrive expecting this service.)

Breakfast, lunch & dinner Monday - Saturday
Brunch Sunday

63

CHICKEN DIVAN

6 uncooked boneless chicken
  breasts, cut into strips
1 12 oz. pkg. frozen broccoli
  spears
2 lbs. Cheddar cheese, grated
1 small can cream of chicken
  soup
1 cup mayonnaise
1/2 cup lemon juice
bread, cubed

Preheat oven to 350⁰
Make a sauce with the soup, mayonnaise and lemon juice.
Layer chicken, broccoli, cheese and sauce, making sure you top with the cheese. Bake for 1 hour. Top with cubed bread and bake 1/2 hour more.

Serve over white rice.

Chef: Tommie Taylor

STUFFED GREEN PEPPERS

4 green bell peppers
2 lbs. ground beef
2 oz. A-1 sauce
2 oz. Heinz 57 sauce
1/2 cup ketchup
2 eggs
8 crackers, crumbed
1 grated carrot
1 diced onion
1 t. pepper
1 t. Johnny's seasoning salt
1 t. garlic salt
SAUCE
2 8 oz. cans tomato sauce
1 t. Italian seasoning
1 t. oregano

Cut top of the peppers and hollow out the inside. Cut the bottom to level and set aside.
Mix in a bowl the ground beef, sauces, ketchup, eggs, crackers, carrot and onion. Add the pepper, Johnny's seasoning salt and garlic salt. When thoroughly mixed stuff the prepared peppers.

Place peppers in a 3" high baking dish. Pour the tomato mixture over the top and around the sides. Bake for 1 1/2 hours.

Serve over white rice.

Yield: 4 servings.

Chef: Robert A. Johnson

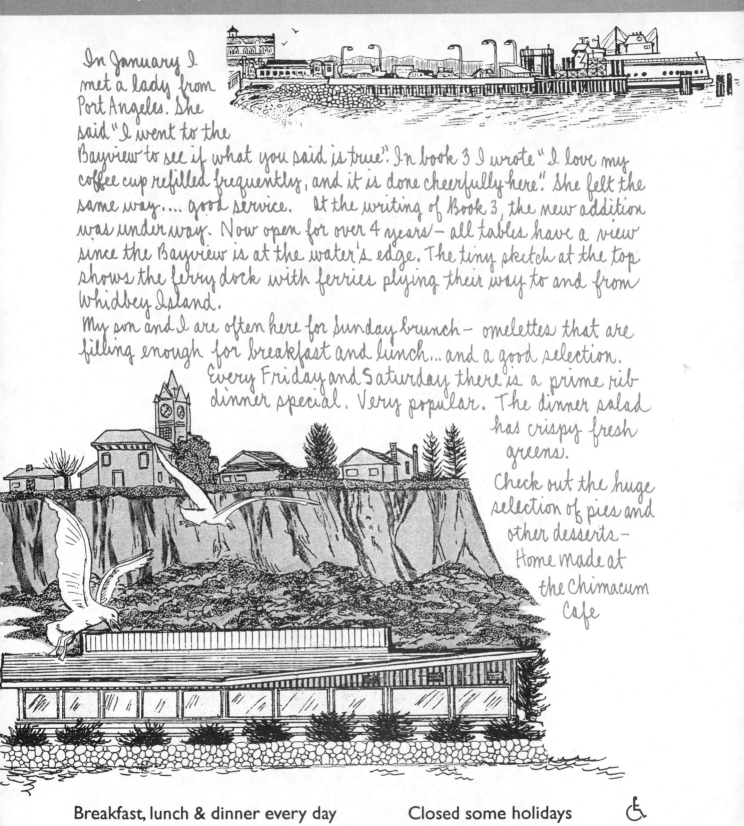

In January I met a lady from Port Angeles. She said "I went to the Bayview to see if what you said is true". In book 3 I wrote "I love my coffee cup refilled frequently, and it is done cheerfully here". She felt the same way..... good service.   At the writing of Book 3, the new addition was under way. Now open for over 4 years — all tables have a view since the Bayview is at the water's edge. The tiny sketch at the top shows the ferry dock with ferries plying their way to and from Whidbey Island.

My son and I are often here for Sunday brunch — omelettes that are filling enough for breakfast and lunch... and a good selection.

Every Friday and Saturday there is a prime rib dinner special. Very popular. The dinner salad has crispy fresh greens.

Check out the huge selection of pies and other desserts — Home made at the Chimacum Cafe

Breakfast, lunch & dinner every day   Closed some holidays

65

CIOPPINO SAUCE

12 oz. celery, diced
9 oz. carrots, diced
12 oz. onions, diced
6 bay leaves
6 oz. garlic
1/4 oz. black peppercorns
1 dash basil

1 dash oregano
2 dashes salt
1 dash parsley
1 dash cayenne pepper
1 pinch saffron
6 oz. white wine
6 oz. dry Vermouth

3 oz. olive oil
38 oz. diced tomatoes in
   juice
22 oz. chili sauce
9 oz. tomato paste
19 oz. tomato sauce
27 oz. clam juice

Mix celery, carrots, onions, bay leaves, garlic, peppercorns, basil, oregano, salt, parsley, cayenne pepper, saffron, wine and Vermouth together. Sauté in olive oil until vegetables are tender. Add tomatoes, chili sauce, tomato pastes, tomato sauce and clam juice and simmer for one hour. Once sauce is done add any seafood you like and cook until seafood is done.

Yield: 1 gallon.

SHRIMP SALSA

1 1/2 lbs. Bay shrimp
2 tomatoes, chopped
1 T. parsley
1 dash Tabasco
1 dash cayenne pepper
1 1/2 T. lemon juice
1 dash white pepper
1 1/2 T. garlic
3/4 cup salsa

Mix all ingredients together and add to the top of a bed of mixed greens. Fan with avocado.

Yield: 6 servings.

When this restaurant changed hands a few years ago, the original name was restored.
I talked to Rick Unrue the owner & he said it would be nice to show the original wharf section of town - about 100 years ago. The local museum had photos. Then compare the new wharf, currently under construction.... locals are watching as it is being built.

Not long ago I told my daughter I'd treat her to lunch - we both chose the Dungeness crab sandwich that includes artichokes, onions, Parmesan, Cheddar and Swiss cheeses over their Italian peasant bread, served open-faced - and with a good green salad. It's such a winning combination that I occasionally order it on the dinner menu as an appetizer dip. That night the Whidbey Island Duck was my entree choice... pan roasted breast, served with Whidbey Island liqueur sauce, plus rice & well-prepared vegetables. Outdoor dining - weather permitting.

(Port Townsend's only remaining 1880's waterfront restaurant.)

Lunch & dinner every day

CHOCOLATE PISTACHIO BISCOTTI

1/4 cup unsalted butter
3/4 cup granulated sugar
3 medium eggs
3/4 t. orange juice
2 1/4 cups unbleached organic flour
3/4 cup cocoa
1 3/4 T. baking powder
3/4 t. baking soda
3/4 cup pistachio nuts, chopped (raw or toasted)
1/2 cup chocolate chips

Preheat oven to 350⁰.
Cream butter and sugar on medium speed. Slow mixer and add eggs and orange juice. With the mixer still on slow add the dry ingredients, then the nuts and chocolate chips.

Shape into 1 log 1 inch high and 4 to 5 inches wide.
Bake for 30 minutes, until firm.
Let cool and slice 1/2" thick. Lay pieces on side and bake an additional 15 minutes, until crisp.
Store up to 1 week in a jar.

MILLET BREAD

1 oz. salt
4 cups water
3 oz. cake yeast
1/2 cup unsulfured molasses
1/4 cup honey
10 1/2 oz. organic whole wheat bread flour
2 lbs. 1/4 oz. organic unbleached bread flour (high gluten)
14 oz. organic unbleached bread flour
2 cups oat bran
2 cups millet
2 cups sunflower seeds

Mix in Kitchen Aid in the order given. Add flour gradually and adjust to create dry but not overly stiff dough.

Let rise to double in size. Scale to 24 oz. per loaf, in rounds, loaves or 4 oz. rolls. Let rise again, covered, in a warm part of your kitchen.
Preheat oven to 350⁰.
Bake approximately 1/2 hour.
To test for doneness, take one loaf and thump on bottom for a hollow sound.
Cool.

Yield: 5 loaves.

What started as a bakery soon expanded to include homemade soups and serving a good variety of sandwiches. Our local weekly Port Townsend newspaper recently ran a nice article about owner/baker Evelyn Dennison. Ev had restaurant experience, but no experience in baking when she purchased Bread and Roses! She had just 6 weeks to learn how to make French bread and other items by hand...no mixes...no machines. Her teacher was strict, but Ev said that time was invaluable. The only heat for the building at that time was the oven heat. If someone came into the building at the wrong time, the French bread would fall.

Now it is the spot that the locals frequent...to relax, have coffee, lunch or pastries. During the winter months when there is a little more time, she experiments. The popular Morning Glory muffin recipe was on the back of a calendar. After reading that oat bran was good for your health, she added several bran muffin recipes.

The baked breads and rolls are now also being served at 5 local restaurants. Currently: Danish pastries piled with fruit, biscotti, scones, croissants (with some having fillings), the famous "Death by Chocolate" cookies...I could go on and on! The staff arrives at 4 a.m. to begin the day's work!

Breakfast & lunch every day

SCOTCH SALMON FETTUCCINE

1/4 cup flaked smoked
  salmon
I t. garlic
I T. butter
I pinch black pepper
I cup heavy cream
1/8 cup green onions,
  chopped
I "good" shot of Scotch
hot fresh fettuccine
Parmesan

Melt butter in pan and sauté salmon, garlic and pepper. Add heavy cream and cook until reduced. Add chopped green onions and Scotch, flame.

Serve salmon mixture over hot fresh fettuccine and top with Parmesan cheese.

Yield: I serving.

SUPER GINGERY GINGERBREAD AKA GANGSTA' BREAD

I 1/2 cups sugar
3 eggs
I 1/2 cups melted butter
7 1/2 cups flour
4 1/2 t. baking soda
I T. cinnamon
I 1/2 t. salt
I 1/2 cups molasses
I 1/2 cups honey
3 cups hot water
I 1/2 cups fresh ground
  ginger

Preheat oven to 375°
Beat together the sugar and eggs. Add melted butter.
Transfer sugar, egg and butter mixture to a large bowl.
Mix together the flour, baking soda, cinnamon and salt.
Mix together the molasses, honey and hot water.
Add the dry mixture and liquids to butter mixture alternately. Stir in ginger until all ingredients are blended.

Spray muffin tins with non-stick spray. Fill tins 2/3 full with mixture and bake for 20 to 25 minutes.

We serve with homemade custard and real whipping cream. ENJOY!

What started as a bakery soon expanded to include homemade soups and serving a good variety of sandwiches. Our local weekly Port Townsend newspaper recently ran a nice article about owner/baker Evelyn Dennison. Ev had restaurant experience, but no experience in baking when she purchased Bread and Roses! She had just 6 weeks to learn how to make French bread and other items by hand... no mixes... no machines. Her teacher was strict, but Ev said that time was invaluable. The only heat for the building at that time was the oven heat. If someone came into the building at the wrong time, the French bread would fall.

Now it is the spot that the locals frequent... to relax, have coffee, lunch or pastries. During the winter months when there is a little more time, she experiments. The popular Morning Glory muffin recipe was on the back of a calendar. After reading that oat bran was good for your health, she added several bran muffin recipes.

The baked breads and rolls are now also being served at 5 local restaurants. Currently: Danish pastries piled with fruit, biscotti, scones, croissants (with some having fillings), the famous "Death by Chocolate" cookies... I could go on and on! The staff arrives at 4 a.m. to begin the day's work!

Breakfast & lunch every day

SCOTCH SALMON FETTUCCINE

1/4 cup flaked smoked
  salmon
1 t. garlic
1 T. butter
1 pinch black pepper
1 cup heavy cream
1/8 cup green onions,
  chopped
1 "good" shot of Scotch
hot fresh fettuccine
Parmesan

Melt butter in pan and sauté salmon, garlic and pepper. Add heavy cream and cook until reduced. Add chopped green onions and Scotch, flame.

Serve salmon mixture over hot fresh fettuccine and top with Parmesan cheese.

Yield: 1 serving.

SUPER GINGERY GINGERBREAD AKA GANGSTA' BREAD

1 1/2 cups sugar
3 eggs
1 1/2 cups melted butter
7 1/2 cups flour
4 1/2 t. baking soda
1 T. cinnamon
1 1/2 t. salt
1 1/2 cups molasses
1 1/2 cups honey
3 cups hot water
1 1/2 cups fresh ground
  ginger

Preheat oven to 375°
Beat together the sugar and eggs. Add melted butter.
Transfer sugar, egg and butter mixture to a large bowl.
Mix together the flour, baking soda, cinnamon and salt.
Mix together the molasses, honey and hot water.
Add the dry mixture and liquids to butter mixture alternately. Stir in ginger until all ingredients are blended.

Spray muffin tins with non-stick spray. Fill tins 2/3 full with mixture and bake for 20 to 25 minutes.

We serve with homemade custard and real whipping cream. ENJOY!

The Fountain Cafe was purchased in the Spring of '96 by Heidi Hall and her mother, Donna Pollack. They lived in the Port Townsend area for 18 years, then they moved away for awhile. After a time in the Southwest, Heidi returned with a collection of recipes with new ideas and flavors.

The cooks at the Fountain Cafe are daring and love to try something different, and will try "almost anything"... and they are proud of their selection of daily specials.

On the lunch menu, here are a few samples:
1. Vegetarian – Santa Cruz marinated tofu, grape-leaf/cashew pesto and spinach wrapped in a whole wheat tortilla. 2. Panini – grilled vegetable with Myzithra and sweet potatoes. 3. Meat – Guadalupe Quesadilla – smoked chicken, cilantro pesto, roasted garlic and sharp Cheddar grilled in a whole wheat tortilla.

4. Smoked chicken and Brie with mustard, red bell peppers, purple onion and spinach on yeasted cornbread.

I mention these menu selections to show you the ways the cooks are being creative.

Lunch & dinner every day

71

PASTA FOGOLORE

2 cups fresh mushrooms, sliced
1/2 cup onion, diced
1 cup ham, diced
2 cloves garlic, minced
1/4 cup white wine
1/2 t. oregano
1 lb. fettuccine
5 eggs
1/2 t. black pepper
1/3 cup Parmesan cheese
2 T. parsley, chopped
1 tomato, diced
1/4 cup olive oil

Sauté onion, mushrooms, ham and garlic in olive oil and white wine. In a large bowl combine oregano, eggs, pepper and Parmesan cheese. Mix.
Place fettuccine into boiling salted water to cover and cook to desired doneness.   This should not require more than 8 or 9 minutes for al dente.
Add sautéed vegetables and meat together with the pasta and mix well.
Add tomatoes and parsley as garnishes. Serve hot.

Yield: 4 servings.

SMOKED SALMON AND PASTA

1 cup cold smoked salmon,
    flaked
1 t. olive oil
1/2 cup mushrooms
1/2 cup frozen green peas
1 egg
1/2 cup cream
pasta, cooked

Sauté salmon in olive oil. Add mushrooms and green peas and cook until warmed through.
Crack 1 egg into above and stir in along with cream.

Toss in bowl with hot cooked pasta.

Serve.

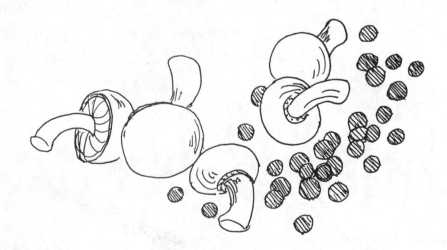

Last week at lunchtime while working on this book, I couldn't stop thinking about my favorite sandwich at the Landfall - the oyster sandwich with a crispy coating, served with a good green salad. I put my pen down and soon was enjoying it, then ready to return to work.

It was winter and I chose a table near the toasty warm wood-burning stove. This a very casual place, as you can tell by the sketch.

In the summer months, if the wind is blowing towards town, you can tell when it's barbecue time... using alder, the Landfall barbecues prime rib steaks, halibut and salmon. Available year-round are fresh seafood, great burgers and homemade desserts.

Go through the downtown district on Water Street as far as you can go without going in the water - it is on the left side of the street.

Rob and Patricia welcomed my son and me when we moved to Port Townsend 11 years ago and made it feel like home right away.

Breakfast & lunch Monday - Thursday
Breakfast, lunch & dinner Friday - Sunday Summer

MI PATRONA

4 oz. chicken breast, skinned
   and cut in long strips,
   dusted in flour
3 oz. Italian sausage
4 oz. quartered artichoke
   hearts
2 oz. diced tomatoes
3 oz. fresh spinach
6 oz. heavy whipping cream
3 oz. dry white wine
1 oz. fresh garlic
dash salt
dash pepper
2 oz. olive oil
8 oz. penne pasta, cooked al
   dente

Sauté garlic in olive oil. Add chicken, sausage, artichoke hearts, salt and pepper. Sauté for 5 minutes until chicken and sausage are almost cooked. Deglaze with wine. Add whipping cream and simmer until thickened. Add cooked pasta, tomatoes and spinach. Toss until spinach begins to wilt.
Top with Parmesan cheese.

Yield: 2 servings.

STEVE'S CHILEAN SEA BASS

10 oz. fresh Chilean sea bass

10 Kalamata olives, pitted
2 oz. red onions
3 oz. fresh tomatoes
2 oz. balsamic vinegar
2 oz. olive oil
1 oz. garlic
1 oz. butter
salt
pepper
2 oz. white wine

Preheat oven to 375°.
Bake sea bass with wine, 1 oz. butter, salt and pepper for 10 minutes.
While fish is baking, sauté garlic in oil. Add red onions, and olives. After one minute add tomatoes and balsamic vinegar and 1 oz. of butter. Cook until onions are transparent.
Remove sea bass from the oven and place on plate. Pour the onion and olive mixture over and enjoy!

Yield: 2 servings

Lanza's, located Uptown Port Townsend has been a family restaurant since 1982.

In February of 1996 Lori Lanza (the youngest of the 8 Lanza children) and Steve Kraght took over. They are partners and best of friends. They work well together. Lori told me that they want to keep the menu items "traditional" and to keep the prices down. She said "It should be like coming home and having a family dinner."

My son and I ordered two different entrées, so that I could sample his. Mine: "Mi Patrona", the recipe is shared here on the opposite page. The second entree: The Specialita, "Florentina". This is chicken tenders, mushrooms, spinach and goat cheese. I could highly recommend either of these.

Live music is mostly local talent and is offered on Friday and Saturday nights.

Dinner Monday - Saturday

PAN SEARED KING SALMON WITH BLOOD ORANGE AND GREEN PEPPERCORN AIOLI

2 T. Kosher salt
1/4 cup sugar
2 T. grated blood orange zest
1 t. fresh ground black pepper
6 salmon fillets, 7 oz. each

1/2 cup blood orange juice
3 large egg yolks
1/2 T. fresh lemon juice
2 cups olive oil
1 T. garlic, finely chopped
2 T. grated blood orange zest
1 T. Dijon mustard
2 T. lightly crushed green peppercorns in brine (rinsed of brine)
salt to taste
olive oil

The salmon is first lightly "cured" by mixing the salt, sugar, orange zest and pepper and rubbing the mixture on both sides of the fillets. Put the seasoned fillets into a stainless pan and refrigerate for about 3 to 4 hours.

Aioli: Heat the orange juice in a small sauce pan until reduced to 2 T., set aside to cool.

Combine egg yolks and lemon juice in electric mixing bowl. Very slowly drizzle in the olive oil while whisking at high speed. The mixture should thicken like mayonnaise. Stir in remaining ingredients, including the reduced orange juice. Chill.

Heat oil in a large sauté pan until very hot then place fillets in the pan and sear on both sides. You are trying to achieve an almost blackened or caramelized crust on the outside of the fish. Cook fillets rare to medium rare inside. Place on serving plates and garnish with dollops of the aioli sauce, orange slices, mint sprigs and whole green peppercorns.

Yield: 6 servings.   *Chef Tim Roth*

SLOW ROASTED PLUM TOMATOES

2 dozen Roma tomatoes
1/2 cup olive oil
3 T. balsamic vinegar
2 t. chopped garlic
1 t. dry basil leaves
1 t. dry oregano leaves
1 t. dry thyme leaves
1 t. ground fennel seed
salt
fresh ground black pepper

Slice tomatoes lengthwise and arrange close together on a heavy cookie sheet. Mix the olive oil, vinegar, and garlic and brush evenly on the tomatoes. Mix the dried herbs and fennel together and sprinkle evenly over the tomatoes. Dust tomatoes generously with salt and fresh pepper.

Place these in an oven set at the lowest possible temperature, and leave them for at least 12 hours. Tomatoes will lose about 70% of their volume, but be much more moist than sun dried tomatoes.

Lonny's simple technique with fresh tomatoes is revolutionary! Use these anywhere you might use sun dried tomatoes.

With over 25 years on the Olympic Peninsula, Lonny Ritter's reputation for fine dining is well established. His newest restaurant "Lonny's", is also his best.

When I heard that he had taken on remodeling an old garishly painted restaurant, it seemed impossible that he attained the results he did! We're talking changing walls, creating new spaces, creating an open kitchen to the dining room and enticing customers with the smells and sounds of this top quality establishment.

But let's talk about the food. An example of his ingenuity: His grilled vegetable salad, with fire-charred eggplant and zucchini, roasted red peppers and plum tomatoes served with tossed baby greens, French goat cheese and polenta croutons. (See what I mean, not your usual fare.)

One of the entrees is Grilled chicken alla Lido. This is free range boneless breast of chicken char-grilled with toasted pistachio nut pesto, and served with a Gorgonzola Dolce demi-glaze sauce. A winner!

Soups are one of Lonny's specialties, made daily, and you can count on them being very good.

Lots of pasta choices.

I'll let the desserts be a surprise!

Dinner Wednesday - Monday

77

MUSHROOM VELVET SOUP

4 T. butter
1/2 lb. mushrooms, sliced
1 med. onion, coarsely
   chopped
1 can beef broth (14 oz.)
1/2 pint sour cream

Melt butter, add mushrooms and onion. Cook, stirring until mushrooms are soft and juices have evaporated (about 5 minutes). Stir in 1/2 of the broth. Blend sour cream and remainder of broth with a whisk and add to soup.

Sprinkle a little parsley over the soup.

ALMOND CHERRY CRUNCH PIE

3 to 4 cups already made
   cherry pie filling
1 T. corn starch
2 drops almond flavoring

Topping:
1/2 cup finely chopped
   almonds
1/2 cup brown sugar
1/2 cup all-purpose flour
4 T. butter, melted

Preheat oven to 350°
Mix pie filling, corn starch and almond flavoring. Pour into unbaked pie crust.
Combine almonds, brown sugar and flour. Stir in melted butter until mixture is crumbly.
Crumble mixture on top of pie.
Bake about 30 to 40 minutes, until topping is golden brown.

At how many places are you able to order a milk-shake any more and have them bring what's left... almost another glass full? I love to order a rootbeer shake with just a little bit of chocolate added.

But the Plaza (located in Don's Pharmacy) is much more than just a fountain. Always a good cook on duty. Not long ago potato pancakes were added to the breakfast menu. You must try them! Fresh muffins and other baked goods are very popular.

Lunches often include daily specials. Example would be Thursday "this spud's for you"... a large baked spud with more than a dozen add-ons. To name a few: ham, cheese, shrimp, guacamole, cheese, bacon bits, onion, sour cream. Choose 3 and add a green salad for a very good price. In the summer months when the fountain is open longer, locals come here for what they call "early dinner".

This is definitely a home-town favorite spot. The counters angle in and out, allowing the waitress to serve 3 sides. Occasionally the cook will be creative and do a new special... recently on St. Patrick's Day, she used an old Irish recipe for a kind of pot-pie. Fresh hand made crust, very tender and flaky. Inside chicken, ham, and vegetables in a cream sauce. I hope she doesn't wait a year to offer this again!

Two large blackboards list the soups, salads, specials daily. Always 2 to 4 homemade soups. You'll often find me here.

Breakfast & lunch Monday - Saturday
Closed some holidays

SEAFOOD CHOWDER

32 Mediterranean mussels (cleaned and debearded)
32 Manila clams
1# fresh Atlantic or King salmon (cut into 1 oz. pcs.)
1# white fish (cod, halibut, sole) whichever is freshest (cut into 1 oz. pcs.)
1 lb. Dabob oysters, shucked
16 21/25 black tiger shrimp (peeled and deveined)
6 stalks celery, diced small
1 large red onion, diced small
12 Red Bliss "B" potatoes (cooked and quartered)
1 tomato, peeled, seeded and diced
8 strips bacon, cooked and chopped
8 oz. fresh seafood stock or bottled clam juice
4 oz. dry white wine
3/4 T. garlic, chopped
1 large bay leaf
8 oz. heavy cream
10 leaves fresh basil (chifonad)
10 - 15 springs fresh thyme leaves (lightly chopped)
salt and cracked black pepper to taste
a bit of olive oil

Obtain a high sided pan, large enough to hold all the seafood and that can be covered.

Heat the pan on the stove on high heat for 4 to 5 minutes until very hot. Add enough oil to lightly coat the bottom of the pan.

Add the onion and celery, stirring constantly to sweat the vegetables, (just about 1 minute).

Add the garlic and sauté lightly being careful not to burn the garlic. Add fish stock or clam juice, white wine and bay leaf and bring to a boil.

Add all the seafood with the bacon, tomato and potatoes.

Cover tightly and steam until the shellfish have just started to open. Add heavy cream, basil and thyme and reduce until slightly thickened.

The finished product will be both creamy and brothy.

Season with salt and cracked black pepper and a few splashes of your favorite hot sauce.

The great thing about this chowder is that it is made to order, the seafood is cooked and served, never having the chance to get tough. This dish comes together very quickly, so wait until after your guests have arrived to start. Serve with a nice salad and brown bread with plenty of Honey Almond Butter.

Yield: 8 servings

Construction began in 1890 and bricks were laid 4 stories high. Work was stopped in 1893 because of financial unrest with the U.S. Economy. The top 2 floors remained a shell. The first two floors were used by an auto dealer, then later it was a tire store. Later a bowling alley, followed by a shopping mall, then a sporting goods store. It has been "The Public House" for about 5 years now. Finally in the '40's, the 2 top floors were removed, and the bricks were put on a barge and dumped into the Port Townsend Bay. (If you need some bricks....)

New owner Joanne Saul is making menu changes, and the changes are good. For lunch I had the grilled chicken and zucchini sandwich, with mustard onions and fresh herb mayonnaise... I thoroughly enjoyed it.

For dinner another day I ordered the grilled ribeye that was served with oven-roasted garlic mashed potatoes and julienned vegetables.... a very enjoyable meal.

Just inside the front door are 1 or 2 chalkboards listing the day's specials - just take a look and you'll be hooked!

The selection of hand-crafted Northwest microbrews is good.

Lunch & dinner every day

♿

HALIBUT WITH HAZELNUT CREME

4 8 oz. halibut fillets
1 t. white pepper
1 T. olive oil
1 T. butter
1 cup dry white wine
1 t. salt
4 T. toasted hazelnuts,
   chopped
3 T. hazelnut liqueur
3/4 cup whipping cream

Dust the halibut fillets with pepper. In a large skillet on medium-high heat, melt the butter with the olive oil. When hot, place halibut in pan and sear, about 3 minutes. Turn the fillets over and braise with white wine, covered. Cook until wine is reduced to almost a glaze, about 10 minutes. Remove halibut and place on a warm plate.

In skillet, add the hazelnuts and salt. Sauté until hazelnuts are quite toasted. Add the liqueur and reduce to a glaze. Add whipping cream and reduce to a thickened consistency. Pour over the halibut.

ZUCCHINI ROQUEFORT SOUP

8 cups grated zucchini
1 onion, finely chopped
1/4 cup olive oil
5 1/2 cups milk
1/3 cup flour
3/4 cup crumbled Roquefort
   cheese
salt and pepper to taste

In heavy bottomed pot, sauté zucchini and onion on medium heat for 20 minutes, stirring frequently. Sift flour over the mixture and stir well. Continue to cook until well mixed and thick. Add milk. Heat gently on medium heat until hot, but not boiling. Add the cheese and mix thoroughly. Continue to heat until it begins to thicken. Adjust seasoning with salt and pepper.

Owner/chef Alison Hero's devotees followed her to the new location. Locals have watched as extensive remodeling was being done. A mezzanine was opened up, boarded store front received large new windows, and much more.

Built in 1889, first a store, then the Elk's Lodge in the 40's. The huge plants were carefully transported several blocks to their new home. Some have over 10 ft. vines and have been "in the family" for years. I believe they must thrive with all of the wonderful aromas.

Alison is a creative chef and finds interesting ways to use herbs.

It seems as if half of Port Townsend eats here – it's "Meet me at the Silverwater".

On the day I did this sketch my lunch was a vegetarian dish: Rotini with Gorgonzola, julienne spinach and toasted walnuts in a rich cream sauce. No room this day for a dessert, but they are tops!

In the summer months later hours allow for a walk on the beach or an early movie next door before dinner here.

Lunch & dinner every day
Sunday dinner only in Winter

Brunch Sunday

DISCOVERY BAY OYSTERS

1 empty oyster shell
1 raw oyster
5 pine nuts
1 t. garlic butter
dash brandy
Parmesan cheese
rock salt

GARLIC BUTTER

2 lbs. whipped butter
1 t. fresh garlic, chopped
pinch of parsley
1/2 cup brandy
3/4 cup lemon juice
pinch of pepper
4 dashes Tabasco
4 dashes Worcestershire

Preheat oven to 400°.

Place single oyster in clean oyster shell. Put in pine nuts, then drop T. garlic butter to cover the whole oyster. Sprinkle Parmesan cheese to cover, then drizzle brandy over the cheese so it soaks in.

Bake in a bed of rock salt for about 10 to 15 minutes.

Note: Garlic Butter will be enough for at least 20 to 25 oysters.

BAKED SALMON WITH SMOKED SALMON HORSERADISH CRUST AND LEMON BUTTER SAUCE

1 filet fresh King salmon

CRUST

1 horseradish root, finely
   shredded
1 bunch green onion
3 cups bread crumbs
1/2 lb. smoked salmon

LEMON BUTTER SAUCE

1 cup heavy whipping cream
1/2 oz. lemon juice
1/2 oz. white wine
1 T. butter
seasoning salt

Preheat oven to 400°.

Crust: place all ingredients in food processor and mulch. (Enough for 10 filets).

Sauce: Combine ingredients and reduce until thick.

Cover top of filet with crust and bake for about 8 to 10 minutes.

Serve with sauce under the filet.

Not many people enter a restaurant through the kitchen door, but I came here early to prepare the sketch. The sun was shining and sparkling on the waters of Discovery Bay. The ropes of garlic and red peppers were silhouetted and seemed to frame this great view.

The Original Oyster House is settled on the shores of the bay. My last book noted the fact that at low tide you will be rewarded with the sight of hundreds (maybe thousands) of clams squirting (or is it spitting?)

I overheard the lady at the next table ask about the plastic owl outside. The waitress replied that it was put up 3 years ago to scare the seagulls, but often the gulls sit on the owl's head... and one minute later a gull did!

The early bird dinners from 4 to 6 p.m. week days are the best. Many places offer 1 or 2, but the Original Oyster House offers 5 choices: chicken, fish, seafood, fettuccine or steak were tonite's selections. They came with soup or salad and a baguette of French bread. The wild rice couldn't have been better and the vegetables were cooked firm, the way I like them.

Too full for dessert, but ordered the Chocolate Kahlua Cheese Cake "to go", promptly eating it when home.

Dinner Monday - Saturday   **Lunch & dinner Sunday**

SESAME CHICKEN SALAD

Bed of crisp greens (mixture of
  green leaf, romaine & iceberg)
16 cherry tomatoes
1/2 cup sliced California black
  olives
1/3 cup sliced almonds
1 can mandarin oranges (14 oz.)
2 avocados, sliced
4 broiled 6 oz. skinless-boneless
  chicken breasts

SESAME DRESSING

1 T. sesame oil
1 T. olive oil
1/2 cup white wine vinegar
1/2 cup granulated sugar
1 t. salt
1 T. fresh ground black, red
  peppercorns

Dressing: Whip sesame and olive oils together.
Add white wine vinegar and sugar. Whip until
sugar is dissolved. Add seasonings.

For 4 salads: Garnish each bed of fresh greens with
4 cherry tomatoes, black olives, almonds and mandarin oranges. Slice 1/2 avocado and lay out on top
of salad. Top with thin slices of warm broiled
chicken breasts. Drizzle with dressing and sprinkle
with whole sesame seeds.

SWEET AND SOUR CABBAGE SOUP

1 lb. pork or beef ribs
2 onions, chopped
1 can tomatoes, 28 oz.
2 cups granulated sugar
1/2 cup lemon juice
1 T. olive oil
1 t. paprika
1/2 t. salt
1/2 t. freshly ground pepper
1 large head cabbage, chopped
4 cups water, to start
DUMPLINGS
2 cups flour
2 eggs
1/2 t. salt
1 T. water (enough to make
  dough sticky)

Brown meat and onions in olive oil. Add all other
ingredients and simmer for 1 1/2 hours. Add
dumplings and serve.

Dumplings: Beat eggs and water together. Stir in
the flour and salt and drop off spoon into boiling
water. Cook until they come to top. Drain.

Yield: 8 servings

The gardens at the Oak Table Cafe draw crowds every year... someone has a magical green thumb. Of course the crowds are here for the "special" food as well. Breakfasts are served all day, and when you see the very extensive and creative menu, you see why. You will hear bells ringing...it is to announce that the kitchen crew has just prepared another order of their famous Apple pancakes. The sketch on the opposite page shows it... made in the tradition of a soufflé, baked in the oven until it is at least 3" high, filled with fresh apples that were peeled and cut up in the Oak Table Cafe's kitchen.

All of this is then covered generously with a pure cinnamon glaze.

Lots of house Specialties: Chef Kim's porridge of whole rolled oats, cooked with all your favorite fruit-apples, blueberries and strawberries- and served with fresh cream. Also French baked Omelettes, Crepes, many egg dishes.

Not much room to talk about lunches, but they're noteworthy. Soup is made fresh each morning from scratch. They can boast about the sandwiches, Specials of the Day, salads. (It's only a 30 minute drive from my home) I'm hungry just writing about all of this good food.

Breakfast & lunch Monday - Friday
Breakfast only Saturday & Sunday

LEMON BARS

1 1/2 cups (12 oz.) salted butter
1 cup powdered sugar
3 cups flour

Filling:
8 eggs
3 cups granulated sugar
1/2 cup flour
juice of 4 lemons (1/2 to 3/4 cup)

Preheat oven to 350⁰
Place powdered sugar and flour in food processor. Add cold butter and pulse until mixture is a pea size crumble. Press into an 11" x 17" pan and bake approximately 12 minutes until crust is a light golden brown.
Whisk together eggs, sugar, flour and lemon juice until thoroughly mixed. Pour onto cooled crust.

Bake until set and just beginning to brown.

Cool and cut into bars.

APPLE OAT SCONES

1/2 cup flour
1 cup oats
1/3 cup brown sugar
2 1/2 t. baking powder
1/2 t. salt
1/2 cup unsalted butter

1 large egg, beaten
1/4 cup milk
1 T. molasses
1 t. vanilla
1 apple, peeled and chopped

Preheat oven to 375⁰
Place flour, oats, brown sugar, baking powder and salt in food processor. Add unsalted butter in small amounts and pulse until it forms a pea size crumble.
In another bowl mix filling ingredients, add the crumble and mix thoroughly.
Form into a 7" circle and place on greased baking sheet. Score into slices.

Bake 22 to 27 minutes.

Yield: 8 scones.

The plaque in the lower left reads "President Lincoln, June 19, 1862, ordered a reservation here for lighthouse and military use."

Bonny's was, until recently, located in the town's oldest church. This new place was an early fire house that had 3 fire poles. Later, it was a police station with jail cells in the back (still there), city council chambers, a YMCA youth center, and lastly a senior citizen center. After standing empty for several years, it now has a new and exciting life.

Old fire equipment was rescued for display, and the interior greatly restored to set the decor. The front is now a patio with umbrella tables and chairs for summer outside dining.

Bonny's has built a good reputation and patrons are ready to follow her to this new location. Soups are homemade and were really appreciated this past cold winter... have some with a few slices of bread or rolls. I was intrigued watching Bonny decorate a large wedding cake while I enjoy some soup and a turnover. The menu includes many sandwiches, espressos, beverages and soup. There are varied breads, savories, pastries, desserts and more.

Breakfast & lunch until 5:30 Monday - Saturday
Extended hours in Summer

BAILEY'S IRISH CREAM CHOCOLATE MOUSSE

8 eggs
2 cups whipping cream
4 T. sugar
1 1/2 oz. unsweetened choco-
    late
4 squares milk chocolate from
    bar (use jumbo chocolate
    bar) or 1 1.55 oz. chocolate
    bar
1/2 to 3/4 cup Bailey's Irish
    Cream Liqueur
3 T. water
6 T. sugar

Separate eggs. Cook yolks with 3 T. water in a 4 quart pan on low heat, constantly whisking. Beat until yolks thicken and turn pale yellow. Add Bailey's and continue to beat until thick. Remove from heat. Melt chocolate, stir until smooth and add to egg mixture.

Whip cream with 4 T. sugar, fold into egg mixture. Beat egg whites with 6 T. sugar until peaks form. Fold into mixture.

Refrigerate for 4 to 6 hours before serving.

Yield: 13 to 15 servings.

SHRIMP AND SCALLOP A BUBBLE

10 to 12 oz. pasta (fettuccine,
    linguine or angel hair)
1/2 lb. shrimp
1/2 lb. scallops
6 oz. whipping cream
6 oz. champagne
2 oz. clam juice
2 oz. Parmesean cheese
2 T. dill
1 lemon (1/2 for garnish)
salt and white pepper to taste

Boil pasta al dente, drain and cool.

Clean and devein shrimp. Sauté shrimp and scallops in olive oil with chopped garlic. Cook until half done and then add champagne, cooking for 2 more minutes. Add clam juice and cook for 1 to 2 minutes. Add whipping cream and reduce. Add pasta to the reduced sauce and squeeze the juice of 1/2 of fresh lemon in. Add dill, Parmesan cheese, salt and white pepper. Cook for 2 to 3 minutes. Mix and serve topped with freshly grated Parmesan.

Goes great with homemade garlic bread.

About 25 years ago the Bushwhacker moved from the wilds of Montana where they had a good reputation for their prime rib and char-broiled steaks.

The Bushwhacker was transplanted to the east end of Port Angeles and is continuing to please their customers, and have developed a menu around the fresh seafood from local waters: Puget Sound oysters, Sequim Bay clams, halibut from Neah Bay, local King Salmon and Puget cod fillets.

On my last visit I was pleased to see that changes had been made to the waiting area (previously a smaller space) and that the old staircase that had been blocked off was reopened. See sketch. Very nice!

They state on the menu "We carefully select Mid-western corn fed beef, season and slow-roast for at least 8 hours in our Alto-Shaam oven. Carved to order."

Dinner every day
Closed Thanksgiving, Christmas Eve & Christmas Day

PEANUT BUTTER PIE
CRUST
1 cup graham cracker crumbs
1/4 cup packed brown sugar
1/3 cup melted butter
1/2 cup finely chopped peanuts
FILLING
2 cups crunchy peanut butter
16 oz. cream cheese, softened
2 cups sugar
2 T. butter, softened
2 t. vanilla extract
1 1/2 cups whipping cream,
  stiffly beaten
CHOCOLATE TOPPING
4 oz. semi-sweet chocolate
  chips
4 T. hot coffee
coarsely chopped peanuts

Combine all the crust ingredients and press into the bottom and slightly up the sides of a springform pan. Chill.
Beat peanut butter, cream cheese, sugar, butter and vanilla until smooth. Fold in the whipped cream. Spoon into crust and refrigerate 6 hours or overnight.

For topping, melt the chocolate with coffee until smooth, spread over the chilled pie. Garnish with a wreath of chopped nuts. Refrigerate until firm, about 30 minutes. Can be frozen, does not freeze solid.

Yields: 16 servings.

Note: Best to cut when slightly frozen.

BLACKBERRY MARSALA BBQ SAUCE
6 cups blackberries (frozen is ok)
1 1/2 cups Marsala wine
1 t. ground ginger
1/2 t. black pepper, medium grind
1 cup sugar
2 cups barbecue sauce
1/4 cup brown sugar

Cook blackberries and wine until berries break down, about 20 minutes.
Add other ingredients and simmer 20 to 30 minutes.
Strain through a fine strainer, adjust thickness with water.

Great on broiled Salmon or Pork Loin.
Garnish with toasted almonds.

Chef: David Reynolds

92

I have followed Dave Reynolds over the years from downtown to the current location on East First street. I watched the garden develop and most recently this addition of the brick walls, boxes and gateways. Well named, the Cafe Garden has a beautiful garden.... plus a big variety of garden salads on the menu! And to crown the salads, 7 homemade dressings. The salads are a meal in themselves, but add the honey wheat bread. Three of us dined today and (of course) I insisted on a taste from each lunch...all in the interest of informing you, my readers, of the fare. At least that's what I told my friends. First: the seafood croissant; a light crab, shrimp and seafood sauté that was placed open-faced on a grilled croissant. Second: the honey mustard chicken sandwich, a grilled chicken breast, topped with bacon and Swiss cheese - on a Kaiser roll with the honey mustard dressing that gave the sandwich a little "zing". My order was chicken marinara, fresh pasta topped with marinara sauce and Parmesan. Mmm! Dinners are very popular with good choices across the board, with fish, seafood, chicken, beef (and more) all good.

Breakfast, lunch & dinner every day in Summer
Breakfast, lunch & dinner Monday - Saturday in Winter
Sunday breakfast until 3 PM in Winter

93

SCALLOP SOUFFLÉ

4 T. butter
5 T. flour
1/2 to 2/3 cup milk
pinch of salt
pinch of pepper
pinch of nutmeg
pinch of cayenne
5 egg yolks
1/2 lb. scallops
6 egg whites

SCAMPI OR CRAB SAUCE

1/4 cup white wine
3 or 4 scampi, finely
   chopped or crab
   meat
salt and pepper
green pepper corns
1/2 cup fish stock or
   clam juice
1/3 cup heavy cream

Preheat oven to 350⁰.
Melt butter and stir in flour for 2 to 3 minutes on medium heat. Add milk, stirring until it thickens. Add salt, pepper, nutmeg and cayenne.
Stir yolks into mixture one at a time. In food processor, grind scallops and add to the mixture.
Just before cooking, whip the 6 egg whites until soft peaks are formed, then fold into mixture.
Butter soufflé dish and pour mixture into dish.
Bake until soufflé rises, checking after 15 to 20 minutes. Soufflé should be 1 to 1 1/2" over top of pan and have a nice color.
Garnish with scampi or crab sauce.
Cook ingredients for sauce, reducing until thick. Stir in scampi or crab. Serve as a side dish or garnish for soufflé.

ALMOND TARTE

Paté Brisée Sucré
2 cups flour
5 oz. butter
2 T. sugar
2 to 3 T. ice water
FILLING

2 cups heavy cream
2 cups sliced almonds
1 cup walnuts,
   ground
2 cups sugar
2 T. vanilla
1 t. almond extract

Preheat oven to 350⁰.
Cut butter into small pieces in the flour. Add sugar and mix until flaky. Add water and mix again to form a ball. Set aside.

Mix all filling ingredients and let rest for 2 hours.

After forming your shell over a removable tart form, bake the shell until lightly browned. Cool shell.
Preheat oven to 375⁰.
When shell is cool, add filling and bake for about 1 hour.

Serve cold.

C'Est si Bon has a good reputation, and they have earned it. Owners Norbert and Michele Jukasz came here from Lyons, France years ago.... all to the benefit of their patrons. Many French recipes, as well as seafood, beef and lamb dishes are some of their specialties... or try their escargot or the oyster appetizers. I've never had better onion soup; it is served in a large bowl, bubbling and covered with a golden crust of cheese. Mmm! (I can't help dunking my bread into it.)

The main dining room is light and airy, high ceilings, art on the walls, a grand piano, and high multi-paned windows that look out onto wonderful rose gardens. Try to sit in this area during the rose season. Beyond the roses, the sun sets behind the Olympic mountains.

C'est si Bon it is.... très bon! Plan a stop here. Mr. and Mrs. Jukasz have a reputation for the best dinners for many miles.

Dinner Tuesday - Sunday

GREEK PASTA

1 lb. fettuccine
3 cloves garlic
1 bunch fresh basil leaves
3/4 cup sour cream
1 1/4 cup Feta cheese
pinch of pepper
2 T. olive oil
1 bunch green onions, sliced
  on the diagonal
1 red pepper, diced
6 mushrooms, thickly sliced
1 tomato, sliced into wedges
1/4 cup zucchini, chopped
1 cup Greek olives, pitted

Cook pasta according to directions.
Prepare sauce by blending garlic, basil, sour cream, Feta and pepper in a food processor or blender. Set aside.

Heat olive oil in a large skillet. Quickly sauté the onions, pepper, zucchini and mushrooms. Toss with pasta and stir in the sauce.
Toss with tomatoes and olives.
Serve.

DEEP DARK CHOCOLATE CAKE

1 3/4 cups flour
2 cups sugar
3/4 cup cocoa
1 1/2 t. soda
1 1/2 t. baking powder
1 t. salt
2 eggs
1 cup milk
1/2 cup vegetable oil
2 t. vanilla
1 cup boiling water

Preheat oven to 350° Grease and flour cake pan.
Sift dry ingredients 2 to 3 times and place in a large mixing bowl. Add remaining ingredients except boiling water. Beat 2 minutes on medium speed. Stir in boiling water.
Pour into greased and floured pans and bake for 35 to 40 minutes in a 9 x 13" pan   or 30 to 35 minutes in 2 9" pans.
When cake is done, cool for 10 minutes, then remove from pans onto rack to completely cool.

The Cottage has a warm and welcoming atmosphere. As shown in my sketch, the exterior of the building is brick, with French doors and lots of windows. The landscaping and flowers are extra-special.

Inside there are wood floors and lots of antiques on the walls.
I always request a table by the windows to be able to fully enjoy the garden.
On my last visit I ordered "Jesi's Omelette" with fresh spinach, mushrooms, bacon, cashews, Swiss cheese and cream cheese. The cashews add a nice touch!

A good choice: light lemon pancakes with raspberry pureé...or try the apple walnut French toast, thick sliced Vienna bread dipped in a rich custard batter, then grilled until golden with Korintji cinnamon and walnuts. Finally, it's topped with fresh sautéed apples.

At lunch they serve humungous salads, homemade soups, delicious pastas.. I love the fajitas that arrive sizzling along with piles of onions, guacamole, cheeses, lettuce, tomatoes, and more.
There's espresso, beer and wine.
I have only touched on a few of the extensive possibilities. The freshly baked desserts, muffins, apricot walnut scones, fruit streudel plus are home made.

Breakfast & lunch every day   Closed Thanksgiving & Christmas day   ♿

THREE BERRY COBBLER
CRUST
1 1/4 cups flour
1 1/2 t. baking powder
1 T. sugar
1/4 lb. butter, cut into cubes
  and keep cold
1 egg
1/3 cup milk
FILLING
1/2 lb. each, frozen blueberries, blackberries and strawberries
2 T. water
1 1/2 T. sugar
1 1/2 T. cornstarch
1 T. lemon juice

Preheat oven to 350⁰
Prepare individual baking dishes by spraying with non-stick coating.
Crumble together the flour, baking powder, sugar and butter until they have the texture of coarse cornmeal. Blend in egg and milk, mix and form into a ball.
Roll dough on a floured surface to 1/8" thickness. Using something round, (a touch smaller than the bowls), press out circles.
Combine all the ingredients for filling in a saucepan and bring to a boil, stirring frequently. When the mixture is thick and syrupy, remove from heat. Spoon the mixture into prepared baking dishes. Cover loosely with the dough circles and bake for about 15 minutes or until the crust is lightly browned and the berry filling is bubbling out around the edges. Allow to cool before serving.
Serve warmed with vanilla ice cream.
YUM!!!!

LEMON POPPYSEED MUFFINS
3 cups flour
1 1/2 cups sugar
1 1/2 T. baking powder
3/4 cup sour cream
2 eggs
1/2 cup butter, melted
3/4 cup milk
peels of 3 lemons, grated.
  (save lemons for glaze)
1/2 cup poppy seeds
GLAZE:
juice of 3 lemons
1/2 cup sugar

Preheat oven to 350⁰
Mix dry ingredients together. Set aside.
Mix wet ingredients together. Pour into dry ingredients and mix until moistened. Fold in poppy seeds.
Pour into greased muffins tins and bake for about 30 minutes, or until tester inserted comes out clean.
Glaze: Heat juice and sugar until it is dissolved.
Glaze muffins when they come out of the oven.

The First Street Haven is located on a one-way street going through the center of the downtown district. Look on the left side... don't blink or you could miss it. If you do, go back around the block. A must!

Remodeling was recently completed, with ceiling being removed, opened skyward, with the wonderful results as shown here. What a difference! Owner Diane Nagler and her husband, Ken Nemirow were then inspired to add new choices to their already good menu. My son, Gene, was with me on this visit. We split a giant omelet with fresh spinach, sautéed mushrooms, bacon, cheese and cashews. This meant we could add a giant piece of sour cream streusel coffee cake, served warm. Mmm! Then couldn't resist taking home some apple walnut scones.

In this lower sketch, on the left is Diane with brother, Billy Nagler, owner of Sequim's Oak Table Cafe, and on the right, their parents, Ann and Henry Nagler, owners of Ann's Cottage Gifts, located in the Oak Table parking lot.

The Haven is a stop worth making. In business for over 20 years.

Breakfast & lunch Monday - Saturday
Breakfast until 2 PM Sunday

CHICKEN WITH PAPRIKA

1 lb. boneless chicken breast
   or thighs
salt
pepper
paprika
2 T. oil
1 red bell pepper, julienned
1 onion, julienned
1/2 lb. mushrooms, sliced
1 T. paprika
1 cup heavy whipping cream
1 cup stock (bouillon cube
   okay)
2 T. cornstarch
2 oz. dry sherry
salt and pepper to taste

Dry breast or thigh with paper towel, rub with salt, pepper and paprika. Heat oil in heavy skillet, add chicken pieces, brown on all sides for about 8 minutes. Remove chicken and set aside to drain, keep warm. Sauté bell pepper, onion and mushrooms lightly in pan. Add paprika and heavy whipping cream and stir. Add the stock and let simmer for about 10 minutes. Mix some water and the cornstarch and add to the simmering vegetables. Add only enough cornstarch to lightly thicken the mixture. Add sherry, salt and pepper to taste. Return the chicken pieces to the sauce. Heat through.

Serve over rice or noodles.

Yield: 4 servings.

CHOCOLATE MOUSSE

7 oz. semi-sweet chocolate
1/2 cup whipping cream
1/2 cup sugar
4 eggs
1/4 cup Frangelico

Melt chocolate in double boiler until fully melted. Separate eggs, add 1/4 cup sugar and 1/4 cup Frangelico to egg yolks. Beat until fluffy and creamy. In a bowl, beat whipping cream with mixer until stiff. In another bowl, beat egg whites with mixer until stiff peaks form, then add 1/4 cup sugar.

Pour melted chocolate into egg yolk mixture. Add whipped cream to chocolate mixture. Lightly fold in egg white mixture.

Refrigerate for 2 to 3 hours before serving or pipe into wine glass. Garnish with fresh fruit and enjoy!!

This quote on the menu at Toga's says a lot, and it's a good way to start telling you about what's happening here.

"From my apprenticeship in the Black Forest of Germany to cooking on a 5 star cruise ship, journeys have brought me back to my hometown of Port Angeles. Now, owning a restaurant, I can put the culinary skills I have learned around the world to work. Your chef, Toga Hertzog."

I was pleased to see the results of the remodeling done on this building (formerly a gift shop.) This pleasant setting offers a view of the Olympic Mountain range with a splash of the Strait of Juan de Fuca.

Fondues are offered: original Swiss cheese Fondue, a Northwest Seafood Fondue containing scallops, prawns, halibut, salmon and clams, or the "Meat Lovers Fondue" with beef, pork, chicken and turkey sliced into thin strips. Not just a delicious feast, but a social event, making this an entertaining experience for you and your friends.

Also "Jagerstein" (an ages old way of cooking on a hot stone), where the hot stone is brought to the table ... you cook to the preferred "doneness", several choices of meats. Reservations are recommended for either the Fondues or the "Jagerstein". Of course, there's a full menu for those not interested in "doing it yourself".

Dinner Tuesday - Sunday   **Reservations recommended**

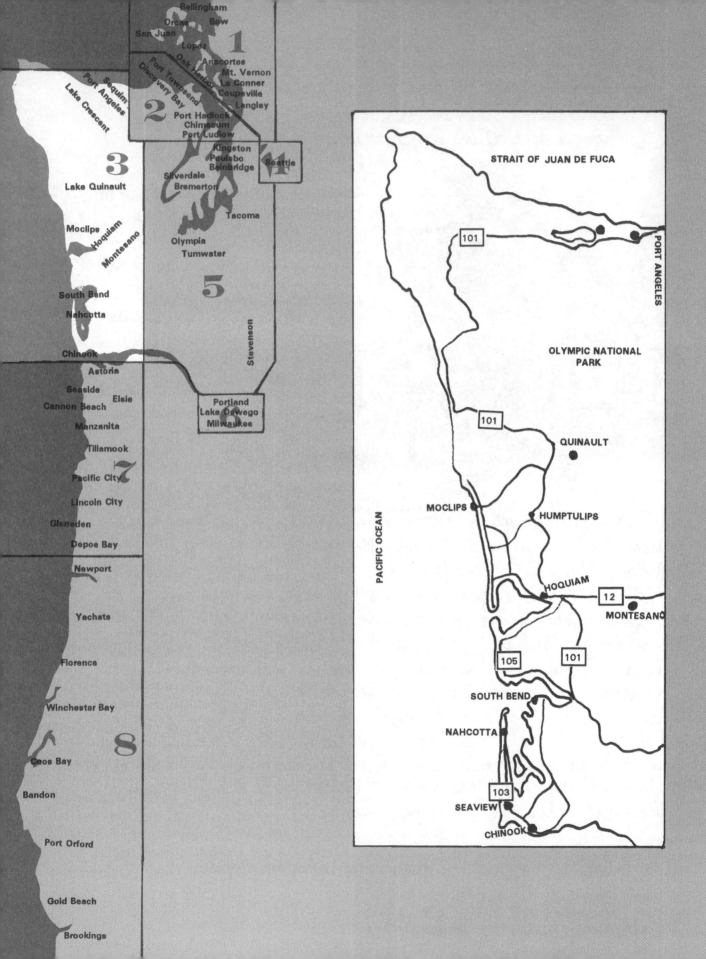

Bellingham
Bow
Orcas
San Juan
Lopez
Oak Harbor
Anacortes
Mt. Vernon
La Conner
Coupeville
Port Townsend
Langley
Discovery Bay
Port Hadlock
Chimacum
Port Ludlow
Kingston
Poulsbo
Bainbridge
Silverdale
Bremerton
Seattle
Tacoma
Olympia
Tumwater

Sequim
Port Angeles
Lake Crescent

Lake Quinault

Moclips
Hoquiam
Montesano

South Bend
Nahcotta

Chinook
Astoria
Seaside
Cannon Beach
Elsie
Manzanita
Tillamook
Pacific City
Lincoln City
Gleneden
Depoe Bay
Newport
Yachats
Florence
Winchester Bay
Coos Bay
Bandon
Port Orford
Gold Beach
Brookings

Stevenson

Portland
Lake Oswego
Milwaukee

1
2
3
4
5
7
8

STRAIT OF JUAN DE FUCA

101

PORT ANGELES

OLYMPIC NATIONAL PARK

101

QUINAULT

PACIFIC OCEAN

MOCLIPS

HUMPTULIPS

HOQUIAM

12

MONTESANO

105

101

SOUTH BEND

NAHCOTTA

103

SEAVIEW

CHINOOK

PORK AND SAUERKRAUT

8 pork chops
3 T. vegetable oil
2 (32 oz.) cans or jars
   sauerkraut, drained
I large apple, grated
I large onion, sliced
I t. Worcestershire sauce

Preheat oven to 350⁰.
Brown pork chops in the vegetable oil in a roaster pan.
Drain off fat.
Mix sauerkraut with the apple, onion, and Worcestershire sauce.
Bake all together for I hour or until chops are tender.

CABBAGE PATCH SOUP

1/2 small cabbage, chopped
I lb. ground beef
I 28 oz. can whole tomatoes,
   chopped
I 15 oz. can tomato sauce
I t. chili powder
2 cloves garlic, chopped
I t. salt or to taste
I t. pepper or to taste
2 stalks celery, chopped
2 carrots, chopped
I cup ready made chili with
   beans
I small potato, chopped
2 quarts water, or more as
   desired

Combine all ingredients and cook until vegetables are tender, approximately I hour.

I have known "Granny" Marian for over 10 years and her brother, Richard. I've watched changes being made... adding dove pens at one end of the patio dining room, a glassed-in wall, antiques, etc. — and redoing the main room — now a beautiful pagoda (pictured here) and a collection of bird houses. If you have children, there are chickens, ducks and a donkey named "Hoaty" out-back. (Say out loud "Donkey Hoaty.")

As I write this, brother Richard said that there's over 5" of snow everywhere. The parking area had to be scraped clear.

"Down home" cooking here with home made soups and a life-size cut out Granny holds up a Daily Specials board.

Now over 20 years here. This is a gathering place of a lot of the locals... a very informal place, and friendly. In the summer months there is often a line for cones (it's right on highway 101).

Breakfast, lunch & dinner every day

105

CHILI SOUP

1 lb. ground beef chuck
1 large onion, finely chopped
2 (2 lb.) cans Italian plum
  tomatoes
2 t. salt
1/2 t. freshly ground black
  pepper
1 T. chili powder (or to
  taste)
1/2 t. thyme
1 bay leaf
1 (20 oz.) can red kidney
  beans, drained
cayenne pepper to taste
beef broth or water, if
  necessary

Brown the beef in a skillet, stirring frequently. Add onion and cook 5 minutes. Add tomatoes, salt, pepper, chili, thyme and bay leaf.
Bring to a boil, cover and simmer about one hour. Add the beans and simmer 15 minutes longer. Season with cayenne. Add beef broth or water if soup is too thick.

Yield 6 servings.

MUD PIE

3 boxes Nabisco chocolate
  cookie wafers
3/4 cup canola oil
3 gallons ice cream
Hershey chocolate syrup
whipping cream
maraschino cherries

Crust: Roll out chocolate cookies to fine crumbs. Mix crumbs with canola oil. Mixture should hold firm when pressed in hand. Spray springform pan 9 x 3 inch high with vegetable food spray. Press crumb mixture on sides and bottom. Freeze for 1 hour.

Pie: Soften ice cream (suggested Mocha Almond Fudge or Mint Chocolate Chip) or a flavor of your choice. Pack ice cream into springform pan and mound high in the center. Freeze for 24 hours (or longer) before serving.

Yield: 8 servings

Note: When proofing this recipe, the staff couldn't believe that a pie with 3 gallons of ice cream and 3 boxes of cookies could be eaten by only 8 people, so a phone call was made to the Log Cabin Resort Restaurant. They laughed and said that often customers share one piece.

The post in the upper left hand corner of this sketch shows how close the Log Cabin restaurant is to Lake Crescent.

This is a very popular destination in summer because there are A-frame chalets, lodge rooms, cabins and R/V trailer sites. If you like to fish, many trophy size Beardslee and Crescent trout have been pulled from the clear blue waters of the lake. Explorers were doing this in the 1800's. All around are giant old growth firs and cedars, with nearby trails to spectacular waterfalls, snow-capped mountains and Mount Storm King rises above the lake to the south.

The Rice and Butcher families recently took over the lodge and they continue with a good selection of meals. Geoduc is featured prepared in different ways. Chicken and beef kabobs are also featured with speared vegetables and rice. (No, the rice isn't speared!) They are proud of their clam chowder and the seafood sauté salad with scallops and shrimp in a butter and wine sauce.

The resort was established in 1895 and is located on the "sunny side of the lake... a 17 acre resort in the Olympic National Park.

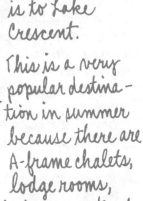

Open Seasonally

HOT and SPICY PRAWNS STIR FRY

4 or 5 prawns, for lunch or 6 or 7
    prawns for dinner (size 16 to 20) -
    per entrée
1 t. garlic, crushed - per entrée
1/8 cup onion, chopped - per entrée
1/8 cup green and red bell peppers,
    sliced - per entrée
1/8 cup mushrooms, sliced per
    entrée
3 dashes Tabasco sauce - per entrée
cayenne pepper to taste

Over medium heat combine all items in a oiled
sauté pan.   Cook until prawns are done.
Prawns should change color to white; they
should not be shriveled.

BAKED SALMON

1 salmon fillet cut into dinner
    size portions (apx. 8 oz.)
lemon juice
pepper
garlic powder
seasoning salt
onion slices
lemon slices

Preheat oven to 400⁰.
Spray a baking sheet with cooking oil. Remove skin
from salmon. Place salmon on sheet. Sprinkle salmon
with lemon juice
Season lightly with pepper, garlic powder and seasoning salt. Place a few onion slices and a lemon slice on
top of salmon. Cover with aluminum foil.
Bake for 15 minutes or longer depending on thickness
of salmon. The salmon is done when the middle just
starts to change color.
Pour juices over salmon before serving.

If you're looking for boating, sailing, hiking, horseback riding, fishing, hunting, bicycling, wildlife viewing, driving range, kite flying...or just plain old relaxing, with the only crowds being "crowds" of trees, this is the place. I chose to stay in the fireplace cabin because of the whirlpool and being able to enjoy a fire in the evening. Although the cabin had kitchen facilities, my dinner plans were for a steak at the "Salmon House" Restaurant. It was prepared perfectly! The view from the dining room looks out across Lake Quinault, inspiring views. And what a sunset that evening... golds, orange and streaks of red! Before dining I walked over to see what is said to be the world's largest Sitka spruce tree....
← this view showing the enormity.

The Rain Forest Resort Village is located on the south shore of Lake Quinault: three and one half miles off Highway 101.

Breakfast, lunch & dinner Summer
Dinner every day

109

FLORENTINE SALMON

2 T. butter
1 cup fresh mushrooms, sliced
1/2 cup green onions, chopped
1/2 bunch fresh spinach
1 oz. brandy
4 salmon filets (8 oz. ea)
salt and pepper to taste
1/2 cup white wine

Preheat oven to 400°.
Quickly sauté mushrooms, green onions and spinach in butter. Add brandy, flame and remove from heat.
Cut pocket in salmon filets and stuff with the sauté mixture.
Place salmon in pan and season to taste with salt and pepper. Add 1/2 cup of white wine.
Bake for 10 to 12 minutes, depending on the thickness of the fillets.

Yield: 4 servings.

DUNGENESS CRAB CAKES

1 1/4 lbs. crab meat
1 green pepper, diced small
1/2 medium white onion, diced small
2 eggs, beaten
1 cup mayonnaise
1/8 t. dried thyme
1/2 t. Tabasco
1 1/2 cups dried bread crumbs

Combine all ingredients in bowl. Using small scoop or spoon, form 3 inch round by 1/2 inch thick cakes. Drop into hot oil and cook until nicely brown on each side.

Serve with sauce of choice

Yield: about 18 cakes.

Last year a friend stopped me and asked "Where would you choose for a special 3 days away? My husband and I want a place with good lodging, good food and good hiking... and maybe swimming. Oh yes, not too far away." I answered without hesitating "Ocean Crest Resort at Moclips on the coast." The  next time I saw her she thanked me. They walked on the beach for miles. Snuggled into a natural forest setting, the buildings are surrounded by a variety of evergreens, ferns and wild flowers. A long series of stairs zig-zags down to the beach. There are benches along the way to stop and take in the beauty of it all.

It has always been very busy in the spring and summer, but now is a getaway destination off season... plus special prices then. It will soon be their 50th year! In the recreation center: indoor heated pool, therapy spa, Finnish sauna, fully equipped exercise room, aerobic and aquasize and tanning bed.

The Ocean Crest restaurant has ocean view dining for breakfast, lunch and dinner. The couple at the table next to mine told me that they've been coming here for over 20 years – always happy with the meals. I've been stopping here for about 8 years and can say the same. Quinault River salmon is fresh daily... or try the fresh Penn Cove mussels.

Breakfast, lunch & dinner every day　　　　♿

CHOCOLATE RUM RAISIN BREAD PUDDING

1 1/2 cups dark raisins
1/3 cup rum
4 cups dry rustic bread
1/2 cup sugar
1 quart milk
3 large eggs, beaten
zest of one orange
zest of one lemon
2 t. cinnamon
1 t. nutmeg
1 cup dark chocolate shavings

Preheat oven to 350°
Soak raisins in rum until plump, about 1 hour.
In a large bowl, combine bread, sugar, milk, eggs, orange zest, lemon zest, cinnamon and nutmeg. Refrigerate 1 hour or until bread is soft. Stir in raisins, rum and chocolate. Pour into buttered 9 x 9 inch pan. Bake 45 minutes to 1 hour until set and golden brown.

Yield: 8 servings

CAPITALE ESPRESSO BAR

1 1/2 cups all-purpose flour
4 t. cardamom, ground
1/2 t. salt
1/2 t. baking powder
1 cup unsalted butter, melted
1 cup brown sugar
1 cup granulated sugar
2 eggs
3 cups quick cooking oats
1 1/2 quarts coffee ice cream

Preheat oven to 350°
Coat 2 baking sheets with a nonstick cooking spray. On a sheet of waxed paper, sift together the flour, cardamom, salt and baking soda. Set aside.
Process together butter, brown sugar and 1/2 cup of the granulated sugar. Beat in the eggs, one at a time. Add flour mixture and process. Slowly add oats, mixing well. Put the remaining granulated sugar in a bowl.
Scoop up 2 tablespoons of the dough, roll into a ball, then into the remaining sugar. Place on a cookie sheet about 2 inches apart. Flatten to about 3 inches in diameter. Bake 12 to 14 minutes. Transfer to a cooling rack.
For each bar place a 1/2 cup scoop of ice cream between 2 cookies, bottom inward. Press together so the ice cream spreads to the edge.
Wrap in plastic wrap and place in freezer until ready to serve.

Yield: 11 servings

Lots of changes at the Levee Street Restaurant by new owners Lela Cross and Tina Musser. Walls were knocked out, new doorways, larger windows, and a new room that will allow for parties, meetings, special occasions. Lela told me that when I return in June or July the new outside patio will hopefully be ready for lunches.

Lela and Tina are bubbling with new ideas, but they said "we will continue to spoil people"... sounds good to me.

Lela comes here following years in Santa Fe, New Mexico and brings many new recipes from that part of the country. She trained in Seattle and presently also has a bistro in Olympia. Look for new flavors.

As pictured on the opposite page, two of a line of oils (some spicy hot) are being sold now, plus about 25 to 30 pastas. Their product name is "Pastabilities".

The word has gotten out. The Levee Street Restaurant is becoming busier now. I plan to sit outside and watch the boats go by after this book is printed in June.

Oh, yes, almost forgot that if you have special diet needs they will work with your request. I can highly recommend their bread pudding... served piping hot, topped with cream.

Lunch & dinner Tuesday - Friday   **Dinner Saturday**   ♿

CANDI'S PIE CRUST

2/3 cup cold butter, cubed
2/3 cup cold shortening
4 cups all-purpose unbleached
   flour
1 1/2 t. salt
2/3 cup cold water

In a processor bowl put flour, butter, shortening and salt. Process with on/off switch until the mixture resembles heavy corn meal. I usually hit on/off switch about 10-12 times. Add water all at once and process until it forms a ball. Be careful not to over work!! Stop when it is just barely pulling together.

Place dough on a floured surface and cut into 4 pieces. Roll out as needed or refrigerate or freeze, wrapped in plastic wrap.

Yield: 4 crusts.

CREAM PIE MASTER RECIPE

2 cups whole milk
3/4 cup sugar
4 egg yolks
1/4 cup cornstarch
1 t. vanilla

Place all ingredients in a heavy bottomed saucepan. Mix well. Place over medium heat and stir constantly until thickened.

VARIATIONS

Coconut Cream:
1 cup coconut
whipped cream
toasted coconut

Add coconut to pastry cream. Pour into a pre-baked 8" pie shell and refrigerate until cool. Top with whipped cream and sprinkle with toasted coconut.

Banana Cream:
4 bananas, sliced
whipped cream

Slice 4 bananas into pastry cream. Pour into a pre-baked pie shell and refrigerate until cool. Top with whipped cream.

Chocolate Cream:
1/2 cup chocolate chips or
   shaved semi-sweet chocolate bar
whipped cream
chocolate curls

While pastry cream is still hot, stir in chocolate until smooth. Pour into baked pie shell and refrigerate. Top with whipped cream and chocolate curls.

Yield: 6 servings.

Candi Bachtell's reputation continues to grow. Each time I visit Savory Faire there are more waitresses, more customers and more offerings on the menu. I wonder if Candi had any idea how this business would grow? Years ago all of this began when she taught cooking classes.

Candi told me "it's home-style cooking using all of the freshest ingredients in everything... all made from scratch and all of the baked goods are made here."

If you visit Savory Faire at breakfast time, the omelets are an excellent choice -

and you can count on fresh baked bread and muffins.

If you're here for lunch, salads and pastas are popular.

You'll also find extra-special sandwiches.

Always fresh desserts, so take a look at the choices in the refrigerated display case as you enter.

Breakfast & lunch Monday - Saturday

FISHERMEN'S STEW

2 T. extra virgin olive oil
2 cloves garlic, minced
I med. red onion, julienned
4 ribs celery, sliced 1/4 inch
   thick
2 T. chopped fresh parsley
2 cups fish stock
2 12 oz. cans diced stewed
   tomatoes
2 T. tomato paste
I lb. white fish, cubed
pinch of fennel
pinch of oregano
pinch of thyme
salt and pepper to taste

Sauté garlic, red onion and celery in olive oil over medium heat until translucent, about 4 minutes. Combine remaining ingredients in stock pot and add sautéed vegetables. Bring to a boil over medium high heat. Reduce heat and simmer uncovered I hour.

Serve with a loaf of your favorite bread.

Enjoy!

SEAFOOD HOLLANDAISE

4 slices toasted garlic bread
   (thick)
8 oysters
4 2 oz. pieces cod
4 2 oz. pieces salmon
2 lemon wedges
I bay leaf
several whole peppercorns

4 eggs, soft poached

HOLLANDAISE

3 egg yolks
I oz. white wine
1/2 cup firm butter
I T. lemon juice
dash Tabasco
salt and white pepper to taste

Prepare Hollandaise and keep warm over low heat.

Hollandaise: Place butter in measuring cup and microwave on high for I minute. Meanwhile, whisk egg yolks and wine in a small saucepan over medium heat, being careful not to scramble. Add butter slowly, constantly whisking, until sauce becomes creamy. Season with lemon juice, salt and white pepper.

Poach seafood in saucepan with seasonings over medium heat until firm, about 4 minutes. At the same time, in a separate saucepan, poach eggs in lightly vinegared water until soft, about 3 minutes.

Arrange poached seafood over garlic bread. Place I egg on top of each slice. Ladle Hollandaise over all.

Enjoy!

Yield: 4 servings

Arrived in pouring rain in November; I couldn't believe the brilliant rainbow and sunshine 5 minutes later! It touched down on the opposite side of the Willapa River. South Bend is the historic county seat of Pacific County and calls itself "Oyster Capitol of the World". Fine views whether in the coffee shop, dining room or on the open patio during the summer.

Lots of activity to watch, and during the busiest times, customers often arrive at 6 a.m. Salmon gill netters: the first men set the nets. There are oyster barges, wood chip barges, sports fishing. Also ducks, geese, seals or an otter could be playing near the docks... or a stately blue heron standing nearby. A new dock offers waterskiing and other boating activities.

When a restaurant has been operating for almost 30 years (started in 1969), you know they are doing the right things.
Breakfasts include the regular items, but oysters may be ordered grilled or raw. The Gray family work together here, with son John arriving at 3:30 a.m. to make pies, brownies, cookies, turnovers, and more. Also breads: sourdough, French, 8 grain, rye and their own hamburger buns. Ellie tries to keep the prices reasonable, and a lot of the dinners may be ordered as "half orders".

Breakfast, lunch & dinner every day

LAMB LOIN WITH APPLE-DATE STUFFING

STUFFING	SAUCE
1/2 lb. butter	6 to 7 cloves garlic, minced
1/2 cup garlic, finely chopped	3 shallots, minced
7 apples, finely chopped	1 T. fresh mint, chopped
2 cups fresh mint, chopped	3 T. flour
2 yellow onions, finely chopped	3/4 cup Madeira
1/2 cup Madeira	3 cups lamb stock
2 cups pitted dates, ground	fresh-cracked pepper and salt to taste
4 - 1/2 to 3/4 lb. lamb loins	

Preheat oven to 425°

Sauté in butter the garlic, apples, mint and onions. With the mixture still in the pan, deglaze with Madeira.

Add the dates and set stuffing aside.

Work a steel through the center of the loins to make one lengthwise hole in each. Fill a pastry bag without a tip with stuffing; pipe into loins. Sear loins in butter to brown them. Reserve juices. Bake in oven for 15 to 20 minutes.

Sauce: Add garlic, shallots and mint to pan juices. Sauté till flavors are full, 1 to 2 minutes, agitating pan so ingredients do not burn. Add flour, stirring constantly to keep from burning. Deglaze with Madeira. Add lamb stock, pepper and salt. Simmer until reduced by half.

Yield: 10 servings.

Note: Extra stuffing might be rolled in blanched spinach leaves and steamed.

CHICKEN STUFFED WITH MUSHROOMS AND SPINACH

1/4 cup clarified butter	flour
1/3 cup white onions, finely chopped	2 to 4 T. clarified butter
1/2 t. garlic, minced	1/2 t. garlic, minced
1 cup mushrooms, finely chopped	1/2 t. shallot, minced
1/2 T. dried oregano	salt and pepper to taste
3 T. Madeira	1 t. grainy Pommery mustard
2 bunches blanched and chopped spinach	2 T. lemon juice
4 to 5 T. Parmesan	3 T. brandy
4 oz. goat cheese	1/4 cup chicken stock
1/2 cup breadcrumbs	1/3 cup heavy cream
4 to 6 half chicken breasts, boned	2 T. Madeira

Sauté until tender in the clarified butter onions, garlic, mushrooms and oregano. Without removing mixture from pan, deglaze with Madeira. Remove from heat.

Add spinach, Parmesan and goat cheese while mixture is still hot. Add breadcrumbs to bind mixture. Set aside for several hours to cool and allow flavors to marry.

Slit pockets into chicken breasts and divide the stuffing among them. Lightly dust breasts with flour. Sauté in butter. Add to the pan garlic, shallot, salt and pepper, grainy Pommery mustard, lemon juice, brandy, chicken stock and heavy cream. Reduce until sauce is slightly thickened.

Finish with Madeira, cooking only until the alcohol evaporates.

Yield: 4 to 6 servings

Note: Chef Lucas suggests that the dressing mixture will keep (refrigerated) for 4 to 5 days.

When you see a giant mound of oyster shells on the right side of the road, the Ark is just beyond... <u>many</u> more shells than on previous trips.

When I asked one of the owners "What's new?" she excitedly told me of their work in the community "Kids feeding kids". A class visits to see where food comes from. For example: cranberries grow nearby, they are studied, then the kids are served cranberries at school.

On the wall at the Ark is a photograph of Nanci and Jimella with President Clinton and a letter personally thanking them for their gift of the Ark cookbook. Their meals continue to be tops. I am often asked if the Ark is going to be in Book 4 and a "yes" is to the satisfaction of the asker.

Inventive combinations of herbs and sauces make for memorable fare. When I read of the salmon entrée with Chanterelle mushrooms and lime, cilantro and sherry, I knew this would be my choice!

<u>Must</u> mention their bakery here, turning out homemade breads and dreamy desserts — save room.

Dinners only   Seasonal hours, call for information
Always Sunday Brunch   From July 4th Lunch Thurs., Fri. & Sat.

HALIBUT WITH GINGER AND BLACK BEANS

8 fillets of halibut
2 to 3 Shitake mushrooms
1/4 cup hot water
2 oz. Chinese fermented
  black beans
2 green onions, sliced fine
1/2 oz. fresh ginger root,
  grated fine
1 cup sherry
1 lemon, zest and juice
3/4 cup peanut oil
1/4 cup sesame oil
1/2 cup soy sauce
1 cup white wine

Preheat oven to 500⁰

Rinse the beans well to rid of salt. Squeeze dry.

Soak the mushrooms in hot water for at least 1 hour. Squeeze out liquid; reserve.   Remove stems and slice mushrooms into ribbons, 1/8" wide.

Combine oils, reserved mushroom liquor, lemon juice and zest and sherry. Whisk, add soy sauce, ginger root, onions, black beans and mushrooms.

Cover halibut with marinade. Refrigerate overnight, or at least 2 hours.

Remove fish to baking dish. Mix 1 cup marinade with white wine and pour over fish. Cover with foil and bake 10 to 12 minutes.

Serve with marinade spooned over.

Garnish with lemon slices.

This recipe works very well with all types of rockfish and sturgeon.

Yield: 8 servings.

CRANBERRY AND CARDAMOM MUFFINS

1 3/4 cups sugar
3 1/2 cups flour
1 t. baking powder
1 3/4 t. baking soda
3/4 t. salt
1/2 t. cardamom
1 cup cranberries
4 oz. sweet butter, melted
4 eggs
1 t. vanilla
2 cups sour cream

Preheat oven to 400⁰

In an electric mixer bowl, mix together all dry ingredients.

Add cranberries and mix briefly to coat.

Add the eggs, sour cream, melted butter and vanilla, all at once, mixing only to moisten completely. Do not overmix!

Scoop into well-greased muffin tins, filling 2/3 full.

Bake in preheated oven for 15 to 20 minutes or until golden.

Yield: 18 to 24 muffins.

Note: This is Ann's favorite "basic" muffin recipe: the muffins are light as a feather. Try leaving out the cardamom and cranberries and substituting instead lemon zest and poppyseeds; blueberries and orange zest; or cinnamon, walnuts and raisins.

The decor is elegant, with stained glass windows (as shown here), antiques, good paintings on the walls and fresh flowers on the tables. Also on some of the tables – a copy of "The Shoalwater's Finest Dinners" by owners Tony and Ann Kischner and Cheri Walker. The restaurant opened in '81, a large professional kitchen replaced the old small one in '86, and in '87 "The Heron and Beaver Pub" brought an informal dining alternative and has its own menu. There's an abundance of the area's seafood. Excellent are the Dungeness Crab Cakes, served with red pepper mayonnaise – a prize winner! Local seasonal products are featured, including wild mushrooms, local berries and freshest of seafoods from this area. A good selection of vegetarian and low-fat cuisine is available.

Their home-made soups are very good... desserts to die for.

So many write-ups – it's no secret: Bon Appetit said "some of the best of Northwest cuisine". Wine Spectator gave them the Award of Excellence. Others add: "skillful preparations", "appealing menus" and more. I agree with them all.

Lunch & dinner every day
Brunch Special Occasions

121

ANGELS ON HORSEBACK (SANCTUARY STYLE)

12 fresh oysters, shucked,
  liquor reserved
12 slices Prosciutto ham,
  thinly sliced
melted butter

In a small sauté pan add oysters and their liquor. Lightly poach. Remove oysters and wrap each one in prosciutto ham securing with a tooth pick. Sprinkle with melted butter and broil or bake until ham is nicely browned. Remove toothpicks and serve on artichoke bruschetta. (Recipe follows)

ARTICHOKE BRUSCHETTA

12 toast points
3 garlic cloves
olive oil (good quality)
1 cup artichoke hearts, diced
3 plum tomatoes, diced
1/4 cup Kalamata olives, pitted
  and chopped
1 to 2 T. basil, minced
1 t. balsamic vinegar
2 cloves garlic, minced with
  salt

Rub toast points with garlic and brush with olive oil. Combine remaining ingredients.

Dine with the angels in a 1906 church building. Angel artifacts and a recently added fresco ceiling now adorn the dining room.

In 1979 when Joanne and Geno Leech purchased this Methodist Episcopal church of Chinook, they had planned to remodel it for their home. Plans changed and (lucky for us) the Sanctuary has become a most popular dinner house. Mother and son are the chefs who prepare an eclectic array of tastefully created dishes. Fresh seafood is a specialty. You'll be pleased with other selections of rack of lamb, beef, chicken, pasta and Scandinavian entrées.

Homemade desserts are heavenly.

Wine selections, beer and cocktails.

(Note: thanks to the Sanctuary for sharing their style of "angels on Horseback".) Yesterday I purchased the recipe ingredients. It will be our dinner tonite!

Seasonal hours, call for information & reservations

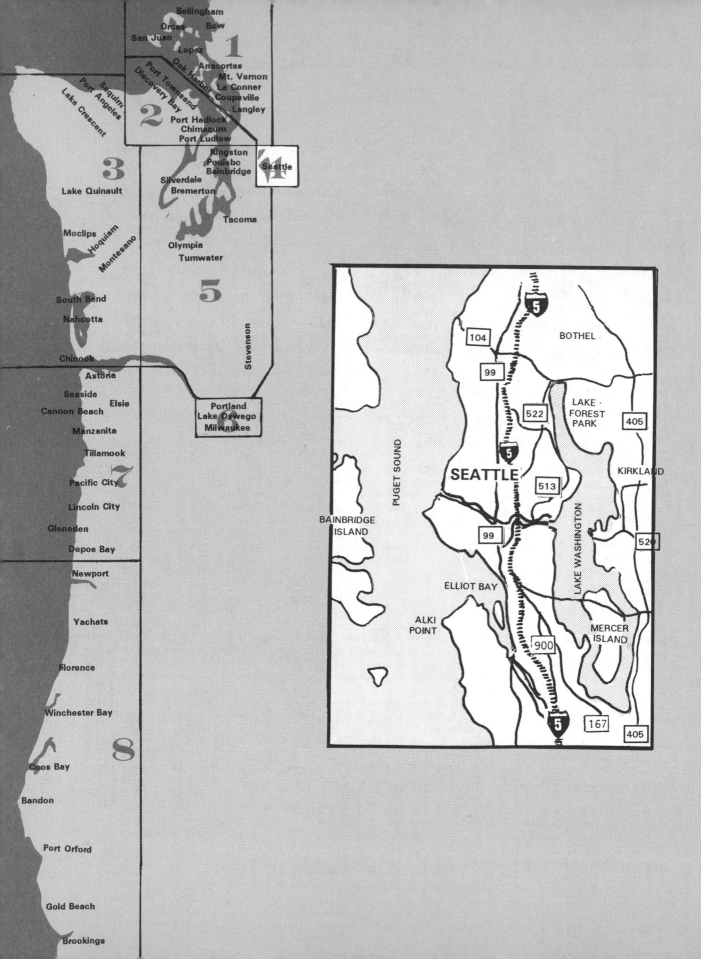

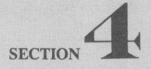 **SECTION** **SEATTLE, WASHINGTON**

The Athenian, Canlis, Chez Shea, The Hunt Club, Maximilien In The Market, The Painted Table, Pink Door Ristorante, Place Pigalle Restaurant and Bar, Ponti, Ray's Boathouse and Cafe, Space Needle Restaurant, Tulio, Waters Bistro

SWEET POTATO TURKEY HASH

2 lbs. sweet potatoes,
  cooked and diced
1 1/2 lb. turkey breast,
  diced
1 cup celery, diced
1 cup onions, diced
2 cloves garlic, minced
2 T. parsley, minced
2 T. cooking oil
1 t. thyme
1 t. marjoram
1/2 t. ground sage
salt and pepper to taste
2 eggs
1 cup flour
1 cup bread crumbs

Preheat oven to 350⁰.
Sauté sweet potatoes, turkey breast, celery, onions, garlic and parsley in the cooking oil. Add thyme, marjoram, sage, salt, pepper, eggs, flour and bread crumbs. Bake for 20 minutes.
Serve with 2 poached eggs on top.

Yield: 6 servings.

SEAFOOD SINIGANG

4 cups water
juice of 1 lemon
1 tomato, diced
1/2 onion, diced
1 oz. fresh ginger, smashed
salt and pepper to taste
1/2 lb. prawns, shelled
1 lb. steamer clams
1 lb. true cod
1/2 lb. mussels
1 bundle fresh spinach,
  washed and trimmed

Bring water, lemon juice, tomato, onion, ginger, salt and pepper to a boil, reduce heat and let simmer.
Add seafood. Cook until clams open.
Add spinach and simmer until tender.

Serve with rice.

Yield: 4 servings.

Scouts for the movie "Sleepless in Seattle" spent 8 months looking for a place with the look of 40 years ago. They chose the Athenian. "Tom Hanks was so nice" said owner Louise Cromwell. She and husband Bob Cromwell came to the Athenian in 1965. They closed for 1 full day's shooting that appeared for 3 minutes in the film. One older customer always eats his dinners here. When he was told of the 1 day's closing, he answered "I know". Louise grinned when she later saw him on the set. He had been hired as an extra. Charles Kuralt included the Athenian for his "On the Road"... also a Friday Night TV movie filmed here; Louise was filmed, but her part landed on the cutting room floor. It was a pleasure talking to her.

Originally opened in 1909 by 3 Greek brothers as a bakery and a luncheonette. The main floor booths are small with straight wooden backs. The bar to the right of this sketch is noisy — the waitress told me upstairs was more quiet. Years ago Urban Renewal closed the Pike Market for 1½ years while everyone was to remodel their businesses, but the Athenian just went on vacation. I remember eating here in the '50's. Now film companies come looking for old Seattle. Here it is!

For breakfast — would you believe <u>5</u> egg omelettes? The menu is huge — heavy with seafood dishes — prices reasonable — portions ample. Only early dinners are served — perfect for pre-theatre diners.

Breakfast, lunch & early dinner Monday - Saturday
Closed Sundays and all Holidays

CHEF'S HAT HALIBUT

1 8 oz. Alaskan halibut filet
3 med. zucchini, seeded and
  julienned
3 medium yellow squash,
  seeded and julienned
1 medium carrot, peeled and
  julienned
1 red bell pepper, sliced thin
1/2 red onion, thinly sliced
1 handful Shitake mushrooms,
  thinly sliced
salt and pepper to taste
lemon juice
butter
parchment paper

Chef Rocky Toguchi

Preheat oven to 400⁰

Mix all vegetables together in a large bowl.

Season the filet of halibut with salt, pepper and lemon juice.

Prepare the parchment bouffer by cutting the piece of parchment paper into a large heart shape and fold it vertically in the center.

Spread two tablespoons of melted butter in the middle of the right side of the paper. Top butter with one handful of mixed vegetables and season lightly with salt and pepper.

Place fillet of halibut on the vegetables and top with another handful of vegetables. Top with 1 T. of butter.

Fold the left side of parchment paper over right to form a 1/2 heart shape. Starting from the top left of the fold, roll the parchment paper in 1/2" around the edge and follow all the way around to seal the bouffer. Turn upside down and bake in oven for 12 to 15 minutes.

Use a knife to cut open the bouffer. Use a triangular spatula and serving spoon to serve halibut, vegetables and juices. Enjoy!

THE CANLIS SALAD

1 or 2 tomatoes, peeled and cut into
  eighths
1 large head romaine lettuce, cut
  into 1" squares
1/2 cup chopped green onion
1 cup freshly grated Romano cheese
1 cup crisp bacon, finely chopped
1/4 t. oregano
2 T. chopped fresh mint
DRESSING:
1/2 t. ground pepper
juice of 1 lemon
1 coddled egg or egg substitute
1/2 cup olive oil
1/3 cup croutons
1/4 cup Romano cheese

Prepare salad.

Put pepper, lemon juice and egg in a bowl, whip vigorously.

Slowly add olive oil, whipping constantly and tasting as you do.

Pour over salad, toss thoroughly.

Add croutons and a sprinkle of Romano last.

This is a special place, from the Japanese treasure house door into this outstanding restaurant, to the 180° view of Lake Union and north Seattle. Canlis is being rebirthed with new energy, new design and new life. In 1950 Peter Canlis opened Seattle's first a la carte fine dining restaurant. In the '80s the original Frank Lloyd Wright-style design was kept, with many interior changes. In 1996 a fall re-opening after $1.5 million remodeling was met with approval. The windows were enlarged and over 1,000 square feet were added for dining.

It would take a page just to list the many recognitions and awards: top service, top view, top overall, best of award of excellence, in the top 250 restaurants in the nation... many more.

Alice Canlis stated "Our objective is to honor the traditions of our past, while creating a look that is refreshing to the eye and compelling to the mind".

Chef Rocky Toguchi began with the Canlis restaurant in Honolulu, then 8 years later, he moved to Seattle and assumed the title of Chef in 1979. He has been turning out some of the finest cuisine in the Pacific Northwest... and hasn't missed a day's

work in 28 years!

Over a dozen chilled or hot appetizers to awaken taste buds are presented with outstanding sauces and herb combinations. Special soups are offered, as well as Canlis chowder.

The Original Canlis recipe is shared with us. The entrées are many...hard to choose just one! Example: chicken-apple sausage, an Ellensburg lamb chop, and tournedos of beef (listed as Mixed Grill).   Desserts are works of art!

Dinner Monday - Saturday

OYSTER STEW WITH LEEKS AND SHERRY

2 dozen extra small oysters,
  fresh or jarred
4 cups milk
2 cups cream
1/4 cup unsalted butter
1/2 cup leek, finely chopped
  (mostly white part)
2 T. dry sherry
salt and freshly ground pepper
2 T. chives, finely chopped

Combine milk and cream in medium saucepan. Shuck or drain oysters, save liquor and add to milk mixture. Heat milk mixture slowly until hot, but below boiling point.

Sauté leeks in 2 T. of the butter until soft. Add oysters and sauté briefly until edges are slightly curled. Splash with sherry and stir to combine. Transfer oyster mixture to milk and add salt and pepper. Cook until oysters are nice and plump, about 3 to 4 minutes.

Transfer oysters to warm serving bowls, ladle liquid over them, dot with remaining butter (in slices). Garnish with chives and Enjoy!

Yield: 4 servings.

ROULADE OF PROSCIUTTO, FIGS, STILTON AND GOAT CHEESES WITH PORT GLAZE

4 fresh figs (or 3 oz. dried black
  figlets, halved)
2 1/2 cups Port
1/3 cup crumbled Stilton cheese
1/3 cup soft fresh goat cheese,
  such as Montrachet, crumbled
3 oz. cream cheese, room temp.
6 oz. prosciutto, thinly sliced
4 fresh figs, quartered (optional)

Soak figs in Port overnight. Blend all cheeses in processor until smooth. Place large sheet of plastic wrap on work surface. Arrange prosciutto slices on plastic wrap, forming an 8 x 10 inch rectangle and overlapping slices slightly. Carefully spread cheese mixture over prosciutto leaving 1/2 inch border on sides. Season with pepper. Drain figs; reserve Port. Finely chop figs. Sprinkle figs over cheese. Roll prosciutto up tightly beginning at one long side, using plastic as aid. Wrap in plastic and refrigerate until firm, about 4 hours. (Can be prepared 1 day ahead.)

Bring reserved Port to boil in heavy small saucepan. Reduce heat and simmer until thick, syrupy and reduced to 1/3 cup, about 15 minutes. Cool to room temperature.

Remove plastic from roulade. Slice roulade crosswise into 18 rounds. Place 3 rounds on each plate. Drizzle rounds lightly with glaze. Garnish with fresh fig quarters.

Yield: 6 servings.

My first thought was "Do I want to climb the stairs to reach Chez Shea? I'm glad that I did! The tranquility of this remarkable place sets the mood for enjoying a great dinner. Leave the hustle and bustle of the market and enjoy... and you will !! Gaze out the high arched windows over the roof tops and across the water of the Sound.

Shea's theory: "If you are walking through the market in the morning, and you see a fresh pheasant, grab it." The spontaneity of using the freshest produce, fish or whatever entices you... Shea takes pleasure in working with the best that is available for that day and creating something special.

For more casual dining... Shea's Lounge features a full bar with a bistro menu, a lighter option.

Chez Shea works magic with lamb and seafood... creative and exciting salads - plus much more.
P.S. I couldn't wait. The oyster stew with leeks (the recipe shared) is a real winner!

Dinner Tuesday - Sunday

HERB MARINATED SALMON CARPACCIO

4 - 3 oz. portions of thinly sliced
   sashimi grade salmon
1 t. salt
black pepper to taste
juice of 2 limes
juice of 1/2 orange
2 T. extra virgin olive oil
2 T. basil chiffonade

4 oz. baby salad greens
toasted bread, preferably sourdough or brioche

Lay the salmon out on chilled plates, sprinkle with salt and pepper. Squeeze the lime and orange juice over the salmon and drizzle with olive oil.
Allow to marinate in the refrigerator for 3 hours. Cut the herbs just before serving and sprinkle liberally on the salmon.
Dress the lettuces with olive oil and a squeeze of lime and season lightly with a little salt and pepper. Serve with toast points.

Yield: 4 servings as an appetizer.

LAVENDER ROASTED LAMB

1 bone-out leg of lamb or 4
   frenched racks of lamb
1/4 cup dried lavender
1/2 cup garlic cloves, crushed
1/2 cup fresh thyme
1/2 cup fresh marjoram
1/2 cup fresh rosemary
1/4 cup virgin olive oil
salt and pepper to taste

Preheat oven to 450^0
Rub the lavender, herbs and crushed garlic into the lamb with the olive oil. Allow to marinate overnight.
Season the lamb well with salt and pepper and sear over medium high flame until deeply browned on all sides. Roast for 10 to 20 minutes. Internal temperature of 125^0 is medium to medium rare.
Allow to rest covered for 5 minutes off the heat.
Carve lamb and serve with Merlot wine.

The Hunt Club restaurant is housed in the Sorrento Hotel that was recently modernized for 1⅓ million dollars.

The ambiance in the Hunt Club: a soft glow of mahogany paneling, candle-type sconce lighting, the brick walls and white table cloths. Two carved lions on pedestals guard the entrance... enter and forget your cares for awhile... enjoy one of the best meals you've ever had. Now listed with 4 ★'s (the very best) in Northwest Best Places as well as raves in several other publications. Chefs Ted Mathesin and Executive Chef Eric Lenard, both with well-earned reputations, have shared the two recipes.

You'll find surprises in the combination of flavors that are sure to please. A favorite here is the Rosemary Rack of Lamb — succulent, very tender. Raves always for their superior treatment of seafood. My selection of salmon could not have been better — a meal to remember!

Then after dinner, the desserts and coffee are served in the lobby.

Or try the afternoon tea that is served with pastries and sandwiches daily in the Fireside Room.

Breakfast & lunch Monday - Friday
Brunch Saturday & Sunday   **Dinner every day**

GREEN TOMATO CHUTNEY

3 lbs. green tomatoes
3 lbs. sugar, (cane, not beet)
I lb. raw peanuts, shelled and
  blanched
2 cups cider vinegar
I cup fresh ginger root,
  chopped (shredded)

Dice green tomatoes into 1/2 inch cubes. Place in a large pot with 1/2 cup water. Boil, stirring to prevent scorching, for 5 minutes. Add sugar and boil, stirring, as for a fruit jam to the "pearl drop" stage.

Meanwhile boil and reduce the vinegar and ginger to 1/3 of its original volume. Let tomato jam rest for 5 minutes, then stir in the peanuts and ginger reduction.

Pour into sterile jam jars. Seal with paraffin or sterile lids or both.

Store on a cool dark shelf.

PAN FRIED GREEN TOMATOES

green tomatoes
1/2 cup olive oil
2 chicken bouillon cubes,
  crushed into powder
3 shallots (medium), peeled and
  chopped
2 cloves of garlic, peeled and
  chopped
1/2 t. sugar
pepper to taste
1/3 cup chopped parsley

Bring in your home grown green tomatoes before the first frost. Two or 3 (1/2") slices per person.

Heat olive oil in a large skillet. Add tomato slices. When slightly brown, turn, season with 1/2 of the bouillon powder. Turn over again and season with remainder of bouillon powder. Simmer for I minute.

Remove tomato slices to broiler plate or oven proof dish. Sprinkle slices with mixture of shallots, garlic, sugar, and pepper. Press down with spatula to coat with juice. Pour remaining pan juices over. Put under broiler for I to 2 minutes until cooked and slightly browned.

Garnish with chopped parsley.

May be used as a garnish for an egg, fish or meat dish.

Yield: 6 servings.

134

This little antique table is an old French butcher's table. Owners François and Julia Kissle have styled this as a French market cafe. Seating looks out over Elliott Bay – beautiful day or night.

"Un restaurant-cafe Français" at Pike Place Market... a real experience in dining.

The menu changes nightly because the chef shops in the Market every day, then plans that night's menu accordingly.

Every morning the brioche is freshly baked. Now <u>here</u> is a special feature... all jams are made here in a 40 quart steam pot the old-fashioned way. Just fresh fruit, sugar and a little lemon juice, then drop-tested to see when it is ready. All year the fresh fruit in season is used: melon, apricot, berry, pineapple.... whatever is available and good. It changes all of the time.

Breakfast, lunch & dinner Monday - Saturday   Brunch Sunday

135

LAYERED GOAT CHEESE AND VEGETABLE SALAD WITH GRILLED EGGPLANT, OVENDRIED TOMATO AND ONION CONFIT

2 medium Walla Walla onions	I bunch basil	2 oz. baby lettuces
I medium eggplant	I cup balsamic vinegar	12 oz. goat cheese
2 vineripe tomatoes	I cup olive oil (chilled)	2 T. lemon juice
	3 sprigs of thyme, chopped	I T. white pepper corns, ground

Basil Oil: Pick basil leaves and blanch for 10 seconds in boiling salted water, then shock in an ice bath. Drip dry the basil leaves and purée in a blender with 3/4 cup of olive oil. Pour purée into a glass and allow to infuse for 30 minutes. Strain purée through some cheese cloth and reserve the basil oil.

Balsamic Syrup: Reduce all but I T. of balsamic vinegar in a sauce pan until it coats on spoon. Reserve.

Vegetables: Peel and carve the onions, halve them and slice lengthwise. Sauté the onions in olive oil caramelizing slightly. Add 1/2 of the chopped thyme, salt and ground white pepper. Cook over low heat for approximately 15 minutes until soft. Next cut the tomatoes into 1/2 slices. Season with salt and ground pepper and rest of the chopped thyme. Lay the tomato slices out onto a well oiled sheet tray and dry them in a 300⁰ oven for 40 minutes, turning frequently. Finally cut the eggplant into 1/2" slices and season with salt and ground pepper, oil slightly and grill on both sides until tender.

Wash baby lettuces and toss with the lemon juice and remaining olive oil and ground pepper.

In a ring mold 2 1/2 inches wide and 2 to 3 inches high layer the onions, then tomato, then eggplant, then goat cheese, repeat once more. Invert onto serving plate. Toss the baby greens in the remaining olive oil and balsamic syrup and place the lettuce on plate. Drizzle basil oil and balsamic syrup around the plate.

PAN SEARED SCALLOPS WITH BRAISED ENDIVE, TOMATO CHUTNEY AND CURRY OIL

CHUTNEY	CURRY OIL	ENDIVE
1/2 cup champagne vinegar	1/2 cup grape seed oil	2 endives, halved
I T. mustard seeds	2 T. madras curry powder	I lemon
4 whole cloves	1/4 cup onion, chopped	2 sprigs thyme
I stick cinnamon	2 cloves garlic, smashed	I T. sugar
1/2 t. nutmeg, grated	**COUS COUS**	2 T. butter
I T. brown sugar	I box cous cous	**MISC.**
I med. red onion, big dice	1/4 cup currants	I 1/2 lbs. sea scallops
I lb. vineripe tomatoes	1/8 cup sliced almonds	I bunch watercress

Chutney: In a sauce pan sauté onions, add tomatoes and the rest of the ingredients and salt and pepper. Simmer 10 minutes.

Endive: Preheat oven to 350⁰. In a baking pan lay the endive flat side down. Sprinkle with sugar, lemon juice, salt and white pepper. Top with butter. Add enough water to almost cover the endive. Cover with foil, and bake for 30 minutes or until tender. Cool in broth.

Curry Oil: Sauté onions and garlic in butter, add curry then grape seed oil. Simmer 5 minutes. Place the mixture in a jar and shake it a few times. Rest uncovered for I day then strain. Reserve the oil.

Prepare cous cous according to package directions.

Heat endive in its own liquid, heat chutney in a sauce pan. Season and sear the scallops in oil. Heat and plate the cous cous. Fan the endive on its side. Spoon some of the chutney by the endive. Place the scallops around the plate. Garnish with watercress.

Yield: 4 servings.

Each time I dine here the art presentation is new, huge and often spreading 30' to 50' across a wall in the dining room.

The Seattle Post-Intelligencer last year wrote of The Painted Table: "If it's fresh, seasonal and fashionable, it's likely to appear on the menu of this witty, art-oriented restaurant, whose kitchen is directed by a New York import, Tim Kelley.

Splashy fun ceramic plates created especially for The Painted Table are on the tables, but not used for the meals. The plates may be purchased.

Let me tell you about a few of the inspired presentations. The local green garden salad uses Duffield Farm edible flowers, Asian pears and honey glazed walnuts. The Peruvian shrimp cocktail includes cucumber, Boniato and mint salad, toasted peanuts and Feta cheese.

One entrée is pan roasted Oregon rabbit with preserved lemon, broccoli rabe, herbed gnocchi, baby carrots and mustard glaze.

Another entrée is lemon pepper tagliatelle pasta with roasted fennel, grilled Shitake, mussels and clams. Another treat is the Ellensburg lamb chops with sun dried tomato ravioli, grilled Japanese eggplant, braised celery, smoked tomato broth with celery oil. What I say is "expect the unexpected — and enjoy"!

Breakfast & dinner every day
(Holiday hours may vary)

Lunch Monday - Friday

♿

137

RISOTTO SFORZESCO con GAMBERI ORANGE and SAGE RISOTTO with SHRIMP

4 T. olive oil
1/2 cup onion, chopped medium
4 cups shrimp stock or water
1 cup white wine
1 1/2 cups Italian rice (Arborio)
zest and juice of 1 orange

1/4 cup fresh sage, chopped into strips
salt and pepper to taste
1 lb large prawns (5 per serving)
2 t. olive oil
1 t. garlic, chopped
1/4 cup white wine

Cut the sage into thin strips (julienne), combine with the zest. Set aside.
In a large heavy bottomed sauce pan sauté the onion with the olive oil. Cook over moderate heat until onions become translucent, about 3 minutes. Do not allow onions to brown. Add the rice to the pot, stirring until the rice is well coated with the oil and onions. Add the wine and stir well. Begin to incorporate the stock or water 1 cup at a time, stirring until it is absorbed. Add more liquid, keeping rice covered with liquid. Continue stirring and adding liquid until the liquid is gone, (about 15 to 18 minutes) and a creamy consistency is achieved. Stir in the sage and zest. During the last few minutes of the rice cooking, heat up a sauté pan large enough to contain all the prawns. Sauté the prawns in olive oil and garlic for about 3 to 5 minutes. Deglaze pan with wine and season with salt and pepper to taste.
Remove prawns from the sauté pan and incorporate the remaining juice into the rice.
Serve risotto in a large shallow bowl, placing the prawns over the rice. Garnish with sage leaves.
Yield: 4 servings.

LINGUINI with CLAM SAUCE

2 T. butter
1 1/2 T. all-purpose flour
2 T. olive oil
2 to 3 cloves garlic, minced
2 oz. white wine
1/2 t. oregano
red chili flakes to taste
1 4 oz. can baby clams
1 4 oz. can chopped clams
salt and white pepper to taste
1 lb. linguini, fresh or dry

Yield: 6 servings.

In a small saucepan over moderate heat melt the butter and stir in the flour to make a roux. Stir the mixture achieving a golden paste. Set aside.
In a 2 quart sauce pan over moderate heat sauté the garlic with the olive oil. When garlic has been cooking for a short time (be careful not to burn), add the wine, chopped and baby clams. When the clam mixture has come to a boil add small portions of the roux stirring continuously to avoid lumps in sauce. Allow the sauce to simmer for 6 to 8 minutes. Add the oregano and chili flakes and allow the sauce to simmer for a few more minutes. Check the seasoning and add salt and pepper to taste. Keep sauce warm and set aside.
In a large pot bring 6 quarts of salted water to a boil. Cook pasta to desired doneness. (2 to 3 minutes for fresh and 10 to 12 minutes for dry).
Drain pasta and return to the pot. Pour over the clam sauce. Combine well and serve.

Ever-surprising, ever-entertaining, the Pink Door offers the tastes of Italia coupled with live cabaret and ever-present life-on-parade ambience.

The Pink Door is well-named because there are no signs... just look for the pink door. Hidden behind this door lies a romantic hideaway similar to those found in Europe. Breezy service and a menu seasoned with impish wit serve to sooth the soul.

An unusual delicious vegetarian Antipasti is their Eggplant Rolls: grilled eggplant roll stuffed with fresh Mozzarella and basil... napped with roasted red pepper sauce. Luscious! A lasagna named for the Pink Door is fresh spinach pasta layered with bechemel, pesto and topped with a marinara sauce. An organic enterprise brings local produce within 24 hours of harvesting.

The Pink Door menu states "It is our wish that the vitality, flavor and freshness of our combined efforts will result in a memorable meal for all of you."

Lunch & dinner Tuesday - Saturday

STEAMED MUSSELS PIGALLE

6 strips smoked bacon, finely diced
2 stalks celery, finely diced
1 oz. shallots, chopped
1 T. parsley, chopped
1/2 t. celery seeds

1 T. Dijon mustard
8 oz. balsamic vinegar
12 oz. olive, soy or peanut oil
2 lbs. mussels, bearded
8 oz. dry white wine

Heat skillet to medium-high heat. Add bacon and brown lightly. Pour off fat. Reduce temperature to medium and add celery. Sauté until it sweats, but remains crispy.

Place shallots, parsley, celery seeds, mustard and 4 oz. balsamic vinegar in a food processor or blender and process until the parsley is finely chopped. Slowly add the oil to form an emulsified vinaigrette.

Add the bacon and celery mixture, the wine and the mussels to a sauté pan and boil covered over high heat until the mussels just begin to open. As the mussels open, remove them from the pan. Reduce the remaining liquid until nearly dry. Add the last 4 oz. balsamic vinegar until nearly dry.

While the liquid is reducing, arrange the mussels in four shallow bowls with hinge side down and the openings facing skyward.

Add the vinaigrette to the reduced liquid and warm through. Care should be taken to avoid boiling as this will "break" the vinaigrette. Pour the warm sauce evenly over the mussels. Sauce should flow into the open mussels. Serve immediately.

Yield: 4 servings.

PLACE PIGALLE'S BRANDIED APRICOT ALMOND TORTE

PASTRY
1 2/3 cups all-purpose
    flour
2 T. sugar
1/4 lb. butter
1 egg yolk
5 T. water

FILLING
2 cups dried apricots,
    chopped
1/3 cup brandy
2 cups sliced almonds
1/2 cup sugar
3/4 cup melted butter
4 eggs, whole

Yield: 12 servings.

Preheat oven to 350⁰.

Pastry: Mix flour and sugar. Cut in one T. butter at a time until mixture is crumbly. Beat egg yolk into water then mix with other ingredients until dough forms a ball. Do not overwork the dough. Press into a 9" springform pan covering the bottom and 3/4 of the way up the sides. Dough should be slightly thinner on the bottom than on the sides.

Filling: Chop the apricots into 1/4" dice and soak with the brandy in a small bowl. Set aside.

Mix almonds, sugar, melted butter and excess brandy drained from the apricots. Thoroughly mix in one egg at a time until even. Sprinkle the chopped apricots into the bottom of the springform, then pour the batter over the apricots.

Bake for approx. 1 hour or until the almonds on top are nicely browned.

Serve with a small pitcher of heavy cream.

As you enter Place Pigalle you first see into the kitchen and this wonderful pile of fresh vegetables .... how refreshing!

Of course the outstanding view is of Elliott Bay with ferries, pleasure boats and huge container ships... a continuous parade just outside. The evening we planned to attend a musical at the Fifth Avenue Theatre, we had an early dinner here. I ordered the seafood in Tamarind broth. Sautéed mussels, prawns, calamari, scallops, oysters and fin fish in

a sauce so good that I sopped it all up with the fresh rolls. Good to the last drop!

The warm asparagus salad made a good starter. It's served with Shitake mushrooms and a red miso vinaigrette. Place Pigalle specializes in seasonal menus combining local ingredients with a variety of culinary traditions. The resulting dishes are artful and fresh.

A sunny patio opens in the summer. When I mentioned to friends that this restaurant would be in my book. They nodded, smiled and said "good".

So have many, including awards from Zagat magazine, North west Best Places, Gourmet magazine, and more!

Lunch & dinner Monday - Saturday

PONTI SEAFOOD GRILL'S PEACH PIE

2 1/2 lbs. peaches, peeled, pitted
    and sliced
1/3 cup all-purpose flour
1/2 cup granulated sugar
1/2 t. cinnamon
1/4 t. nutmeg
1/8 t. ground ginger
grated peel and juice of 1 lime
3 T. butter, cut into pieces

CRUST:

2 1/2 cups all-purpose flour
1 1/2 T. sugar
1 t. salt
1 cup cold butter, cut into
    pieces

TOPPING:

2 t. milk
2 T. brown sugar
1 t. flour
1/4 t. cinnamon

PONTI THAI CURRY PENNE

TOMATO CHUTNEY:

1/2 cup rice vinegar
1 t. grated ginger
1/4 cup brown sugar
2 t. lemon juice
1 (16 oz.) can pear tomatoes,
    drained and chopped
1 stick of cinnamon

CURRY:

1 T. butter
1 t. chopped garlic
1/4 cup diced onion
1 large Granny Smith apple,
    cored and diced
2 t. curry powder
salt and pepper to taste
1 cup Marsala
1 cup chicken broth
3 t. Thai red-curry paste
2 t. Thai fish sauce
1 cup coconut milk
1 cup whipping cream
1/2 lb. penne pasta, cooked
1/4 lb. crabmeat
chopped fresh basil

Preheat oven to 400°.

Filling: Put the peaches in a bowl and toss with flour, sugar, cinnamon, nutmeg, ginger, lime peel and juice. Set aside while preparing the crust.

Crust: Put flour, sugar and salt in a food processor. Add pieces of butter and process a few seconds to attain a coarse texture only. With the processor running, add only enough ice water through the feed tube so that the dough holds together. Roll out crust to 1/8" thickness and allow crust to overhang on a 9" pie pan by about 4 inches.

Place the filling into the pastry-lined pan and dot with 3 T. butter. Fold crust overhand up over the fruit, gather into the center and twist in a decorative bun.

Topping: Brush crust with milk. Combine the brown sugar, flour and cinnamon. Sprinkle over the top of the pie. Place on a baking sheet and bake for 30 minutes. Turn heat to 350° and continue baking 20 minutes more.

Serve warm with a scoop of vanilla ice cream.

Yield: One 9" pie.

Chutney: Combine vinegar, ginger, brown sugar and lemon juice. Simmer 5 minutes. Add tomatoes and cinnamon and simmer 30 additional minutes. Remove from heat and set aside.

Curry: In a large saucepan combine the butter, garlic, onion, apple, curry, salt and pepper. Sauté over high heat until the onions are soft.

Add the Marsala to the apple-onion mixture and reduce by half. Add chicken broth, curry paste and fish sauce; simmer 10 minutes. Let cool and blend to a purée in a food processor or blender.

Transfer mixture back to the saucepan and add the coconut milk and cream. Cook until thickened, about 10 to 15 minutes.

Drain the pasta and combine with the crabmeat and sauce. Divide between two plates and top with the tomato chutney and fresh basil.

Note: There is enough sauce for 3/4 to 1 lb. of pasta.

I really should have a chapter, not just 1 page, to describe Ponti.

"Ponti" means bridge in Italian, but this isn't an Italian restaurant. From the 1st planning, owners Richard Malia and Jim Malevitis decided to recreate the beauty of European canal-side restaurants. In the mid-80's they picked up the option to buy an old wrought-iron works on the south shore of Lake Washington ship canal. Construction began in '89 and Ponti's Seafood Grill opened in 1990.

There is a good view of 2 bridges, but "bridge" refers also to the intention of the kitchen to bridge different foods and styles of cooking.... combining diverse elements of food and cultural influences, especially Asian, but shows influences from several continents. The eclectic menu has evolved from chef Alvin Binuya's creative approach.

From the moment you arrive, the mood is set. Architecturally reminiscent of a Mediterranean villa and tiled courtyard, then into an inviting entry, with many dining rooms, high ceilings, airy. In April over 10,000 tulips are in bloom. Dining on the large deck is very popular in the summer months. While I had lunch, I watched a tug boat, a rowing team, several small boats go by. Then the bridge was raised for a very large sail boat.

From the conception, the artistic approach was important, too. The building plans, the layout, the way the rooms flow one to another, the extensive art on display, the menu design, the food presentation! Many awards. John Hinterberger gave Ponti's 3½★, out of a scale of 4.

Lunch Monday - Friday   **Dinner every day**
Brunch Sunday

143

THAI MUSSELS

2 cups coconut milk
1 1/2 T. red curry paste
juice of 1 lime
1 t. Thai fish sauce
1 cup Sake
2 t. minced garlic
2 t. minced ginger
2 T. chopped basil
1 lb Penn Cove mussels,
   cleaned and debearded

Mix above ingredients together with a wire whip. Put mussels in heavy sauce pan and add enough broth to cover bottom of pan. Cover and steam until mussels open.
"Happy Cooking!"

Executive Chef Charles Ramseyer

BLACK COD SAKE KASU

2 to 2 1/2 lbs black cod
   fillet, skin on, bones
   removed, cut into 4
   serving pieces
1/2 cup kosher or table salt,
   more if needed

6 oz. (3/4 cup) kasu paste*
1/3 cup sugar
3/4 cup water

fresh ginger, thinly sliced
   and blanched, or pickled

*available at Asian markets

Set black cod pieces skin side down in a shallow dish. Sprinkle a generous layer of salt over the fish, cover with plastic wrap and refrigerate for 24 hours.
Rinse salt from the fish and pat dry, return to the cleaned dish.
Stir together the kasu paste and sugar in a small bowl until smooth. Slowly stir in the water. Pour the kasu mixture evenly over the fish, cover and refrigerate for another 24 hours.
Turn on grill or light coals. When grill is very hot, remove black cod from the marinade, allowing excess to drip off. Grill fish until nicely browned and just cooked through, about 5 minutes per side. Transfer to individual plates, top with fresh or pickled ginger, and serve.

In 1939 there was a boat rental business with over 300 boats on this site. 7 years later a coffee shop opened here and was the 1st eatery at Shilshole. For about 13 years many different owners tried, but left. In 1973 a group of local business people jumped in, totally refurbishing the building. Word soon spread, and this was a popular spot, until at the height of Ray's Boathouse popularity, it burned to the ground. In only 5 months, the new building was begun with the new Boathouse opening April '88.

There are now fire sprinklers – even under the rebuilt pier.

It has become a Seattle landmark restaurant. Ray's is an upscale Northwest establishment.

Ray's Boathouse is the formal dining room for dinner located on entry level. Ray's Cafe is a casual comfortable cafe located upstairs (shown in this sketch). Both dining rooms seat 300 and 75 on the outdoor deck.... great views from all of these locations, overlooking Puget Sound and the Olympic mountains. The full bar shares these views, too.

I was pleased to learn of the extent of recycling going on here: paper, cardboard, cans, glass, grease, plastic, and a composting bin for organic food waste. A trend setter and a first for the Seattle restaurant industry.

Their reputation is known far and wide; the food, the service, and the setting are at the top of the charts!

Lunch & dinner every day

SPACE NEEDLE APPLE PIE
TOPPING
1 1/2 cups brown sugar
1 1/2 cups all-purpose flour
1 1/2 cups walnuts, chopped
   coarse
1 cup unsalted butter, room
   temperature

FILLING
1 pre-made 8" pie crust
2 Granny Smith apples
2 Red Rome apples
1/4 cup all-purpose flour
1/2 cup granulated sugar
1 t. cinnamon, ground
1/8 t. nutmeg, ground
1/8 cup lemon juice
1/2 t. vanilla extract

Preheat oven to 275⁰.
Soften butter in mixer at low speed for 3 minutes. In a separate container, mix all dry ingredients well. Gently mix all dry ingredients into the softened butter. Set aside

Peel apples, core, and slice 1/4" thick. Add the vanilla extract and lemon juice to the apples and toss well In a separate container mix all dry ingredients well. Add dry ingredients to the apple mixture and toss well. Place the pie filling into the pie crust and cover with the pie topping. Bake for 1 hour.

Presentation:
Cut the apple pie into sixths. Warm in an oven at 200⁰ for approximately 10 minutes. Remove a slice of pie and place on plate. Drizzle the apple cinnamon caramel glaze (see recipe below) liberally over the top. Garnish with dried cranberries and fresh mint.

APPLE CINNAMON CARAMEL SAUCE
4 cups apple juice
1 oz. (1/4 cup) dried apples,
   minced
1 1/2 cups unsalted butter
ground cinnamon to taste
   (approximately 2 pinches)

In a stainless steel saucepan combine the apple juice and minced dried apples. Cook the mixture on high heat until it is the consistency of a light syrup. It should take approximately 20 minutes.
Remove the pan from the heat and slowly add the unsalted butter. It is best to add the butter in small amounts while gradually stirring. Repeat this procedure until all the butter has been incorporated into the mixture.
Add the cinnamon to taste.

Note: This mixture is very sensitive to heat. Avoid exposing to excessively cold or hot temperatures.

What does every movie, video, story, tourist brochure or calendar about Seattle always include? The Space Needle.

Since 1962, guests dining in one of the Space Needle's restaurants have delighted in the 360° panoramic views of Puget Sound, the Olympic and Cascade mountain ranges, Lake Union, downtown Seattle, Mount Rainier and the waterfront. Guests may dine in the informal main dining area which seats 200 or in the upscale Emerald Suite with seating for up to 50.

Executive Chef Damon LeMaster offers a menu of simple elegance featuring fresh Northwest seafood, local vegetables, fine-aged meats, homemade soups and specially created desserts. The famous signature dessert is the "Lunar Orbiter" which arrives dramatically in a "fog" of dry ice!

For those dining in either restaurant there is no charge for the elevator with admission free to the Needle's Observation Deck. For those not dining, there is a charge.

According to "Restaurants and Institutions" magazine, the Space Needle Restaurant is one of the "top 20 most popular restaurants in the United States".

The rotation is so slow and smooth that passing each of the window frames tells you that you are moving. Between windows a sign states what view you are seeing at that time.

Breakfast, lunch & dinner Monday - Saturday
Brunch & dinner Sunday

♿

COD BRAISED IN PUTTANESCA SAUCE AND CELERY ROOT PURÉE

4 6 oz. portions ling cod	4 cups nage (vegetable stock)
3 fresh red tomatoes, peeled and seeded (retain skin)	8 t. virgin olive oil
	1/8 t. fresh thyme, minced
3 fresh yellow tomatoes, peeled and seeded	1/8 T. fresh rosemary, minced
	1/2 white onion, minced
8 garlic cloves, sliced into thin slivers	4 celery root, peeled
	1/2 cup milk
3 anchovies	3 T. unsalted butter
2 t. capers	1/8 T. salt, black pepper
2 t. Kalamata olives, minced	I T. crushed red chili pepper

Puttanesca sauce: In a sauce pot on medium heat, place 2 T. olive oil. Add anchovies, when anchovies have dissolved, add chili pepper. Sauté the minced onions until soft (don't burn). Add capers and sauté for 1 minute, add red tomato only, sauté for another 2 minutes, add nage, bring to a simmer and let cook under a low heat for 20 minutes. Pass sauce through a food mill and set aside.

Garlic chips: In a sauce pan place 2 T. of olive oil and heat slowly. When oil is hot, just before it smokes, place garlic chips in oil and turn the flame off. Keep a close eye on the garlic and when it starts to brown, remove with a fork and place on a paper towel to drain well. Set aside for garnish.

Celery root purée: In a sauce pot with slightly salted boiling water, place peeled celery root making sure that the vegetable is completely submerged in the water. Turn flame down to a rolling boil for approx. 40 minutes or until celery root is completely soft, drain water well and pass each celery root through a potato ricer into a pot of warm milk and softened butter. When incorporated well, season with salt and pepper and keep warm.

Preheat oven to 375⁰
Braised cod: Season the individual fillets with salt and pepper. Have yellow tomato, olive, thyme and rosemary, tomato sauce and nage ready to assemble the dish. In a medium 3" tall saucepan, heat oil to just before smoking. Place cod in pan belly side down, skin side up. Turn flame to avoid burning. When cod has a nice golden brown color, turn the fish over and discard remaining oil from pan. Add tomatoes, olives, nage, thyme and rosemary, place in oven for approximately 12 minutes. Remove from oven and add your tomato sauce. Cook on the stove for about 15 seconds. Place warm celery root purée in a pastry bag with a star tip.

Presentation: On a warm platter with at least a 2 inch lip, place cod on the center of the dish. Pour warm sauce over the fish and around the platter. If the sauce mixture is too thick, you may need to thin with a little nage before you pour onto the plate. Pipe little stars of celery root purée around the fish, then garnish with crispy garlic chips and serve.

An early arrival for lunch assured me a place at a small counter facing the area by the wood-burning ovens, so I could do my sketch.

The Antipastis were my choices: 1st, Salt cod Baccala, potato and garlic spread, formed into small patties and fried in butter. 2nd, Fried Mozzarella, grilled eggplant and tomatoes with Balsamic vinaigrette. 3rd, Sweet Potato Gnocchi with browned butter, Chateau Dumas local Mascarpone and sage. I complimented the chef on all 3 (he had OK'd my receiving smaller portions). Each arrived like a work of art!

Talking briefly to executive chef Walter Pisano, I learned a little of his extensive background, including classical training in European cuisine, a culinary learning tour of Europe, then returning as an executive chef in the Northwest. Following his meeting Jean-Louis Palladin, he worked 1 year at the prestigious Watergate Restaurant in Washington, D.C. Walter Pisano returned to Seattle to open Tulio in the Fall of 1992. His rustic, yet refined cuisine was an instant favorite ... always a crowd. Near the entrance, an iron spiral staircase leads to an upper dining area, Solaio, a cozy semi-private room.

Breakfast, lunch & dinner every day

CHICKEN POTSTICKERS
FILLING
1/2 lb. chicken breast, ground
1/4 cup green onions, sliced 1/8"
1/8 cup carrot, diced 1/8"
1/8 cup celery, diced 1/8"
1/2 T. ginger, minced
1/2 t. garlic, minced
1/4 cup Shitakes, minced 1/8"
1 T. soy sauce
1 T. Aji Mirin rice wine
1/4 t. red chili flakes
1/2 T. cilantro, minced
1/2 egg white
1/2 t. cornstarch

24 pieces Shui Mai skins
1/2 T. vegetable oil

Combine filling ingredients in a stainless steel bowl. (Be sure to combine cornstarch with egg white before adding.) Beat together until well mixed.

Place Shui Mai skins on dry work area, brush edges lightly with water. Place a rounded tablespoon of filling on each skin. Fold in half to form half moons and pinch together tightly.
Oil perforated pan and lay dumplings in as you complete them. When all are folded, place pan in steamer and steam 7 minutes until cooked through. Refrigerate any leftovers.

To reheat, simmer in clarified butter until golden brown. Turn, continue to simmer, add 1/8 cup water and cover to steam.

GINGER SAKE GLAZE
1 t. vegetable oil
1 1/2 T. ginger, minced
1 t. garlic, minced
1 t. sugar
2 2/3 T. soy sauce
2/3 cup Sake
2 2/3 T. Aji Mirin rice wine
2/3 t. arrowroot
1 t. water

Heat vegetable oil in saucepan. Add garlic and ginger and sauté until golden brown.
Add sugar, soy sauce, Sake and rice wine and bring to a boil.
Dissolve arrowroot in water. Add arrowroot mixture to sauce, whisking well to incorporate. Bring back to a boil, boil 1 minute. Remove from heat and cool.

ROASTED PEPPER CORN RELISH
2 Anaheim peppers
1 red bell pepper
1/4 lb. corn kernels, fresh or frozen
1 2/3 T. olive oil
4 3/4 oz. white onion, diced 1/4"
1/8 T. lemon zest, minced
1 1/4 T. basil, finely chopped

1/3 T. bacon fat
2/3 T. roasted garlic, mashed
2 T. lemon juice
1 t. salt
1/4 t. pepper
1 1/3 T. olive oil

Preheat convection oven to 500⁰.
Deep fry peppers until skin lightly blisters. Peel and seed. Dice peppers 1/4".
Toss corn and onion with olive oil. Spread in thin layer on sheet pan. Roast for about 4 minutes or until lightly roasted.
When cool, toss all ingredients together.

I had never ordered meat loaf at a restaurant, but on a whim I decided to try it, later finding that it is a signature item and one of the most popular. Excellent! Especially noteworthy was the gravy being served in a piping hot small pitcher that allowed me to choose how much or how little to use. The meatloaf was in its own baking pan.... absolutely the best I've ever eaten! Garlic mashed potatoes and seasonal vegetables are included.

As shown in the sketch, the Waters, a lakeside bistro, is located inside the Woodmark Hotel which is the only hotel on Lake Washington. The waterfront promenade walk is directly outside, a 1½ mile path along the waterfront passes through several parks and ends in downtown Kirkland. 7 miles east of Seattle and located in Carillon Point.

Besides the Waters Bistro, a lounge area "The Library Room" featuring afternoon tea service, espresso, cocktails, hors d'oeuvres and evening entertainment is very popular. The European custom of taking mid-afternoon respites between rounds of shopping, appointments, etc. is a daily event here between 2 and 4 p.m. Reservations are appreciated, since this is like High Tea, with much included: fruit scones, salads, date nut breads, raspberry mousse in a chocolate tulip cup, petit fours, lemon bars, etc. with a pot of tea.

Breakfast & lunch every day   Dinner Tuesday - Saturday   ♿

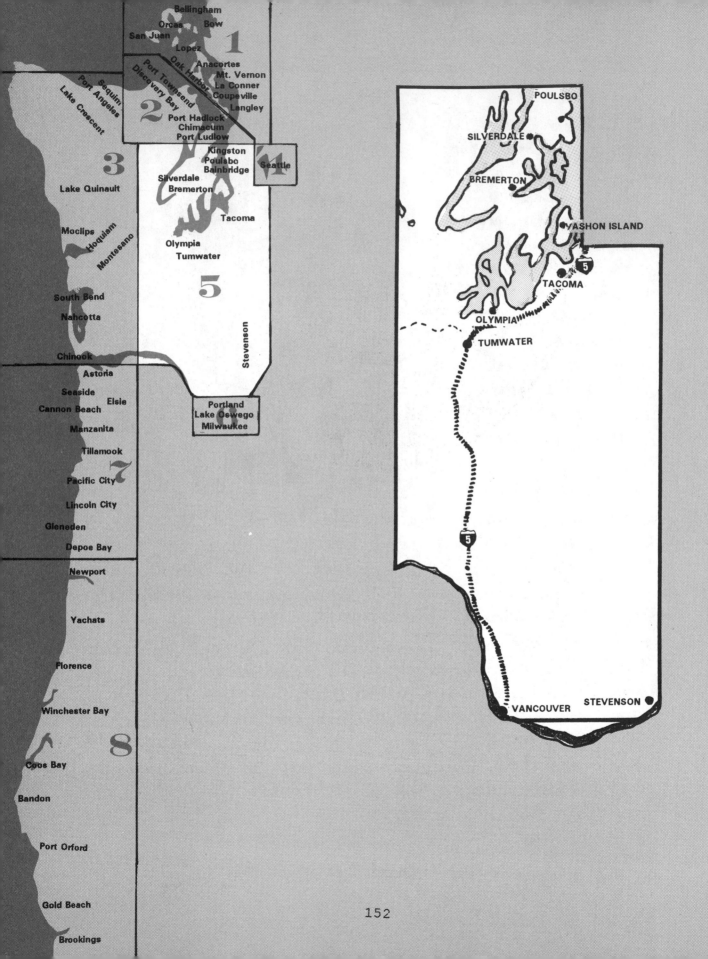

SECTION **5** WASHINGTON

KINGSTON: Old Kingston Hotel
POULSBO: Molly Ward's Garden
BAINBRIDGE ISLAND: The Madrona, Streamliner Diner
SILVERDALE: The Mariner
BREMERTON: The Boat Shed, Pat's Restaurant and Bakery
TACOMA: The Antique Sandwich Company, Bimbo's Italian
               Restaurant, Katie Downs, Luciano's Ristorante, Stanley
               and Seafort's
TUMWATER: Falls Terrace
OLYMPIA: Budd Bay Cafe, Capitale, Fifth Avenue Bistro, Genoa On
               The Bay, Henry C's
STEVENSON: Skamania Lodge

SPICY ANCHO CHILE-FRESH MOZZARELLA TAMALES

18 corn husks
1 1/2 cups butter
1 1/2 t. salt
1 1/2 t. baking powder
3/4 cup milk
3/4 cup whole kernel corn
1 1/2 cups Masa Harina
4 ancho chiles, soaked,
  seeded and puréed
2 cups Parmesan cheese,
  grated
1 lb. fresh Mozzarella, sliced

Soak corn husks in hot water to soften, while preparing the dough.

In a medium-sized bowl, beat the butter, salt and baking powder until light in color and almost doubled in size. Set aside. In a food processor, blend the milk and corn until it looks like pulp. In another medium sized bowl, stir the milk and corn mixture into the Masa until fully incorporated. Continue beating the butter mixture, while adding the Masa to the butter until it is fully incorporated. Stir in the ancho chile purée and grated Parmesan.

Divide the dough evenly among 15 of the corn husks. Flatten the dough and place a slice of fresh Mozzarella in each tamale, wrapping the husk around the dough. Tear the other 3 corn husks into long strips to tie each end of the tamales. In a steamer, cook for 10 to 12 minutes, covered, until they expand or begin to ooze out of their wrapper a little bit. Serve immediately with Two Squash and Parsley Salsa.

Yield: 15 tamales, using 1/4 cup scoop of dough.

TWO SQUASH AND PARSLEY SALSA

1 cup zucchini, minced
1 cup crookneck squash,
  minced
1 cup parsley, minced
2 limes, zested and juiced
1 cup sweet red or green
  peppers, minced
1 cup green onion, minced
1 cup cilantro, rough chopped
3 T. fresh oregano, minced
1/2 t. salt
3 T. sugar
pinch of cayenne or
1 T. jalapeño, minced

Mix all ingredients together. Serve immediately after making.

This salsa makes a good garnish for bean soups, rice dishes, fish or chicken. It is also very pretty.

In 1991 when Judith Weinstock told me she was thinking of opening a restaurant in the Old Kingston Hotel, I knew she'd have a top place... her reputation at the Streamliner Diner was excellent. She took 2 years off between '91 and '93. When I arrived here in June '96, I was pleased with the results.... a lovely garden was created by the Heronswood Nursery. The trellises, benches, wood work were created by David Weinstock.

This day was warm and sunny, and after wandering upstairs, downstairs and in the garden, I chose to have my lunch outside and sketch the garden.

The deck upstairs overlooks the water and the ferries. The rooms are good for birthday celebrations, rehearsal dinners, or small groups .... an intimate setting.

The emphasis is on seafood, vegetables, organic foods. They grow some of their own herbs, and buy lots from nearby farms.

There are daily specials for breakfast, lunch and dinner.

The dessert display is near the front door. I couldn't resist!

Breakfast, lunch & dinner every day Summer
Breakfast, lunch & dinner Tuesday - Sunday off season

155

SPAGHETTI SQUASH with HERBS

3 lb. spaghetti squash,
   approximately
1/2 cup walnut halves
1/2 lb. imported Gorgonzola
   (or domestic)
1 can chicken stock
salt and pepper
Italian parsley sprigs
butter
cream
1 or 2 Bartlett pears

To cook squash: Microwave 5 to 6 minutes per pound turning over after three minutes, or boil 20 minutes or until soft to the touch. Squash is overcooked when it cracks open, so check regularly. Set aside.

Preheat oven to 375⁰.

Lay walnut halves on baking sheet and put in oven for 3 to 4 minutes or until golden. Set aside.

Melt 1 T. of butter on low heat in a sauce pan. Crumble Gorgonzola into pan and add 1/2 cup of chicken stock. Add salt and pepper to taste. Let sauce cook to thicken. Stir. As the sauce reduces, splash cream to keep from burning the cheese.

Keeping an eye on the sauce, slice open the squash lengthwise. Carefully scrape seeds out. With a fork twist into the flesh and pile innards into a bowl. Remember to check sauce ... does it need a splash of cream?

Set out 4 plates and take the sauce and pool evenly onto the bottom of each plate. Crush walnuts in your hand and sprinkle onto sauced plate. Evenly divide the squash into four portions. Mound onto center of plate. Slice pears into thin slices and circle them around the mound. (7 slices per plate.) Garnish with Italian parsley sprigs.

EARLY SPRING SALAD
ORANGE VINAIGRETTE

1/4 cup fresh squeezed
   orange juice
1/4 cup rice wine vinegar
3/8 cup olive oil
splash of quality soy sauce

Mix ingredients in a squirt
   bottle or other dressing
   bottle.

It is truly the dressing that makes this salad the most popular item on our menu.

Gather and clean several heads of spring greens (preferably organic). Either cut the leaves into smaller pieces or leave large for artistic design. Using chilled salad plates, mound greens in the middle using even portions. Clean and slice a selection of fruit. We prefer to use cantaloupe, pears, and berries. Splatter the greens with minced shallot, then display an array of your fruits atop the salad. At this point we enjoy adding the taste of cheese. Aged Parmesan, Feta, goat cheese or Gorgonzola, each is a complement. Finally add the dressing, just a few squirts or drizzles. Keep it light! Our dressing is not a mask, but a delicate enhancer of the fine ingredients you have gathered.

It's like being on a treasure hunt, but finding Molly Ward's Gardens is worth it... it is a treasure! About ½ hour from the Bainbridge ferry, near Manor Farm Inn, on the north side of the road, and with trees near the road, you'll see a big barn with "The Yarn Barn" over the red double doors.

Sam and Lynn Ward have created something special. One corner is a dried flower shop. In good weather the French doors are kept open, giving you a view of the garden.

Organic garden produce is used as much as possible... see recipe on the left - the Garden salad arrives on chilled plates, freshly picked greens with a delicate dressing... and including fresh fruit.

Breakfasts start mid-morning... leisurely.

The dinner menu offers from 5 to 7 entrées... from vegetarian to beef. A standing blackboard tells of that evening's selections.

However, Lynn has also created a handmade menu from heavy oriental papers and her calligraphy – striking!

From a tiny kitchen, great food arrives at your table.

A good selection of beer and wines.

Lunch Tuesday - Saturday
Dinner Thursday - Monday

Brunch Sunday
Reservations advised

TACO SALAD

10 flour tortillas
corn oil
3 cups lettuce, shredded
1/2 cup radishes, julienned
1 (15 oz.) can red kidney beans,
    drained and rinsed
1 lg. tomato, seeded and diced
1 sm. green pepper, diced
1 cup medium-hot salsa
2 T. red wine vinegar
1 lb. lean ground beef
1 sm. onion, chopped
1 T. chili powder
1 (7 oz.) can whole kernel corn
1 cup Cheddar cheese, shredded
1/2 cup sour cream
1 avocado, pared and chunked

Baskets: Preheat oven to 375°. Brush tortillas on both sides with oil. Arrange each tortilla in cone shape in a large glass custard cup, folding under base of cone to set tortilla in cup. Insert a small custard cup inside cone to hold it open. Place on baking sheet for 8 minutes. Remove inside cups and bake 4 minutes longer.

In a large bowl combine lettuce and radishes. In a medium bowl toss beans with tomato, green pepper, salsa and red wine vinegar. Set aside. Cook ground beef, stir in chili powder and corn.

Assemble tacos. Serve with sour cream and avocado.

ROAST TENDERLOIN OF VENISON with CABERNET SAUCE

2 1/2 lbs. tenderloin of axis
    venison or Denver cut
2 large garlic cloves, minced
salt and pepper to taste
2 T. olive oil
1 1/2 cups Cabernet Sauvignon
1/2 cup shallots, chopped
1 small carrot, thinly sliced
1 bay leaf
2 sprigs parsley
1 cup beef broth
1 T. cold unsalted butter

Preheat oven to 450°.

Rub venison with garlic and sprinkle with salt and pepper. Put olive oil in heavy skillet, add venison and sear over high heat until browned on all sides. Place meat in oven and roast for 16 minutes, turning once, until medium rare.

Combine the wine with vegetables and herbs and bring to a boil. Reduce by 1/2 over medium heat, about 8 minutes. Strain out vegetables and discard. In a saucepan reduce broth by 1/2, about 7 minutes over high heat. Combine liquids. Whisk in butter. Remove meat to cutting board, cover loosely with foil. Spoon sauce over each serving of meat.

Yield: 6 servings.

Situated along the shores of Puget Sound on the Kitsap Peninsula, the Silverdale Hotel on the Bay offers a retreat from the fast pace of our lives. Sweeping views from many of the suites. My sketch shows the outside view of the Mariner Restaurant patio dining. Extremely popular in the spring and summer months: sit outside in this patio area, let the cool breezes from Dyes Inlet relax you and try a "Botanical frozen tea infusion". It is a unique frozen product, similar in looks to soft serve ice cream, but it is fat-free, non-dairy, infused with restorative botanical herbs, and the flavors include Peach Serenity and Ginger Mango Vitality.

Now on the menu (new) is a Dungeness Crab and shrimp salad served on a bed of Caesar salad. A definite seafood lover's dream!

Among the pasta dishes — my favorite is the Cajun Chicken Cavatappi. Cajun corkscrew pasta with breast of chicken, green and red peppers, and red onions in a light Cajun sauce.

Two signature items here: their clam chowder to start and Washington Apple Crisp dessert to finish your meal.

Breakfast & dinner every day
Extended breakfast Sunday

Lunch Monday - Saturday

159

STEAMED MUSSELS WITH HERBS

1 lb. of fresh mussels
1 1/2 cups shallots, chopped
3 T. garlic, chopped
2 T. bay leaves, ground
1 T. black pepper
1/2 cup olive oil
2 bunches of parsley
6 oz. butter

1 cup white wine

Melt all ingredients into butter.
In a large stock pot, add white wine and the butter mixture. Steam until mussels open.

POPPY SEED HOUSE DRESSING

2 cups white sugar
2 cups cider vinegar
1 1/2 T. Kosher salt
1 1/2 T. powdered mustard
2/3 cup onion, fine dice
2/3 cup poppy seeds
3 cups salad oil

Blend all the dry ingredients well with the vinegar.
Add oil and mix well.
Blast in blender until creamy.

At water's edge of Port Washington narrows, and almost under the Manette bridge is the "Boat Shed". Originally a marina with boat building and storage facilities, it was charmingly converted in the early '70s to the restaurant it is today. Old plank floors and rough wood walls help create the casual feeling.

Nautical names for the sandwiches: "Longboat", roast beef on a toasted French roll. "Mariner", shrimp, guacamole and trimmings.

"If you decide to order" Pita Chips, cheese and artichoke dip — it's huge! Enough for 2 or 3 people. I was grateful the waitress warned me, because I couldn't finish a ½ order! The pita chips gave a different flavor. A large plate of chips with artichoke hearts in the melted Jack and cheddar cheese — the best!

Lots of choices: seafood, meats, fowl, pasta, soup, salads and sandwiches available, with many items on both the lunch and dinner menus.

Lunch, Mon. - Sat.   Dinner every day.

161

OLD PLANTATION SOUP

5 qts. chicken stock
1 medium onion, chopped
3 cups lima beans
3 cups small red beans
1/2 bunch celery, chopped
1/4 t. pepper
2 bay leaves
6 oz. can tomato paste
2 16 oz. cans green beans
1 1# bag frozen corn
3 cups red potatoes, diced

Combine all ingredients except red potatoes. Bring to a boil, lower heat and simmer for 2 1/2 hours. Return to a boil, add potatoes, bring back to a boil then turn down and simmer for an additional hour or until beans and potatoes are done.

BUTTER PECAN TURTLES

2 1/2 cups flour
3 cups brown sugar, divided
2 2/3 cups butter, divided
2 cups pecan pieces
3 cups chocolate chips

Preheat oven to 350⁰
Combine flour, 1 1/2 cups brown sugar and 2/3 cups butter in mixer until mixed well. Pat into a 12 x 17" cookie sheet (1/2 sheet pan). Sprinkle with pecans, set aside.
Boil 2 cups of butter and 1 1/3 cups brown sugar for 1 minute, stirring constantly. Pour over crust covering evenly. Bake for 15 minutes. Remove pan from oven and sprinkle chocolate chips evenly on top. When the chips start to melt, spread like frosting.
Let turtles sit until chocolate is **firm**, then go around the edges with a knife, (they will come out of the pan easier). Let turtles sit until chocolate is **hard**, then cut into desired size.

While the previous Coasting and Cooking was being printed, Pat's restaurant was being extensively remodeled. A new large dining room plus a meeting room that seats up to 20 was added... new decor, too.

Even with this extra room, the place was packed!

While I had breakfast of the Swiss Frittata of eggs, ham, mushrooms, topped with Swiss cheese, olives and tomatoes, including potatoes and biscuit, I watched the staff carrying large trays of freshly baked goodies for the day.

Pat's opens at 6 a.m. and people begin to fill the place, sleepy-eyed, but ready for "a good way to start the day".

On the counter now is a hand-out monthly sheet that lists the specials for the different days of the week, so if you have favorite entrées, you can note which days these dishes are offered and make plans to return then. Even a list of various soups is on this sheet. What a great idea!

Some specials are listed by the week - some by the day. The atmosphere is very pleasant.

I also noticed while I had my breakfast, that there was a lot of "to go" bakery business — probably for those at-work coffee breaks.

Breakfast, lunch & dinner Monday - Saturday
Breakfast until 3:00 PM Sunday

CILANTRO CHUTNEY

2 bunches of cilantro
1 tomato
1/8 onion
juice of one lemon
1/2 t. salt
1/4 t. chili powder

Break off the big stems of the cilantro and wash the leaves well. I wash the leaves twice by soaking them in a bowl of water.

Place all the ingredients in a food processor and pulse. Chutney can be left chunky or processed until smooth.

We use this on top of our black bean burritos, also as a garnish on top of salads and soups.

GREEK QUICHE

9 inch pie crust
olive oil
1 yellow onion, chopped
1/2 lb. fresh mushrooms, sliced
1 T. oregano
1 T. parsley
1 T. basil
juice of 1 lemon
1 bunch fresh spinach, washed
  and chopped
5 eggs
8 oz. sour cream
12 oz. lowfat plain yogurt
1 clove garlic, crushed
8 oz. Ricotta cheese
1/2 lb. Feta cheese, crumbled
1/2 lb. Mozzarella cheese,
  grated

Preheat oven to 350^0.

In a large pan heat oil on medium high. Add onions and cook until slightly soft. Add mushrooms, herbs and lemon juice. Lower heat. Add spinach and cook until mushrooms are tender. Place mixture in a colander and drain the excess juice.

In a separate large bowl add eggs, yogurt, sour cream, Ricotta, Feta and garlic. Whip vigorously with wire whip until mixture is creamy and thick. Add Mozzarella and blend.

Combine vegetable mixture with egg mixture and blend well.

Pour into pie crust and bake for 60 to 75 minutes.

To test for doneness, quiche should feel firm when tapped lightly or when a knife inserted comes out clean.

Antique Sandwich Co., 5102 N. Pearl, Tacoma 253-752-4069

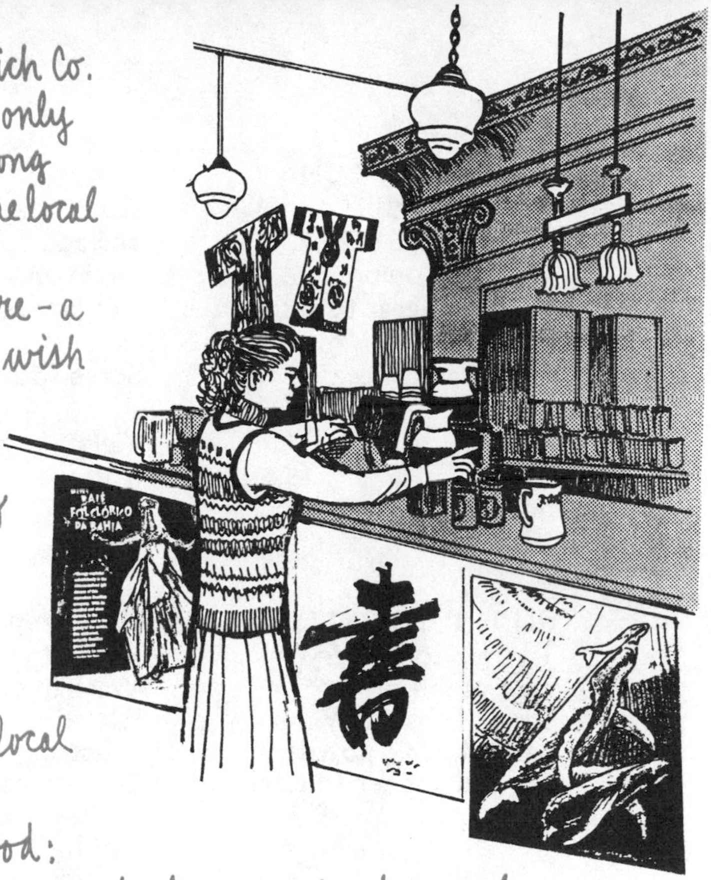

Walking into the Antique Sandwich Co. felt almost as it did 5 years ago. The only thing different is the addition of a long row of posters mostly telling of some local event. Very nice.

There is such a relaxed feeling here - a stack of newspapers for those who wish to slow down for awhile, if only on their coffee breaks. The community is drawn here like a magnet. Tuesday evenings there is open mike, it's folk type music and can be heard on KVTI, radio 90.9. The Sunday music is classical. If interested, call them for the times. A lot of local talent.

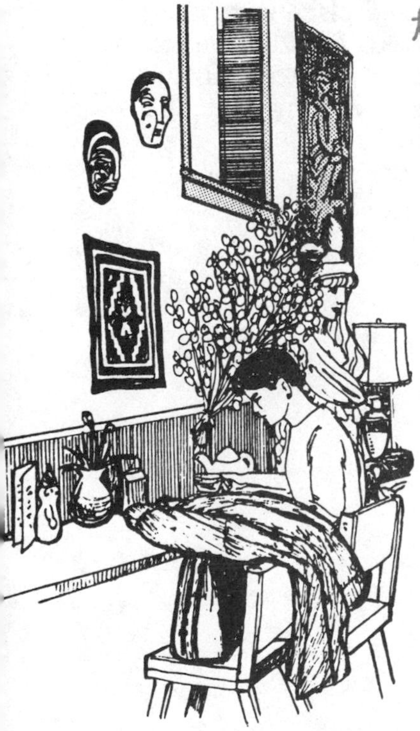

But - about the food:

They are famous for the home made cheesecakes, black bean burritos, turkey and cheese enchiladas, usually two different quiches, and Spanikopita. The emphasis is upon nutritional whole foods in sandwiches, fresh ciders and juices.

How long has it been since you've ordered a quiche? I ordered one on my last visit and am glad that I did.

They are located quite near the Point Defiance Park. What better place to stop off either before or after a visit to the zoo?

Breakfast, lunch & dinner every day ♿

SPAGHETTI TUNA

1 lb. spaghetti
1 can tuna, 6 1/2 oz.
1/2 sliced onion
oil and vinegar to taste
1/4 lb. butter
Parmesan cheese

Cook spaghetti according to package directions. Drain and add butter.
Drain tuna and place in salad bowl. Add onion and oil and vinegar. Sprinkle with pepper and Parmesan cheese.

Serve with hard French bread and white wine.

Yield: 4 servings.

ROAST CHICKEN ITALIAN

1 - 21/2 to 3 lb. fryer
slice of salami
sprig of rosemary
dash of garlic powder
salt and pepper to taste

Preheat oven to 500°.
Wash fryer in cold water. Rinse and dry. Stuff cavity with salami, rosemary and seasonings.
Tie string to tail and tie off both legs crossing each other. Salt and pepper outside of chicken and place in roasting pan with about one inch of oil. Bake for 20 minutes, basting every 10 minutes. Reduce oven to 350° and continue baking for 1/2 hour longer, basting every 10 minutes.
Remove from pan and slice or quarter.
Serve.

Imagine a restaurant in the same spot, cooking the same recipes, by the same family for **75 years**!
The place is Bimbo's. It has been in the family and will soon be in the ~~fifth~~ generation!
Stepping into Bimbo's is like stepping back in time... to the 1920's. The decor has stayed pretty much the same ..... tried and true recipes continue on and on. The traditional style of Tuscany Italian food with meat sauces,

sautéed meats, veal, chicken, rabbit, tripe... all specially prepared. (Although I've been urged, tripe is still one thing that I have never tasted.)

Over the years patrons have raved so much about the excellent meat sauce that it is now for sale here, and now is available in either pints or quarts. Prepared from scratch.

Since my last book more changes are happening in this vicinity, but still needs more. The completely refurbished old Union Depot looks great! And the new Washington State Historical Museum is drawing crowds... just down the street from Bimbo's.
Tacomans don't mind being on juries, because they often can take meal breaks here.

Lunch & dinner every day   **Sunday dinner all day**   ♿

CHICKEN, SAUSAGE AND SHRIMP GUMBO

1 lb. chicken breast
1 lb. spicy sausage
1/2 lb. shrimp meat
1 white onion
2 medium carrots
3 celery sticks
1 green pepper
1 cup white rice
1/4 cup burgundy wine
1 cup okra, chopped
1 cup baby corn
2 oz. fresh basil
1 oz. whole garlic
1/2 oz. nutmeg
1/2 oz. whole cloves
1/2 oz. cayenne pepper
1/2 oz. black pepper
1 oz. whole thyme
squirts of Tabasco sauce,
   to taste
2 27 oz. cans crushed
   tomatoes
2 cups tomato purée
2 cups melted butter

Cut chicken into medium dice, set aside. Cut celery, onions, carrots and green pepper into medium dice and set aside.

In a stew pot, add melted butter along with the chicken, vegetables and all the spices.

Cook at medium high for 10 to 15 minutes.

Return to low heat, add the wine and the sausage, and cook for another 5 to 7 minutes.

Add all the tomato products and bring to a boil. Return to low heat and add shrimp and the chicken base to the gumbo, continue to simmer on low heat until thick.

Remove and serve in soup bowls.

SHRIMP AND ARTICHOKE SPREAD

2 cups mayonnaise
12 oz. can artichoke hearts
1/2 lb. bay shrimp meat
1/3 cup grated Parmesan
   cheese
1 small onion, quartered
   and sliced
sliced garlic French bread

Preheat oven to 450⁰
Combine all ingredients in large bowl. Mix together and place in a casserole dish. Bake until bubbling. Serve with garlic French bread.

Yield: 6 servings

What would a book about restaurants be without a really great pizza place? Katie Downs is that place! Twice voted "Best Pizza in western Washington" by Pacific Northwest magazine's readers poll.

Established in 1982, Katie Downs is a Northwest theme tavern specializing in award-winning pizza, burgers and seafood. Katie's also offers the best in hand-crafted northwest beers and wines. The fresh seafood includes halibut and chips, steamer clams, charbroiled salmon and black tiger prawns.

I found a pizza combination I'd never seen before: The Mariner has red sauce, shrimp, tomatoes, Provolone cheese and smoked bacon. Excellent.

What a location! (see sketch) Katie Downs is perched right over the water on Tacoma's Commencement Bay. This location offers a commanding view of the Olympic and Cascade mountains as well as the Puget Sound. Be sure to arrive early as this place packs out quickly.

Lunch & dinner every day

LOMBATINA DI VITELLO ALLA GRIGLIA CON SALSA DI SENAPE

14 oz. veal chop

Char broil the veal chop to your liking.

SAUCE
2 T. olive oil
1 clove garlic
1 T. Dijon mustard
2 oz. sundried tomatoes
1/4 lemon
1 oz. white wine
1 T. green peppercorns
1 oz. heavy cream

In a sauté pan heat the oil and braise the garlic. Add sun dried tomatoes and juice of lemon. Add the Dijon mustard and white wine. Add green pepper corns and heavy cream. Reduce slightly and pour over the veal chop.

Yield: 1 serving.

CAPELLINI ALLA MARE CHIARO

4 oz. dry angel hair pasta
6 31/40 prawns
1 oz. olive oil
1 clove garlic, chopped
  coarsely
3 oz. cherry tomatoes
1 oz. white wine
1 t. fresh basil
pinch of salt
pinch of black pepper

Boil water and cook pasta until al dente.

Place olive oil in sauté pan and braise the garlic, add prawns and cherry tomatoes. Add white wine and basil. Add the pasta to the sauté pan and toss. Salt and pepper to taste.

Yield: 1 serving.

If you are looking for an outstanding Italian restaurant, I've found it. It's Luciano's Waterfront Ristorante in Tacoma. Open for just two years, Luciano's executive chef Alfredo Russo is a native of Ciavano, a town near Naples, Italy. Russo has been a chef for restaurants in Chicago, Indianapolis, Seattle and Bremerton since 1981. He brings to Tacoma gusto and a reverence for classical Italian cuisine cooked with the freshest of ingredients. A recent restaurant review by Bart Ripp of the News Tribune states "Luciano's southern Italian menu, tinged in neopolitan hues and bursting with fresh flair, offers some of the best Italian food north of San Francisco. I have a feeling that Russo is just messing around. He hasn't shown all his talents, for Luciano's needs time to win the spaghetti-and-meatballs crowd. Russo, unleashed in full cannonade, could be a five-star chef."

Luciano's is built over the water. The fire boats are just next door. I'm partial to squid, and the Calameri del Pescatore is tops: fresh garlic sautéed in a little wine, tomatoes, crushed red peppers and Italian parsley. Mmm!
Buon Apetite.

Lunch & dinner every day

171

HOT DUNGENESS CRAB DIP

4 cups mayonnaise
1 lb. Dungeness crab meat
8 oz. onion, thinly sliced
1 lb. artichoke hearts, chopped
8 oz. Parmesan, shredded
3 t. fresh parsley, minced
lemon slice

Preheat oven to 350⁰.
Combine and mix the mayonnaise, artichoke hearts, crab meat, Parmesan and onions. Portion crab mixture (6 oz.) into small ovenproof baking dishes. Place the baking dishes into the oven for 5 to 6 minutes, or until the internal temperature reaches 140⁰.
Arrange bread slices on a plate around the crab dip and garnish with minced parsley and lemon slice.

ORIGINAL BURNT CREAM

1 pint whipping cream
1 T. vanilla extract
4 egg yolks
1/2 cup granulated sugar

SUGAR TOPPING

4 T. granulated sugar
1 t. brown sugar

Preheat oven to 350⁰.
Heat cream over low heat until bubbles form around the edge of the pan. Beat egg yolks together until thick, about 3 minutes. Gradually beat cream into yolks. Stir in the vanilla and pour into six 6 oz. custard cups.
Place custard cups in a baking pan that has about 1/2" of water in the bottom. Bake until set, about 45 minutes. Remove custard cups from the water and refrigerate until chilled.
Sprinkle each custard with about 2 t. of the sugar blend. Place on top rack under the broiler and cook until topping is medium brown.
Chill before serving.

Yield: 6 servings.

Stanley & Seafort's is high above the city and is rewarded with an unending panoramic view of Tacoma. They are so committed to the quality and value of everything served that an unconditional guarantee is made for all food, beverage and service. Only custom selected and certified Nebraska beef with specifications exceeding USDA grading standards for choice-grade beef is served.

Prime ribs of beef are roasted very slowly for half a day under a mountain of rock salt to increase tenderness and retain juices. (I began using this method about 7 years ago and wouldn't cook it any other way now.)

Only fish fillets are served, not fish steaks, premium grade, fresh packed on ice and hand cut.

Dressings and sauces are all made on the premises. The coffee beans are ground just before each pot is brewed.

A couple of the signature items are their herb-crusted oven-roasted chicken breast that is rubbed with sage and rosemary, roasted to a golden brown and served with red jacket mashed potatoes and a light shallot-vinaigrette sauce.

Another is a bowl of housemade French onion soup served with 1 of 5 excellent salads.

Lunch Monday - Friday   **Dinner every day**

173

ESCARGOT BUTTER

1 lb. butter
1/2 cup garlic, chopped
1/4 cup green onions, chopped
2 T. Worcestershire sauce
2 T. seasoned salt (Johnny's
   Dock)
2 T. white wine (Chablis)

Soften butter -- do not melt!
Mix remaining ingredients all together.

Put generously on escargots and bake in hot oven. This recipe will make about 1 1/2 lbs. of mix. You will need 1 oz. per snail.

NOTE: This recipe is really the butter. You can use it on bread, steaming clams, prawn sauté or on other sautés. It will keep about 1 month in the refrigerator.

BAKER'S CREAM

2 pints whipping cream
10 egg yolks
1 cup sugar
2 T. vanilla extract
1/2 cup brown sugar (sifted)

Preheat oven to 350⁰
Heat cream over low heat until bubbles form around edge of pan.
Beat egg yolks and granulated sugar together until thick, about 3 minutes. Gradually beat warm cream into egg yolks. Stir in vanilla.
Pour into 6 oz. baker dishes or shallow, fluted soufflé dishes. Place in baking pan that has about 1/2 inch of hot water in the bottom. Bake until set, about 45 minutes.
Remove dishes from water and refrigerate until chilled. Sprinkle each dish with sifted brown sugar, place under broiler and cook until medium brown. Chill again before serving.

Yield: 6 to 8 servings.

Falls Terrace Restaurant is located off of I-5 (take exit 103). It is across from the Olympia Brewery.

Falls: the view overlooking the Tumwater Falls of the Deschutes River.

Terrace: the seating is terraced down towards the view, so that as many as possible may enjoy this while they dine.

About 25 years of tradition here... and so popular that it is wise to call for a reservation. However, there is informal dining in the adjacent bar. When the weather allows – some prefer to sit outside on a small deck.

I was prepared to order something new on my most recent visit, but when I saw the waitress serving Bouillabaisse to the customer at the next table, this was my selection, too. Falls Terrace knows how to excel here... loaded with prawns, lobster, crab, salmon and clams.

If you aren't a lover of seafood, not to worry. The menu offers a wide selection of specialty pasta dishes, steak, lamb, chicken and more. Of course, there's an abundant assortment of all kinds of seafood, including Olympia oysters, naturally.

Members of our State Legislature and many state employees "meet and eat" here. If you have time, daily tours are given of the Brewery.

Lunch & dinner every day
Closed Christmas, New Years and July 4th

175

SCALLOPS FORESTIERE

1 T. olive oil
1 1/2 lbs. sea scallops
4 oz. button mushrooms,
    quartered
2 oz. Shitake mushrooms,
    stemmed and julienned
4 T. fresh garlic
2 T. fresh tarragon, chopped
salt and pepper to taste
2 oz. tomatoes, chopped
1 oz. white wine
dash of lemon juice
2 T. chilled butter

Heat oil until nearly smoking. Add scallops, button mushrooms, garlic, tarragon, salt and pepper. Toss for 2 minutes over high heat. Add white wine and lemon juice. Reduce by half. Add Shitake mushrooms and tomatoes. Cook for 1 minute, remove from heat and add chilled butter to make a creamy sauce.

BUDD BAY CLAM CHOWDER

1 lb. russet potatoes, peeled,
    cut into 1/2" pieces

1/2 cup (1 stick) butter
3 celery stalks, chopped
1 medium onion, chopped
1/2 cup all purpose flour
6 8 oz bottles clam juice
4 6 1/2 oz. cans chopped
    clams with juices
1 T. fresh parsley, chopped
1/2 t. fresh thyme, chopped;
    or 1/4 t. dried thyme
1/2 t. fresh marjoram,
    chopped, or 1/4 t. dried
1/2 t. fresh dill, chopped or
    1/4 t. dried dillweed
1/4 t. powdered garlic
1/8 t. liquid smoke*
2 cups whipping cream
1 cup whole milk

Boil potatoes in a large saucepan of salted water until just tender, about 6 minutes. Drain well.

Melt butter in a large, heavy pot over medium-high heat. Add celery and onions and sauté until onion is translucent, about 6 minutes. Add flour and stir 2 minutes. Gradually mix in clam juice. Simmer until beginning to thicken, stirring frequently, about 2 minutes. Add clams with juices, parsley, thyme, marjoram, dill, garlic, liquid smoke and potatoes. Simmer 5 minutes to blend flavors. Add cream and milk. Bring to simmer. Season to taste with salt and pepper.
(Can be prepared 1 day ahead. Cover and refrigerate. Bring to simmer before serving.)

*Liquid smoke is a smoke-flavored liquid seasoning available at specialty foods stores and many supermarkets.

Can't believe it will soon be a decade since Paul Boardman, Brett Hibberd and John Senner opened Budd Bay! As sketched, the outside dining is very popular... 180° view from the state Capitol to the Olympics. They created the largest deck in the area... it's located in the heart of Percival Landing board walk overlooking Budd Inlet in downtown Olympia. Right in the center of community waterfront activities, such as Capital Lake fair, Harbor Days, the Wooden Boat Fair and their own "Oktoberfest" which lasts for several days in the early Fall.

Executive chef Jason Smith admitted to me that when he dines here his usual choice is the scallop recipe he is sharing with us. Both Jason and the sous chef said they are excited to come to work each day! They're allowed freedom of choice on menu ideas, and are bringing new talent and ideas to Budd Bay. They laughed and said "Sometimes we just go crazy... it's great!" Lots of cultural influences... Asian, Thai, Cajun, Japanese, Basic Pacific Northwest. Always using local ingredients in every possible way.

Bon Appetit wrote asking for their Clam Chowder recipe. Currently also doing a lot of Full-Service Catering. It could be in your home, backyard, boat, or a banquet hall. I forgot to mention that the view from inside is very good, too.

Lunch & dinner daily
Sunday Brunch 9-1

MARINATED ARTICHOKE FARFALLE

2 cups artichoke hearts, cooked
1/4 cup balsamic vinegar
1/4 cup extra virgin olive oil
2 cloves garlic, minced
2 T. dijon mustard
1 1/2 cups fresh spinach, washed
  and dried
1 lb. farfalle pasta
1/4 cup Gorgonzola cheese,
  crumbled
1/4 cup Parmesan cheese, grated
1/4 cup sundried tomatoes,
  julienned
salt and pepper to taste

Quarter artichoke hearts and marinate in vinegar, olive oil, garlic and mustard for at least 30 minutes at room temperature.

Meanwhile, cook pasta in boiling water until tender. Drain, rinse in cold water and drain again.

Shred spinach. Toss pasta with artichokes, marinade, spinach, cheeses and sundried tomatoes. Adjust seasoning with salt and pepper to taste

Yield: 6 servings

ROASTED BUTTERNUT SQUASH SOUP

2 butternut squash
1/2 cup almonds, toasted 3
  minutes
1 lb. butter
1 small onion, diced
1/2 cup carrots, diced
2 T. garlic
1 cup white wine, deglaze
1 cup flour
4 cups chicken or vegetable
  stock
1 t. nutmeg
1 t. cinnamon
2 t. thyme
16 oz. coconut milk
2 cups cream
1 cup cream cheese or goat
  cheese
salt and pepper to taste

Preheat oven to 400°
Cut squash in half and brush with butter or oil. Bake 45 minutes.

Remove seeds, discard. Scoop out squash and mash until smooth.

Sauté in pan onion, garlic and carrots until soft. Deglaze with white wine. Add flour and cook until nutted brown. Add stock, squash, coconut milk and cream. Reduce until thick. Add nutmeg, cinnamon, thyme and cheese. Salt and pepper to taste.

Serve with toasted almonds sprinkled on top.

Yield 6 servings

Last December chef Lela and accountant Tina Messer became partners at the Capitale Espresso & Grill in downtown Olympia. A great idea, as too many endeavors fail for the lack of balance between creative and financial talents.

Their style of cooking is "Pan Pacific", an infusion of Southwest, Mediterranean and Asian flavors.

Frittatas are their most popular breakfast... Italian omelettes with vegetables and herbs. For lunch I can recommend any of their made-

fresh daily pastas. There is a display case so you can pick the salads of your choice. In December I asked for smaller portions and tried 3 different salads and all were so good, that I couldn't pick a favorite! Lela said that in less than a year they have created about 2,000 different combinations. They bottle and sell many oils... see picture on other page. Recipes vary on a whim, trying new flavors.

Local art is displayed on the walls, and occasionally jazz music to enjoy while dining. Desserts are a specialty.

Breakfast Monday - Friday   **Closed Sunday**
Lunch & dinner Monday - Saturday

DUCK IN RED WINE

1 duckling
1 twig fresh rosemary
juice of 1 lemon
3 T. butter
1/4 cup whipping cream
MARINADE
salted water
bouquet garni
2 medium onions
1 bottle good red wine
crushed juniper berries

Preheat oven to 350⁰.
Marinate duck for 6 hours. Drain well and pat dry. Rub with salt, pepper and lemon juice.
Brown duck in butter, when well browned gradually add marinade. Place in oven for approximately 1 1/2 hours.
Strain remaining marinade, add cream and adjust seasoning. Serve sauce separately from duck.
Excellent with spätzle and sweet and sour red cabbage.

Bon appetit!

APPLE TART

flaky pastry from your
  favorite recipe
applesauce
apples, peeled, cored
  and cut into 1/8
  wedges
confectioners sugar
butter

Preheat oven to 450⁰.
Roll flaky pastry to 1/8". Cut round to cover the whole inside of a teflon-coated tart pan. Cover dough with a thin layer of apple sauce. Leave 1 1/4" edge uncovered. Place apples on sauce to cover the sauce completely. Sprinkle tart generously with confectioners sugar and small dabs of butter.
Bake for 20 minutes then add some additional confectioners sugar. Bake 5 more minutes.
Serve while still warm with unsweetened whipped cream on the side. Enjoy!

The chef prefers Granny Smith apples for this recipe, although Golden Delicious lend themselves very well too. Simplicity at its finest.

Entrecôte double with two sauces ♥
Chicken fricassée with saffron rice
Ravioli with artichoke hearts & tomato-basil sauce
Seafood stew with rouille ♥

Here's a section of the Valentine's Day menu and shows the interesting loose style of Wolfgang's calligraphy.

Wolfgang Goller came to Olympia from his former pastry shop in Lacey. The Fifth Avenue Bistro is basically French cuisine, but does include some Italian and German dishes.

Wolfgang said the menu for dinner changes seasonally, and the lunch menu more frequently.

Commenting on the art displayed, I discovered that the art on the walls changes about every 4 to 6 weeks. He also mentioned that anyone may play the piano (if they are more proficient than Chopsticks).

The awning "bit the dust" after one of Washington's storms. The measuring is done, but the new awnings are not at this time installed yet.

If you are a garlic lover (I am) perhaps the garlic soup will be on the menu when you visit here.

On this page is a sample of Wolfgang's calligraphy that he uses for all of the menus. This is from the Valentine's Day menu. Very good is the ravioli stuffed with artichoke hearts and in a tomato-basil sauce.

Because it was Valentine's Day, there were many champagne selections .... anywhere from a magnum at $200 down to champagne by the glass at $6.   Beers from Germany, Alsace, and Belgium, and a good wine list.

Lunch Tuesday - Saturday   Dinner Monday - Saturday   ♿

PRAWN SAUTÉ

16 Gulf prawns, (16/20), peeled
  and deveined
4 oz. olive oil
8 oz. mushrooms, sliced
6 oz. Bermuda onion, julienned
6 oz. zucchini, sliced
1 T. garlic, chopped
6 oz. white wine
2 T. unsalted butter
12 sugar peas
6 oz. Roma tomato, diced
4 oz. green onion, chopped

In sauté pan, heat olive oil. Add prawns and sauté lightly. Add mushrooms, zucchini, onion and garlic. Sauté lightly. Deglaze with white wine. Reduce heat, add butter and toss. Add pea pods, tomato and green onion. Toss until heated through.
Serve over rice pilaf.

Yield: 4 servings.

CRAB WON TONS

4 oz. Dungeness crab meat
1/4 cup cream cheese
1/8 cup Mozzarella, shredded
2 T. green onions, chopped
Johnny's seasoning salt to taste
1 pkg. Won Ton wrappers

Blend all ingredients thoroughly by hand.
Place 1/2 oz. on each Won Ton wrapper. Seal edges with water and fold. Freeze until firm.
Deep fry at 350⁰ for 1 1/2 to 2 minutes until golden brown. Serve with Honey Mustard Sauce.

HONEY MUSTARD SAUCE

1/2 cup dry mustard
water
1 cup honey

Mix dry mustard with water to form a paste. Add honey, blend well and refrigerate for 24 hours before serving. For hot sauce use more mustard or less honey.

Genoa on the Bay was originally a "house of the future" at the Seattle World's Fair in 1962. Round rooms, beautiful sky-lights create a unique effect to enjoy while you dine.

It's built on piers right over the water with panoramic views of Puget Sound and off in the distance, the snow-capped Olympic mountains!

Always a busy spot because they do a good job. and it's This visit I had a very good spinach salad and then an order of the Crab Won Tons served with the honey mustard dipping sauce... so good I just had to order a second serving. I was thrilled to see that this is one of the 2 recipes shared here!

If you dare, order the Suicide Chocolate Cake — very rich and _very_ chocolate.

Lunch & dinner Monday - Thursday
Dinner Friday, Saturday & Sunday   Brunch Sunday

CHICKEN-MUSHROOM FETTUCCINE

3 oz. chicken meat, cut into
  1/2" cubes
4 fresh mushrooms, sliced
1 1/2 cups whipping cream
4 oz. shredded Parmesan
  cheese, (divided)
1 oz. clarified butter
1 oz. white wine
1 1/2 t. fresh chopped garlic
1 t. fresh chopped shallots
2 1/2 cups cooked fettuccine
  noodles

Melt butter in large sauté pan, add sliced mushrooms and cut up chicken, garlic and shallots. Sauté with white wine. Add cream, salt and white pepper to taste. Bring to a boil, then reduce until it starts to thicken. When slightly thickened add 3 oz. Parmesan cheese (reserving 1 oz.). Gently stir in fettuccine using a rubber spatula, simmer until sauce has started to thicken. Taste for seasoning.

Place on plate and top with remaining 1 oz. of Parmesan cheese.

Garnish with fresh chopped parsley and paprika.

BREAST OF CHICKEN RASPBERRY

1 chicken breast, 8 oz.
1 oz. butter
1 oz. raspberries, fresh or
  frozen
2 oz. raspberry schnapps
2 oz. whipping cream
salt and white pepper to
  taste

Melt butter in sauté pan or large frying pan. Dredge chicken in flour and brown. Add schnapps and cream. Bring to a boil, then let simmer for 5 to 10 minutes or until sauce thickens. Add raspberries and salt and pepper to taste.

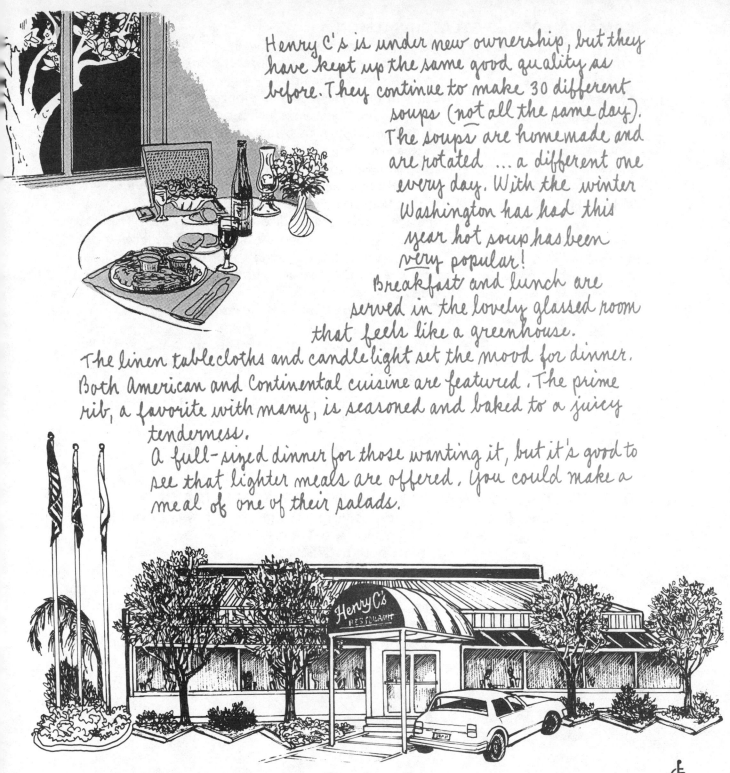

Henry C's is under new ownership, but they have kept up the same good quality as before. They continue to make 30 different soups (not all the same day). The soups are homemade and are rotated ... a different one every day. With the winter Washington has had this year hot soup has been very popular!

Breakfast and lunch are served in the lovely glassed room that feels like a greenhouse.

The linen tablecloths and candlelight set the mood for dinner. Both American and Continental cuisine are featured. The prime rib, a favorite with many, is seasoned and baked to a juicy tenderness.

A full-sized dinner for those wanting it, but it's good to see that lighter meals are offered. You could make a meal of one of their salads.

Breakfast, lunch & dinner Monday - Saturday
Breakfast & dinner Sunday

185

SKAMANIA LODGE POTLATCH SALMON

4 t. kosher salt
2 t. paprika
1 t. cayenne pepper
2 t. dry sweet basil, crushed
2 t. oregano
2 small hot peppers, pulverized
4 seeds of coriander, pulverized

1 side of salmon (4 lbs., skinless)

Blend seasoning ingredients well.

Season salmon 3 hours before cooking. Rub seasonings on both sides of the fish.

Using an alder plank two feet long and 7 1/2 inches wide, drill small holes every six inches on each side of the plank so that an eight-inch bamboo skewer can go through. Place a seasoned side of salmon on the plank and criss-cross skewers to go over the salmon side. (The salmon should **not** be skewered through the meat; bend skewers so that they go over the salmon.)

Prepare a cone-shaped fire of hot charcoal. The coals should be a foot high and a foot in diameter. Place planks of salmon in a circle around the fire about a foot away from the hot charcoal and standing in an upright position, the salmon facing the fire.

Cook for 20 to 30 minutes or until flaky.

If you prefer, salmon may be made into steaks and grilled over charcoal in the usual fashion. They should cook in 12 to 15 minutes.

Yield 8 servings.

ROASTED STURGEON MARINATED IN GINGER WASABI VINAIGRETTE

4 fillets of sturgeon (6 oz. each)
MARINADE
2 T. rice wine
2 T. soy sauce
1 T. garlic, chopped
1 T. Hoisin sauce
1 T. Wasabi
1/2 T. ginger, chopped
1/2 T. sesame seed oil
2 T. canola oil
1 T. coriander, ground
1 T. salt

Mix marinade ingredients in a small bowl. Marinade sturgeon filets for 2 to 3 hours.

Preheat oven to 375°.

Remove sturgeon from the marinade.

In a hot skillet, add canola oil and brown sturgeon on both sides, quickly add 1/2 of the marinade, discard remainder.

Place skillet in oven. Cook fish for 15 minutes.

Serve fish with stir fry vegetables and oriental steamed rice.

Skamania Lodge opened in 1993 on a lushly forested crest overlooking the breathtaking Columbia River Gorge. It rises from a point where peaks, forests, canyons and the river come together to offer astonishing vistas at every turn. Inside, the uses of wood, stone, crackling fireplaces, very comfortable seating invite you to relax.... or jump right into some of the activities. Work out in the full service spa, hike the nature trails, or (my favorite) bask under the stars in a steaming outdoor whirlpool. In the Gorge nearby .... sternwheeler rides, whitewater rafting, windsurfing, take in the museums and visitors' center. Also nearby: lava beds, Pendleton Woolen Mills, ice caves, Mt. St. Helens Volcano area, fish hatcheries, river and lake fishing, biking, Mt. Hood railroad excursion train.

DINING...

1. The Dining Room, casually elegant, offers superb NW cuisine.
2. "River Rock" lounge for light dinners, lunch, appetizers
3. Occasionally a potlatch chinook salmon cookout on the grounds.

Breakfast, lunch & dinner Monday - Saturday
Brunch & dinner Sunday

TIRAMISU

1 cup hot coffee
2 double shots espresso
1 shot Kahlua
2 packages lady finger
  cookies
1 cup shredded dark
  chocolate
2 lbs. Mascarpone
  cheese
2 cups whipped cream
6 eggs separated
1 1/2 cups sugar
1 shot brandy
1 shot Frangelico
1 T. vanilla

Combine hot coffee, espresso and Kahlua.
Place cookies side by side in a large pan. Douse lady fingers with coffee mixture and reserve.
Beat egg whites until stiff peaks form, reserve.
Cream the Marscarpone, whipped cream, egg yolks, sugar, brandy, Frangelico and vanilla in a mixer or food processor until smooth. Fold in beaten egg whites.
In a large pan approximately 8 x 12 inches, layer lady fingers, cream mixture and shaved chocolate.

GRILLED EGGPLANT SANDWICH

1 pita (preferably "Kronos
  Italian Pita"), not pocket
  bread
3 1/2" slices eggplant
extra virgin olive oil
2 T. diced sundried
  tomato
2 T. roasted red pepper
2 T. Roma tomato
1 t. roasted garlic,
  chopped
1 t. red onion
1 t. fresh basil
2 slices smoked Mozza-
  rella cheese
1 T. Asiago cheese,
  shredded
chopped parsley

Preheat oven to 350⁰.
Mix vegetables and spices together.
Grill eggplant. Lightly toast pita bread.
Top pita with eggplant, tomato mixture and smoked Mozzarella.
Bake on middle rack of oven until cheese is well melted.
Sprinkle with Asiago cheese and chopped parsley.

Only a few blocks from the ferry landing on Bainbridge Island, the Madrona Waterfront Cafe was designed to take advantage of the water views. Inside seating is on two levels, and outside there are two decks for dining. Also a large area with lawn has tables. Parents with children like this, as children can run around.

I had an informative talk with Lindy, a waitress here. She has been serving food for 18 years and said chef Keith Pasculli is the best. She has watched him at work and said he takes as much effort on his creative vegetable dishes as on the meat.

She recently traveled over 17,000 miles including New England, but had to come back to the Madrona for the best clam chowder.

Popular with the tourists, it is usually likely that another language will be heard at a nearby table.

Keith's Rosemary Focaccia Bread is excellent! The grilled salmon was topped with artichoke hearts, lemon, pinenuts and herb butter.

Desserts of the Week, changing but all mouth watering. A sight for the eyes as well as the palate. My tiramisu was one of the best I've ever had!

Lunch & dinner every day

189

POTATOES DELUXE

2 potatoes, diced
1 onion diced
1/4 t. salt
pinch pepper
pinch paprika
3 T. oil, butter or margarine
4 green onions, finely
　　chopped
4 mushrooms, thinly sliced
1 tomato, diced
1/2 bunch spinach leaves,
　　washed and drained
1 cup grated Cheddar
　　cheese
1/4 to 1/2 cup guacamole
　　(Below)

Steam potatoes until just tender, approximately 10 minutes. Mix the steamed potatoes with the onion, salt, pepper and paprika. In a large frying pan, heat 2 T. oil, butter or margarine until bubbly. Add the potatoes and fry them over a high heat until golden brown, flipping frequently, for approximately 5 minutes. Turn heat to low and cover to keep hot.

In a small frying pan, heat the remaining T. oil, butter or margarine until bubbly. Add the green onions and mushrooms and sauté until tender, approximately 3 minutes, stirring frequently. Add these vegetables to the pan with the potatoes. Mix well with a spatula.

Top the potato mixture with the tomatoes, spinach and Cheddar cheese. Cover and cook on low heat for 3 to 5 minutes, until the spinach has wilted and the cheese melts.

To serve, top each portion with a heaping T. of guacamole.

Yield: 2 to 4 servings.

This charming art is from their menu.

GUACAMOLE

2 ripe avocados
4 T. Streamliner salsa (or
　　any good salsa)
juice of 1/2 lemon
1/4 t. salt
1 T. sour cream
1/2 t. cumin

Scoop out the avocados and mash them with a potato masher or fork. Mix together the avocados with the salsa, lemon juice, salt, sour cream and cumin.

Yield: 1 1/2 cups.

Guacamole is best freshly made, but can be refrigerated and served the following day.

Bart and Sioux Ogburn, the new owners since my last visit, continue the good reputation of the Streamliner Diner.

A very busy spot in the summer months, the locals take over the rest of the year. Bart and Sioux know many by name. Some have invited the Ogburns to their homes for dinner.

This is also a good weekend day outing for Seattle residents...hop on the ferry, come to Bainbridge Island, then walk just a few blocks to the Streamliner Diner.

Almost everything is made from scratch right here, except bread and pies that are made exclusively for the Diner.
10 different omelettes are offered; one is the "Misto" with Italian fennel sausage with red and green bell peppers, fresh tomatoes and Parmesan.

Their spinach salad is 4★: spinach, red onion, toasted pinenuts, mushrooms, avocado, Feta cheese and tossed with herb vinaigrette.

Breakfast & lunch every day   ♿

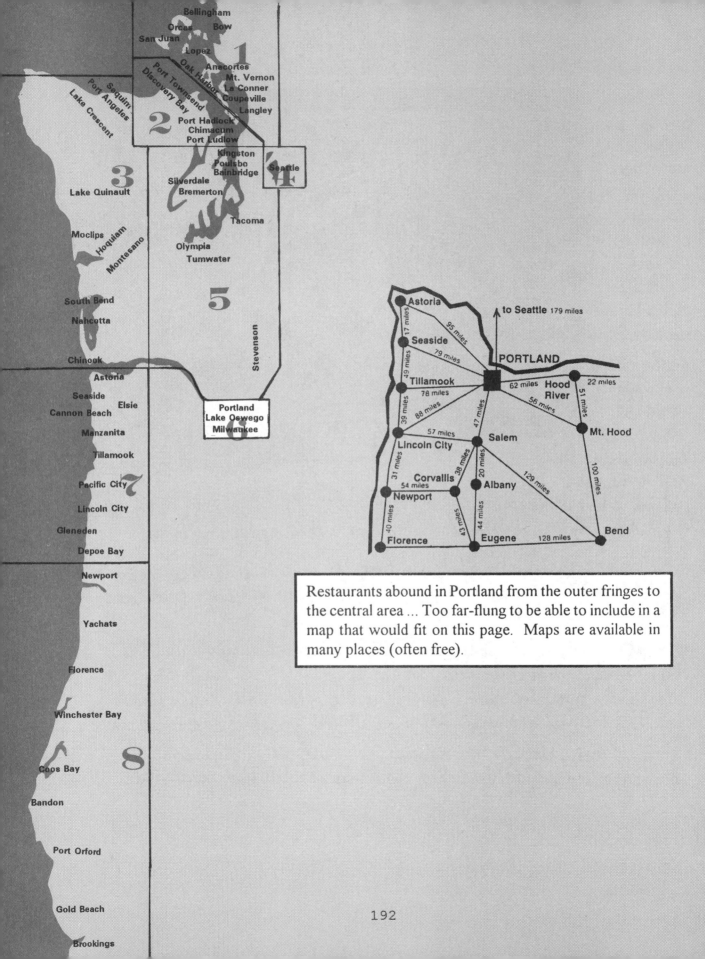

Restaurants abound in Portland from the outer fringes to the central area ... Too far-flung to be able to include in a map that would fit on this page. Maps are available in many places (often free).

SECTION **6** OREGON

MILWAUKEE: Amadeus at the Fernwood
LAKE OSWEGO: Amadeus
PORTLAND: Avalon, Bread and Ink Cafe, Cafe des Amis, Genoa,
Il Piatto, Montage, Ron Paul Charcuterie,
Waterzoies, Zell's - An American Cafe
LAKE OSWEGO: Dancing Bear, Lake Grove Bistro
BEAVERTON: Swagat Indian Cuisine

FILLET of PORK over POTATO PANCAKES

1 lb. fillet of pork
salt and pepper
2 T. mustard
oil
touch of flour
2 scallions, chopped
splash of white wine
1/2 cup sour cream or
   crème fraîche

Rub fillet with salt, pepper and mustard. Cover with touch of flour and sauté in hot oil.
Preheat oven to 390°.
Transfer fillet to oven for 15 minutes. Add scallions, mixing with the cream.
Cut fillets into portions and set on top of pancakes.
Usually served with watercress or spinach salad.

Yield: 2 servings.

POTATO PANCAKES

1 lb. potatoes
1 egg
salt and pepper
onion, grated
oil
flour

Grate raw potatoes and drain off extra liquid. Mix in egg, salt, pepper and onion with just a touch of flour. Heat oil in skillet. Spoon in pancake mixture in small portions and fry until brown on each side.

Often served with applesauce or compote.

Seven years ago Kristina Poppmeier opened her first restaurant. Now there are two. One is Amadeus at Lake Oswego. The other is Amadeus at the Fernwood. There is a good feeling the minute you walk thru the door. A touch of Vienna.

Amadeus at the Fernwood overlooks the Willamette River and the mountains beyond... a beautiful setting for special occasions, weddings, etc. Fireplaces, flowers, candlelight and live classical piano music nightly. Please don't be in a rush... enjoy a symphony of expertly prepared courses. (You will recognize Mozart's music as you dine.) One of the first course offerings is a paté of chicken livers prepared with bacon, onions, crushed pepper and flavored with cognac. Several other selections, including Escargot. Very popular on the Main course list is Rack of Oregon lamb, roasted and topped with garlic, seasoned bread crumbs, and served with Sauce Robert. The Viennese Schnitzel Amadeus is a classic. Pastries are home made. How about Coffee Cloud, Irish Cream or Hazel nut Liqueur to top off the evening?

Dinner every day   **Sunday Brunch**

195

DUNGENESS CRAB CAKES

1 yellow onion, finely diced
1 red Bermuda onion, finely diced
1 yellow bell pepper, finely diced
1 poblano pepper, finely diced
2 lbs. Dungeness crab meat, picked clean
1 3/4 cups bread crumbs
3/4 t. kosher salt
1 1/2 t. white pepper, freshly ground
2 dashes Tabasco sauce
1/2 cup heavy cream
1/2 cup peanut oil
2 eggs, separated

Sauté onions and peppers in a preheated skillet with the olive oil until the onions are translucent, set aside in a colander to drain and cool.

When vegetables have cooled (approx. 20 minutes) and all excess liquid has drained off, combine vegetables with crab, egg yolks, bread crumbs and heavy cream. Blend carefully to avoid breaking up the crab meat too much. Add salt, Tabasco and pepper and mix gently and evenly.

Preheat peanut oil in heavy pot. Roll into 2 1/2 oz. portions, place into beaten egg whites, allowing excess to drain off, then place in flour and pan fry in peanut oil for approximately 2 minutes on each side. Serve with sun dried tomato remoulade.

SUN DRIED TOMATO REMOULADE

3 stalks celery, minced
1/2 cup red and green bell peppers, minced
1/4 cup red Bermuda onion, minced
1/4 cup parsley, chopped
1/2 cup green onion, minced
2 1/2 cups mayonnaise
1 1/2 cups creole mustard
1/4 cup paprika
1 1/4 t. cayenne pepper
1/2 t. white pepper, freshly ground
1/3 cup sun dried tomatoes, oil-packed, drained and minced

Mince all vegetables in a food processor or by hand and place into a large bowl. Mix with a thin wire whip until well mixed. Place into a sealable container, label, date and refrigerate.

Note: Whole-ground mustard or brown mustard may be substituted for creole mustard.

Yield: 25 servings.

Located at Johns Landing only minutes from the city center, the Avalon Grill and Cafe has a choice location.

The design by Lee Winn captures the effect of early 1900's luxury liners... multi-level with ship-style open stairways. The windows are wide horizontal bands. The cuisine is American Regional.

In the summer months the outdoor deck is very popular... boats, waterskiers.

We arrived just as the doors opened for lunch and within minutes the place was a-buzz with activity.

The daily specials are very good. However today I wanted to try their Black Bottom Banana Cream pie... it has become a Portland legend, skillfully executed by the fine dessert chef, Darla Swanson. She makes the shell using chocolate chips, fills it with sliced bananas, tops these with fudgy chocolate, then custard; then whipped cream. Wait – not finished yet! The top is then sprinkled with curls of light and dark chocolate. A banana shape made of chocolate is laid across the top.

This brought to my mind a sign that I saw in my traveling:

"Eat dessert first. Life is uncertain."

Lunch Monday - Friday   Dinner everyday   Sunday Brunch
Closed Christmas Day

TORTA DI CIMABUE

6 egg whites, room temp.
small pinch of salt
1/4 t. cream of tartar
1 1/2 cups superfine sugar
6 oz. bittersweet chocolate,
  melted and cooled
1 1/2 cups filberts, coarsely
  chopped (or other nuts)
2 t. vanilla
1/2 t. almond extract

4 cups heavy cream,
  whipped
1/4 cup powdered sugar
chocolate curls

Preheat convection oven to 200⁰.
Whip egg whites, cream of tartar and salt until frothy. Gradually add sugar and beat until very stiff. Fold in chocolate, nuts, and flavorings. Pipe onto parchment paper in 4 inch diameter circles. Bake for about 40 minutes, or until meringues are almost dry. They should crisp after removing from oven.
Whip cream with powdered sugar to piping consistency.

To serve: Sandwich meringues with whipped cream. Top with whipped cream and chocolate curls

Yield: about 12 servings.

WINTER SQUASH SOUP

2 1/2 onions, thinly sliced
1/4 lb. butter
1 bay leaf
1/4 t. thyme
1/4 of a whole nutmeg,
  crushed
2 lbs. winter squash, peeled
  and diced
2 russet potatoes, peeled
  and diced
water to cover
1 cup cream

Sweat onions in butter until soft without browning. Add bay, thyme, nutmeg, sweet meat squash and sweat again, stirring frequently just until squash is starting to soften a little. Add potatoes, water to cover and bring to a boil. Reduce to a simmer and cook until vegetables are very tender, about 20 minutes.
Purée in batches, and return purée to clean stockpot. Add cream, salt and pepper, and simmer briefly.
Garnish with lightly whipped cream, or chopped chives, or toasted almonds.

Yield: 10 servings.

The Hawthorne District in Portland is where you'll find Bread and Ink. It's an unusual name and makes it easy to remember. Near the entrance the window ledges have stacks of newspapers and magazines to read while you're waiting for your food. Some dining alone find it pleasant to read while dining.

This is a casual urban eatery with dishes being offered from many countries.... French country, Mexican, Jewish, Mediterranean, regional Italian and neo-American. Three or four people could choose entirely different types of food, and all be happy. It would be hard to not find something that appeals to you... and they do a good job of it all!

The soups are very popular, and please note that they've shared their recipe for Winter squash soup, one of the many they offer.

They make "primo" hamburgers... a hefty patty grilled to perfection, served on a fresh onion bun, accompanied by home-made mustard, mayo and catsup. Add their own spicy Guacamole and Cheddar or Gruyere cheese. The brunch, a 4-course Jewish meal includes chopped liver, scrambled eggs with lox and onions.

Breakfast, lunch & dinner every day

ROAST DUCK WITH A WILD HUCKLEBERRY SAUCE

2 ducks
1/2 cup huckleberry vinegar
1/2 cup honey
1 cup port
6 cups duck, veal, or beef stock
3 cups huckleberries
salt and cayenne pepper to
    taste

HUCKLEBERRY VINEGAR

1 gallon white wine vinegar
2 cups sugar
4 cups huckleberries

Simmer together in a non-
    reactive pan for about 1/2
    hour. Put in a jar and store.

Preheat oven to 350°

Truss ducks. Prick all over with a large fork or point of a knife. Roast for two hours. Remove from oven and set aside.

Pour fat from the roasting pan. (You can save it for another use if you like.) Deglaze the roasting pan with stock, scraping up all the drippings and little bits. Put stock in a non-reactive sauce pan. Add the honey, vinegar, port and two cups of huckleberries. Bring to a boil and reduce by half.

Strain through a sieve to remove the seeds. Purée the sauce in a blender or food processor. Return the sauce to a sauté pan. Add the reserved cup of berries. Season with salt and cayenne pepper.

Reheat sauce and finish with 3 to 4 T. unsalted butter. Taste and adjust seasonings if needed.

Quarter ducks, place on a warmed platter and nap with the sauce.

Yield: 8 servings

PORTOBELLO MUSHROOM SOUP WITH COGNAC AND LEEKS

1/2 stick butter
2 onions, diced
1 bunch leeks, split, washed
    thoroughly and diced with a
    small part of the green
1 lb. portobello mushrooms,
    sliced
1 potato, peeled and diced
1/4 cup cognac
6 cups chicken stock
2 cups half-&-half
white pepper to taste

Sauté the onions and leeks together. Add mushrooms and sauté together. Add cognac. Add potatoes and stock. Simmer until done.
Purée.
Add half-&-half.
Pepper to taste.
Thin with additional chicken stock if needed.

Yield: 8 servings.

Chef: Dennis R. Baker

Having dinner with 2 friends at Cafe des Amis was the highlight of this trip to Portland!

By arriving before the dinner opening, I was able to talk to chef/owner Dennis Baker. When I asked him what was new, Dennis brought out this picture of the baby daughter Dennis and his wife traveled to China to adopt. This was taken the first time baby Katherine was placed in his arms. Katy's look says "Here I am... my life is in your hands"... a look of love and trust! Because this isn't about cooking, he wondered about my using it. I pleaded, saying "It has a most important place in your life. I know others will love it as much as I do."

The Cafe des Amis is an extra-special Bistro and has amassed many awards and rightfully so! Gourmet magazine wrote that Cafe des Amis was chosen "Best Food in the City" by reader and customer poll. Zagat survey said "Best in the City" and "Best Bistro in the Northwest." I agree. Baker offers usually four or five entrées each night along with good French appetizers. One entrée is so popular that it's always on the list: the duck with blackberry sauce.

Excellent selection of wines.

Dinner Monday - Saturday

201

RED CLAM CHOWDER

1 lb. Manila clams, washed soaked and picked over, no minced clams
4 oz. cooked red potatoes, diced
1 oz. onions, diced
1 oz. leeks, diced (white and light green part)
1 oz. celery, diced
3 oz. diced tomatoes in juice (canned)
1 T. tomato puree
large pinch of mixed herbs
1 oz. olive oil
1 T. garlic, ground
12 oz. clam juice or fish stock
red pepper flakes
salt and pepper to taste

Sauté onions, leeks, celery, garlic and herbs and pepper in olive oil. Add clams, toss to get them hot. Add potatoes, tomatoes and clam juice and bring to a boil, simmer about 5 minutes. Potatoes should be cooked well enough that at the end they begin to break down and slightly thicken the soup.

HANGTOWN FRY

3 oz. fresh shucked oysters (coarsely chopped)
2 strips bacon
1/4 T. ground garlic
1/4 cup green onions, chopped
3 to 5 drops Worcestershire sauce
3 eggs
1 oz. Swiss cheese, shredded

Cut bacon into thin strips and place in a 10" fry pan with a little oil. Render bacon until it browns.
Turn heat to high and add oysters, cooking them until they begin to curl. Add garlic, and green onions tossing until tender. Add the eggs and Worcestershire, toss to mix all the ingredients. Toss on high heat until the eggs begin to set, flip once. Add the cheese and cook until as done as you prefer. Fold out onto plate. If you like your eggs cooked well done, lower heat and cook slowly to cook thoroughly.

Arriving between meal-times, I had a chance to talk to owner-chef Eddie Cohen. This is his first very-own place. He was chef in Sausalito, Ca for 9 years, and several years with "Rich's" in Tualatin. His sister is a physician in Portland's Good Samaritan Hospital.

He visited her, and was convinced that this should be his home too. He looked a long time before choosing this location. The decor is fun, with possibly a bear ready to keep you company while you dine. Many children (of all ages) put their height and names on the column, as shown on the sketch... returning to see how much taller they are.

The menu at Dancing Bear describes this as "Cuisine from the Eastern Edge of the Pacific Rim." A few specialties for breakfast: "The Blues" (from-scratch buttermilk pancakes with wild Maine blueberries). Or Apple cinnamon swirl French toast... or an excellent selection of omelettes. Lunch: salads include "Northwest Spinach" with smoked salmon, mushrooms, egg, tomatoes and toasted hazel nuts. "Chinese Chicken Salad" fried noodles, red cabbage, carrots, peanuts, his own Soy Sesame dressing on crisp lettuce. (No room left, but dinners are special, prices good.)

Breakfast & lunch Tuesday - Sunday
Dinner Tuesday - Saturday

BERRISSIMO
PASTRY SHELL
2 cups flour
2 T. sugar
1 t. vanilla
1 t. lemon peel
1/4 t. salt
1 cup frozen butter, cut into
   bits
1 egg
2/3 cup sugar 3/4 t. cinnamon
4 cups berries (blueberry,
   blackberry, raspberry, etc.)

1 cup sour cream or crème
   fraîche
3 egg yolks
2 T. honey
dash of vanilla extract

Preheat oven to 400⁰

Preheat oven to 400^0
Place in food processor and blend together the flour, sugar, vanilla, lemon peel and salt. Add frozen butter and egg. Process until just blended. Press into a 11" tart pan and chill.
Mix together sugar and cinnamon sprinkle a little of this over the tart shell and bake for 15 minutes.

Fill tart shell with berries and sprinkle with the rest of the sugar. Bake another 15 minutes.

Pour filling over tart and bake until set, about 15 minutes.

QUAGLIE AI TARTUFI (*"TRUFFLED" ROAST QUAIL*) FROM CATHERINE WHIMS
6 quail, dressed
4 small black truffles
salt and pepper
1 cup whipping cream
2 cups chicken stock
1 T. butter
duck fat or butter for sautéing
cognac

Begin the day before by wiping the quails carefully and patting them dry. Slice a truffle thinly and carefully place a few slices between the breast meat and breast skin of each quail. (This is done by carefullly working your fingers between the skin and breast meat to loosen skin.) Coarsly chop another truffle and divide among the cavities of the six quail. Season each cavity with salt and pepper. Refrigerate overnight.
Slice the remaining two truffles and soak them in the whipping cream, refrigerate overnight
The next day: Preheat oven to 450^0.
Heat butter or duck fat (about 2 T.) in a large sauté pan. Sauté the quail on all sides until golden.
Remove from heat, pour in cognac, and carefully ignite with a match. When flames subside, remove quail to a roasting pan and place in oven to roast until done, about 10 to 12 minutes.
Meanwhile add the chicken stock to pan and reduce to 1/4 cup. Add cream and reduce to a good consistency. Swirl in butter and correct seasoning with salt and pepper.
Serve quail on a bed of creamy polenta with sauce poured over.

Now a quarter of a century that Genoa has been offering their classical Italian cuisine. The menu changes every two weeks. They offer a 7-course fixed price dinner (or a 4-course meal is available).

This night the antipasto course was sausage of foie gras, veal sweet breads and chicken, sautéed and served with slices of poached apple in a port sauce. Especially nice: the server explained each dish — what it will be and how it is prepared. Next was "Zuppa di pesce", a light puréed fish soup flavored with leeks, onions, tomatoes, dry white wine, herbs, orange peel. The pasta course I really loved! It combined flakes of cold-smoked trout with a light reduction of cream tossed with homemade egg pasta and garnished with golden whitefish caviar.

Since our visit was just before Christmas, the traditional insalata was of lentils because they resemble coins, a promise of prosperity in the coming year. It was served warm with cucumbers and red onions accompanied by a "crostini" spread with goat cheese. The 3 of us each ordered a different entrée, and we had a taste of each. Only 3 choices were offered, and all were excellent.

Then, almost two hours later, the dessert choices were explained. The final course was a good selection of fresh fruit.

No room to elaborate on the desserts, but we each raved! I'm still raving. This is an event, not just a dinner.

Dinner Monday - Saturday   ♿

BUTTERNUT SQUASH RAVIOLI with MOSCATO, GORGONZOLA SAUCE

FILLING:
1 1/2 lb. butternut squash
1 T. shallots, chopped
2 T. garlic, chopped
1/3 cup thyme, chopped
1/3 cup toasted hazelnuts, chopped
2 T. butter
salt and pepper to taste
4 oz. gorgonzola

SAUCE
1/2 cup shallots, chopped
2 T. butter
2 T. garlic, chopped
1/3 cup chopped thyme
1 cup moscato wine
1 cup vegetable or chicken stock
3 cups half-n-half
1 cup heavy cream
4 oz. gorgonzola
1 T. balsamic vinegar
salt and pepper to taste
1 1/2 lbs pasta sheets
3 egg yolks

Prepare butternut squash by cutting it in half, removing seeds and roasting, face down on a sheet pan in a 400° oven. When squash is soft, remove from oven and let cool. Scoop cooled squash from peel using a large soup spoon. Crush squash with a whisk and set aside.

Sauté shallots, garlic, thyme in butter, add to the crush squash. Add crumbled gorgonzola, hazelnuts and salt and pepper. Refrigerate and begin sauce.

Sauce: Sauté shallots, garlic and thyme in butter. Deglaze pot with the moscato. When the wine is 2/3 reduced, add your choice of stock. Reduce again to 2/3 and add the half-n-half, let this reduce by 1/3. Add the cream, gorgonzola and balsamic vinegar and simmer until the gorgonzola is melted into the sauce. Set aside.

During the time that the sauce is reducing, start to make your raviolis. Place the pasta sheet flat on a table and place about 1 T. of squash mixture 2 inches apart. I use an ice cream scoop for the filling. If the sheets are between 4 to 5" wide place the mounds in the center of the lower half, that way all you have to do is egg wash around the mounds and fold the top half over the bottom. Seal pasta with a blunt object and press firmly so that the pasta seals properly around the edges. Add raviolis to a pot of boiling water and simmer for several minutes or until that are al dente. Place either in ice water or directly into the sauce and heat.

Yield: 6 to 8 servings.

PUMPKIN GNOCCHI in a ROASTED VEGETABLE PESTO CREAM SAUCE

2 lb. potato
1 cup onion, chopped
2 T. garlic, chopped
2 t. butter
2 eggs
3 cups flour
4 oz. baked, pureed, or canned
  pumpkin
1 T. salt
1 t. nutmeg
1 cup flour for rolling dough
PESTO:
8 oz. peeled carrot
8 oz. peeled onion
3 red peppers
3 T. oil for roasting
3 1/2 T. garlic, chopped
2 oz. grated Asiago cheese
1/2 cup olive oil
heavy cream, half-n-half, milk,
  chicken stock or white wine

Boil potatoes with skin on. Sauté onions with garlic and butter. When potatoes are soft, drain and peel. Purée potatoes with a ricer, or a whisk. Add eggs, flour, pumpkin, salt and nutmeg. Knead the mixture into a firm dough.

Coat a work surface and your hands with flour. Break the dough into large pieces and, using the palms of your hands, roll each piece into a log about 1" in diameter. Cut logs into 1" lengths. Place the cut Gnocchi on a tray that has parchment paper on it and set aside.

Pesto: Roast vegetables and add the chopped garlic, cheese and oil. Puree. (This is more than you need for this recipe)

Bring your cream to a boil, let simmer for 10 minutes and stir in your Vegetable Pesto. Season with salt and pepper to taste. Keep warm.

Bring a large pot of salted water to a boil and drop the gnocchi, a few at a time. As soon as they rise, place them directly into iced water. When all the Gnocchi have been cooked, drain water and reheat sauce in a large saucepan. Place the gnocchi into the sauce and simmer for several minutes.

Serve immediately. Yield: 6 servings.

At first glance the thought might be "Oh, this doesn't look like much." Don't be fooled. This former old natural food store was gutted by the new owners, Eugen and Lenor Bingham, changing the interior dramatically. Lenor, an artist, began by painting the walls yellow, then blending in cranberry paint. Lots of little shelves, sconces, candles and bric-a-brac were pleasing, added along with some of Lenor's paintings from her studio.

Eugen spent his early years and apprenticeship in Germany and was cooking in Switzerland.

The name of each item on the menu is in Italian, but the description is in English .... a good menu.

One of the pasta meals: Lasagne di Verdure is lasagne layered with roasted Swiss chard, oven-roasted yams and Ricotta cheese.

Another inventive offering: Crespelle alla Ricotta is crepes stuffed with wild mushrooms, spinach and ricotta, with a smoked pear crème fraîche.

Rabbit dishes are appearing more frequently on restaurant menus. Il Piatto serves Coniglio in Salmi. This is a marinated rabbit cooked slowly in a sauce of red wine, raisins and prosciutto and is served with polenta and a vegetable.

Lunch Tuesday - Friday   **Dinner every day**

OSSOBUCCO MILANESE (*Ossobucco con Gremolata alla Milanese*)

6 meaty veal shins, 4" long
1/2 cup butter
flour

1 large onion, chopped
1 large carrot , chopped
2 stalks of celery, chopped
2 cloves garlic, mashed

1 sprig each of marjoram,
  thyme and rosemary
1 cup dry white wine
5 ripe tomatoes, peeled,
  seeded and chopped
2 cups veal demi glace (veal
  stock)
1 T. orange rind
1 T. lemon rind
salt and ground pepper to
  taste

Heat 4 T. of butter in a heavy pot over medium heat until golden. Dust the veal shins with flour and brown them on both sides. Add the Gremolata (chopped mixture) marjoram, thyme, rosemary, salt and pepper and stir for 4 minutes. Add the wine and cook until evaporated. Add tomatoes and veal stock and bring to a boil.

Cover the pot, reduce heat to low; simmer for about 1 hour.

Ten minutes before serving, remove lid and raise the heat to medium high, reduce the sauce slightly.

As a garnishment, sprinkle the lemon and orange rinds on top of the meat before serving.

This dish is traditionally served over Risotto alla Milanese.

RISOTTO MILANESE (*Risotto alla Milanese*)

2 cups Arborio rice
1 1/2 cups of butter
1 small onion, chopped
1 cup dry white wine
1/3 t. saffron soaked in 3 T.
  warm water
5 to 6 cups of chicken broth
  or more as needed
1 1/2 cups grated Parmesan
  cheese
salt and pepper to taste

Melt 5 T. of butter in a large heavy pot over medium heat. Add onions and a pinch of pepper. As soon as the onions turn tender, add the wine and cook until wine has evaporated. Add the rice and season with salt, stirring for 4 minutes until every grain is coated. Add the saffron with water and 3 1/2 cups of the chicken broth. Bring to a boil and cook stirring all the time until the rice thickens and dries, add more chicken broth from time to time and continue cooking over medium heat stirring frequently until the rice is *al dente*.

Remove from the stove and add the rest of the butter. If you wish add several tablespoons of Parmesan cheese. Save the remaining cheese for the table.

Buon Appetito!

The Lake Grove Bistro offers French and Italian cuisine in a very charmingly decorated bistro. The walls in the bar have been painted with the feeling of Van Gogh's "Night Cafe" with owner/chef Carlo Rostagni and his charming wife Donna painted into it. The lower picture shows their son Marcello on the right. He is now 17 years old. (Sorry that I didn't get a picture of Angela, their daughter who is now 14. When you are at the bistro, you'll see her in the mural holding a violin. The mural is from floor to ceiling.)

I had heard many good comments on this place... their reputation is excellent. I can recommend the duck ravioli as a starter... it's made with tender juicy roast duck and served in a creamy walnut sauce. Their Caesar salad is traditional... you couldn't ask for better!

This was my night for "stuffed" food, first the ravioli, then Poulet Bistro, a baked chicken breast stuffed with Swiss cheese, sage and prosciutto. This was served over angel hair putanesca with dried porcini mushroom sauce. So many good choices here!

Lunch Tuesday - Friday   **Dinner Tuesday - Saturday**

GUMBO BASE
3 gallons water
5 oz. fish bouillon
1/2 container beef base

1 lb. butter
2 cups red onion, small dice
2 cups celery, small dice
2 cups chopped garlic
3 cups Italian seasoning
3 T. black pepper
1 cup chopped parsley
20 jerks Tabasco
3 cups flour
6 oz. corn starch

Set water aside. Weigh bouillon and beef base, combine and set aside.

In a large stockpot, melt the butter. Add onion and celery, sauté. Add garlic, seasoning, pepper, parsley and Tabasco. Mix with a whip. Using the whip, mix in flour, moving constantly to prevent sticking, for about 2 to 3 minutes. Add the water mixing thoroughly, cover stockpot and bring to a boil.

Mix corn starch with just enough cold water to make a thick slurry. Add slurry slowly while whisking until incorporated.

Simmer for 15 to 20 minutes, cool in water bath and store.

Yield: 3 1/2 gallons.

ALLIGATOR PATÉ
2 1/2 lbs. pork sausage
5 lbs. alligator meat
6 T. garlic, chopped
2 cups red onion
8 jalapeños
1 cup chopped parsley
1 cup cajun seasoning
1 capful Worcestershire
12 jerks Tabasco
3/4 cup Commander St. John
  brandy
1 1/2 cup crouton crumbs
10 whole eggs
1 t. crushed red pepper

Preheat oven to 425⁰.

Grind with big hole blade the sausage and alligator meat, garlic, red onion, jalapeños and parsley.

Mix in by hand very thoroughly the seasoning, Worcestershire, Tabasco, brandy, crouton crumbs, eggs and red pepper.

Fill a paté pan 3/4 full with raw mixture. Bake on sheet pan for approximately 1 hour 15 minutes, or until internal temperature reaches 125⁰.

Chill completely before slicing into 22 portions from each loaf pan.

Yield: 3 pans.

"First come, First served"
   -no reservations
     at the

Montage Bistro. Under the Morrison Bridge, open till very late, quite noisy, but in a friendly happy way. On certain orders, the waiter yells from across the room (so noisy that I couldn't make out what was said). Seating is at long tables and we were joined at our table by 4 people unknown to us. I could write a page just about the unusual menu! My appetizer was Alligator Paté — really. (See recipe on the opposite page). It was served with mango chutney and black bread. It is good! Many students and/or young adults come for dinner — many staying for a long time. The Dec. 1996 prices: Macaroni in garlic, Parmesan, served with corn bread and vegetables $4. Mixed green salad, Caesar dressing (or 3 other dressings) & home made croutons $2.50. Budget pleasers.

The full dinners include N.Y. Steaks, blackened catfish fillet, Jamba-laya, crawfish, chicken and rabbit sausage + more. Desserts are notorious.

Dinner every day
Lunch until 2:00 Monday - Friday

GOAT CHEESE GALETTE WITH BLOOD ORANGE COULIS

BLOOD ORANGE COULIS

1 cup strained blood orange
  juice
1 T. + 1 t. corn starch
2 t. lemon juice
3 T. sugar

GOAT CHEESE GALETTE DOUGH

1 egg yolk
2 T sour cream
1 to 2 T. ice cold water
1 cup unbleached flour
1/4 cup yellow cornmeal
1 T. powdered sugar
1/2 t. salt
7 T. cold butter, in small
  pieces

FILLING

5 oz. log Chevre, room temp.
4 oz. cream cheese, room
  temp.
1/4 cup sugar
1/4 t. vanilla extract
1/2 t. lemon juice
1 egg, room temp.
2 T. flour

Add enough juice to cornstarch to make a slurry. Add slurry to blood orange juice, add lemon juice and sugar. Heat in small stainless steel saucepan over medium-high heat, stirring constantly until thickened. If the blood oranges are too tart, add more sugar. Chill until needed. Makes 1 cup.

Combine egg yolk, sour cream, water and set aside. In stainless steel bowl combine flour, cornmeal, powdered sugar, salt. Add cold butter to flour mix using a pastry cutter until it resembles the size of small peas. Drizzle liquid slowly over flour mixture, and stir together with a fork until dough is gathered together. Do not overwork. Pat into a flattened ball and chill for 1 hour.

Filling: In a mixer with a paddle, beat goat cheese and cream cheese on low speed until smooth. With mixer running, add sugar slowly. Combine egg, lemon, vanilla and pour into cheese mixture. Scatter flour over mixture and mix until just incorporated.

To assemble: Roll out dough to an 11" circle if making one galette, or divide into 4 pieces and roll out for individual galettes.   Preheat oven to 350⁰.

Place rolled dough onto a baking sheet lined with greased parchment paper. Use a spoon to place goat cheese filling in the middle of the dough, spreading out from the middle with the back of spoon, leaving 2" of dough uncovered. Fold the 2" of dough up over the mixture and crimp each fold over the next. It must be crimped tightly to avoid seepage. If making 4, repeat this procedure. Sprinkle with sugar if desired and bake for 30 to 35 minutes until crust is golden and dough does not look raw where it is crimped. Cut. Serve with blood orange coulis.

Arrived when Ron Paul's was opening, set up a table on the first section shown here, then moved along – however a line soon began to form in front of the cases, making it hard to see.... so I bought several items, including one of their famous triple chocolate Black Angus cookies, huge and sinfully delicious!

Starting in a small neighborhood store in 1983 - to the present, with the 4th establishment opening soon, Ron's culinary talents have the perfect showcase. The emphasis is on innovation, with each dish individually designed and reflecting seasonal fresh items. Catering remains a significant part of the business, with the customer's wishes and the event influencing the menu ...in addition, matching the client's cellar or from Ron's extensive selection. Ron has been invited to be a guest chef at the James Beard Foundation in New York City, guest chef at Pacific Northwest Wine Exhibition for 5 years, featured in "Bon Appetit", "The Wine Spectator", "Portland Downtowner", "Portland Best Places" and more.

I had been working on my sketch for less than an hour when staff began to bring out more and more new offerings, the cases now crammed with choices of every kind.... making it hard to find display room, but somehow managing. Wow! what choices!

1. B, L & D until 11 PM Mon. - Thurs. B, L & D until 12 Midnight Fri. & Sat. B, L & D until 9 PM Sunday	2. B, L & D until 9 PM Mon. - Sat. B & L until 4 PM Sunday
3. Open 11 AM until 9 PM Mon. - Sat. Closed Sunday	4. Open 7 AM until 6 PM Mon. - Fri. Open 9 AM until 5 PM Sat. Closed Sunday

BIRIYANI RICE

3 cups Basmati rice
1/2 cup butter or margarine
1 t. salt
2 green chiles, chopped
1 onion, chopped

4 cardamom
4 cloves
4 cinnamon stick
1 T. ginger
1 T. garlic paste

In a frying pan heat the butter and add all the ingredients, (except rice.) Cook them well. In a rice cooker, put rice and 4 cups of water and the cooked product. Cook according to your cooker's directions.
Cover rice with mixture.

Yield: 4 to 6 servings.

DAL CURRY

2 lbs. yellow split peas
1 bunch spinach, washed and chopped
2 medium tomatoes, chopped
2 oz. tamarind fruit
1 t. chili powder
1 t. salt

1 t. turmeric powder
2 T. olive oil
1 t. mustard seed
1 t. garlic powder
1 t. black lentils

Boil the peas in a saucepan with 4 cups of water until it comes to a boil. Add spinach, tomatoes, tamarind fruit, chili powder, salt and turmeric powder and cook well. The peas have to become paste when it is ready.
In a frying pan heat olive oil. Add mustard seeds, garlic powder and black lentils, heating gradually. Add spices to the cooked product. Stir and taste for salt and chili. Add extra if desired.

Yield: 4 to 6 servings.

MEAT CURRY

2 lbs. skinless, boneless chicken, lamb, pork or beef (cut into small pieces)
2 medium onions, chopped
2 jalapeño chiles, chopped
2 medium tomatoes, chopped
1 t. cumin powder
1 t. coriander powder
1 t. Garam Masala

2 t. poppy seeds, lightly roasted and blended
1 T. ginger
2 T. garlic paste
2 t. diced coconut, blended into powder
1 t. chili powder
1 t. salt

In a sauce pan heat 1 T. oil. Add chiles and onions and brown. Add the meat and cook thoroughly. Add remaining ingredients and let it cook well.
Check the meat adding a little water if needed to cook well done before serving.

Yield: 4 to 6 servings.

Swagat, specializing in cooking both North and South Indian dishes, has been pleasing Portland people for about 5 years now. I arrived at 11:20 for lunch (opening is 11:30) and found 30 to 40 people waiting for the doors to open.

The line moves quickly... it is buffet style. A nice touch is the stacks of small bowls to keep sauces from running into unwanted items. Many flavors to try (18 at lunch time). You may go for seconds, but save room for the rice pudding... not sure what spices, but just right!

This has been a family business, with brothers in California who are running several restaurants there. This is the only one in Oregon. None yet in Washington, but it would be a good idea. (I know that I'd be in line.)

The prices are amazingly reasonable. Very good for working people on their lunch hour, or to take home for dinner. Even at lunch time they do a big "to go" business.

I told my friend that I planned to ask for the name of the "crispy crunchy...?...."—discovered they're called pakoras. (I did go back for seconds on the pakoras plus 2 others.)

It's located on a street of 1940's or '50s tract style homes. A little difficult to find, but make the effort. You'll be glad that you did!

Lunch buffet every day   Dinner every day

BAKED SCALLOPS

3 oz. scallops
1/4 cup mirepoix, cooked
2 oz. shrimp
2 oz. shredded Jack cheese
1/4 cup heavy cream
salt and pepper to taste
1 t. chopped parsley

Dredge scallops in flour; sauté 1 minute each side. Add mirepoix and shrimp, cook 1 minute. Add cream and reduce by half. Add chopped parsley and cheese. Cook 1 minute more.

Pour into a small bowl or baking dish. Pipe mashed potatoes around the edge of bowl. Sprinkle cheese on top and broil or bake until brown and bubbly.

WATERZOIE

2 T. unsalted butter
1/2 cup finely diced mixed
  vegetables (1 part carrot,
  1 part celery, 2 parts
  onion)
2 cups fish or clam stock,
  homemade preferred
2 oz. halibut cheeks, cut
  into 2 inch cubes (see
  note)
2 oz. snapper fillet, cut into
  2 inch cubes
2 oz. salmon fillet, cut into
  2 inch cubes
6 fresh steamer clams,
  scrubbed and cleaned
6 fresh mussels, cleaned
  and bearded
2 oz. rock shrimp, peeled
  and deveined
salt and pepper to taste
1 T. chopped fresh parsley

Combine the butter and mixed vegetables in a saucepan or stock pot over medium heat. Sauté the vegetables until they begin to soften. Add the fish stock and simmer on low heat for 30 minutes. Add the halibut cheeks, snapper, salmon, clams, mussels and rock shrimp. Briskly simmer for 5 to 10 minutes or until all the seafood is cooked. Do not overcook. Salt and pepper to taste
Remove to individual bowls and garnish with parsley.

Note: If halibut cheeks are not available, scallops can be substituted to give a similar texture.

Variation: For the classic Belgium Waterzoie, add 1/2 cup diced boiled potatoes and 1/2 to 3/4 cup heavy cream during the last 10 minutes of cooking time.

Yield: 2 generous servings

From: Chef Bill McCarty

I had a policy of not asking for any special recipe, but leaving it to the chef to choose. I broke this after tasting the baked scallops here.

"Waterzoies" is the name for a Belgian fish-based soup and the recipe is about 200 years old!

Bill and Donna McCarty have taken one of Portland's lovely old homes and created a setting for their creative talents from the kitchen. There's well-chosen art on the walls, gleaming hardwood floors in several rooms of this old home ready for dining. Bill told me that the breads and desserts come from their own kitchen and vary with the whim of the chef. There is no freezer, so they make heavy use of local ingredients seasonally. Salad dressings are also made here, and are available for purchase (as well as their breads and marinades).

I was told that the weekend Saturday and Sunday brunches are very popular, but I haven't been in Portland on a weekend.

Lunch Tuesday - Friday   Dinner Tuesday - Saturday
Saturday AM & Monday evening cooking classes
Saturday AM, Sunday & Monday available for private parties

PUMPKIN PANCAKES

2 3/4 cups cake flour
3/4 cup cornmeal
2 T. + 1 t. granulated sugar
4 1/2 t. baking powder
1 1/2 t. baking soda
1/2 t. salt
2 t. ground allspice
4 eggs
3 3/4 cups buttermilk
1 1/2 cup canned pumpkin
1/2 cup melted butter (1 stick)

vegetable oil
butter
real maple syrup

In one bowl, stir all dry ingredients. In a second bowl lightly beat eggs. Add milk, pumpkin and melted butter. Mix well.
Add wet ingredients to dry, stir to mix well.
Let rest 15 to 30 minutes. Add water to mix if it is too thick.
Heat griddle to medium heat until a little water rolls off in drops. Lightly grease with vegetable oil. Add 1/2 cup batter and cook until bubbles appear and the edges appear dry. Turn and cook 2 to 3 minutes until brown. Serve with butter and real maple syrup

Note: For a more traditional pumpkin flavor; substitute 1 t. ground cinnamon, 1/2 t. nutmeg, 1/2 t. ground ginger for the allspice.

Yield: 16 - 6 oz. pancakes

TUSCAN MEATLOAF

1 1/2 lbs. ground beef
1/2 lb. ground pork
2 eggs 1/2 cup milk
scant 1/2 cup fresh bread crumbs (reduce amount if using dry crumbs)
1 1/2 t. salt
1 cup onion, finely chopped
1/2 cup, fresh parsley, chopped
1 t. fresh garlic, minced
1 t. coarsely chopped black pepper
1 t. oregano, dried
1 t. basil, dried
1/2 t. fennel seeds, crushed

Preheat oven to 350⁰
Mix together the beef and pork. In a second bowl mix the eggs, milk and breadcrumbs. Add remaining ingredients to the liquid.
Add mixture to the meat and mix thoroughly. Form into a loaf (mixture will be soft) on a slotted broiler pan to allow juices and fat to flow away from the meat loaf. Do not cook in a bread pan.
Bake about 1 hour until internal temperature reaches 160⁰. Let rest.
Serve hot or cold.

About 50 years ago, this was a drugstore. The vintage soda fountain remains and is still being used ... beautiful tile counter and huge beveled mirrors.

And now along comes Judy Sacheck, former owner of Besaw's cafe in N.W. Portland, and she is breathing new life into an already notable Cafe. She is maintaining the house favorites of German pancakes and scones, but has added exciting egg creations such as Artichoke and Leek Frittata, Scrambled eggs with Brie, tomatoes and scallions (named after cousin, Maurice, in Paris). Also Prosciutto, asparagus and Asiago cheese omelette... smoked salmon and Gruyère scramble plus the traditional Eggs Benedict and Salmon Benedict on the weekends.

At lunch, New Orleans-style pan fried oysters and their Hangtown Fry, as well as other fresh fish entrées.

Delicious soups and salads round out this menu. An extra feature: breakfast is available during all their open hours.

Outdoor seating is available during the summer months.

Breakfast & lunch every day
Breakfast served all hours open

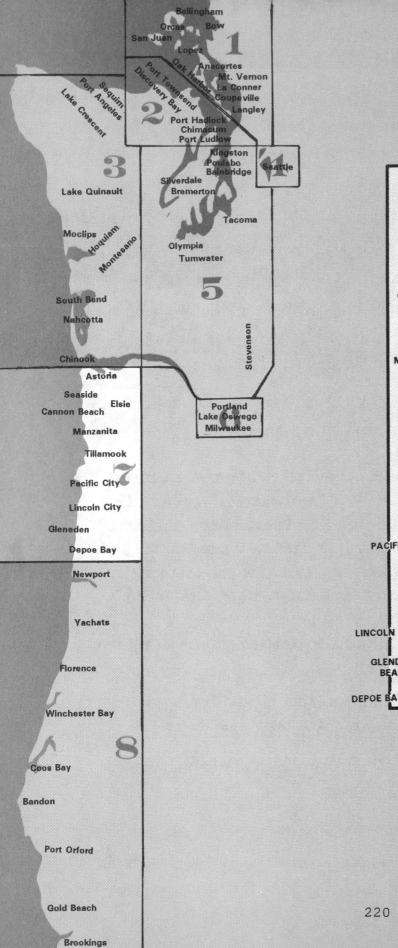

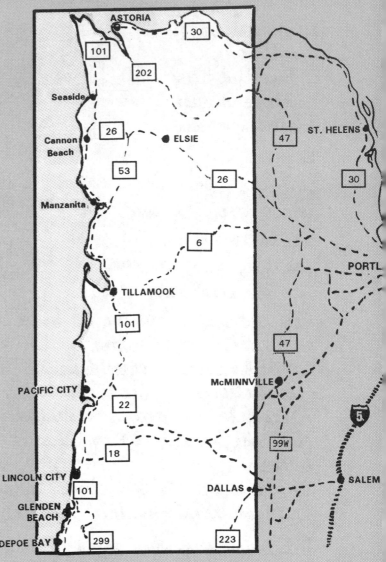

SECTION 7 OREGON

ASTORIA: Columbian Cafe, Pier 11 Feed Store, The Ship Inn
SEASIDE: Dooger's
CANNON BEACH: Midtown Cafe, Dooger's
ELSIE: Camp 18
MANZANITA: Blue Sky Cafe
TILLAMOOK: Tillamook Cheese Company
PACIFIC CITY: Grateful Bread, Riverhouse Restaurant, Bay House
LINCOLN CITY: Kyllo's, Salmon River Cafe
GLENEDEN BEACH: Salishan Lodge
DEPOE BAY: Gracie's Sea Hag, Tidal Raves

ISLAND SALSA

3 to 4 cups fresh fruit (such as
   pineapple, strawberries,
   melon and mango), peeled,
   seeded and diced
1 to 2 oranges, peeled, seeded
   and diced
2 large jalapeño or cayenne
   chilies , seeded, julienned,
   and finely minced

Place in large bowl and mix by hand.

Note: Bananas and apples do not work well in this.

NEW MEXICO LASAGNE

2 lbs Ricotta cheese
4 eggs
3 cups Parmesan, grated
3 lbs. 3 cheeses mixture
   (Cheddar, Mozzarella, and
   Provolone
1 cup cilantro
2 t. salt
2 t. pepper
pasta, cooked
black beans, cooked
corn
1/2 cup mild salsa
corn tortillas

Preheat oven to 350⁰.
Mix Ricotta with eggs until creamy. Add cheeses
cilantro, salt and pepper.
Lightly oil the bottom of a 10 x 14 inch pan. Cover
bottom with pasta, spread with a layer of cheese
mixture, then a layer of black beans and a layer of
corn. Pour 1/4 cup or so of mild salsa over corn
layer, cover with tortillas. Repeat layering. Cover
with pasta and sprinkle with three cheese mixture.
Bake for 30 minutes.

URIAH HULSEY

I saw the business card for
the Columbian Cafe with this
charming sketch that Max
(Uriah's son) did of his dad
one morning at breakfast.
Max was 9 years old when
he did this sketch.

I planned my day so that I'd arrive about 45 minutes before closing time and hopefully be able to talk to owner/chef Uriah Hulsey and to watch his wizardry at the stove. (Actually he uses 2 electric burners and one griddle!)

I asked him "How did anyone have the nerve to open a restaurant next door and decorate it so much like your place?" He laughed and said it was an addition to the Columbian... needed more space.

Out of this kitchen Uriah is able to turn out some great meals... each done to order, even chopping up mushrooms as they're needed. In a back room a staff person will put freshly made pasta through the slicer just before popping it into boiling water. The pasta is made daily.

This cafe is still pretty much the same as it was over 70 years ago... swivel stools at the counter and old straight-backed wooden booths.

A few years ago the Oakland Tribune wrote that Uriah... "is curmudgeonly, contrary, occasionally charming and always eccentric".

But what mouthwatering dishes he whips up. My red snapper in a Thai style nut sauce on pasta... the best!!

Breakfast, lunch & dinner Monday - Saturday
Closed Sunday

BAKED BLUE CHEESE HALIBUT

DRESSING
1/4 lb. blue cheese crumbles
1/2 quart buttermilk
1 1/2 cups mayonnaise
1 cup water
1/2 t. black pepper
1 t. garlic, crushed
1/2 t. white pepper

2 lbs. halibut, cut into 5 oz.
  servings
1 red onion, sliced
blue cheese crumbles

Mix all dressing ingredients, add water to thin if needed. Chill. Or: use blue cheese dressing of preference.

Preheat oven to 350⁰.
In a large serving bowl or baking pan layer a thin amount of the blue cheese dressing. Put fish in and add another thin layer of dressing on top. Cover with sliced red onion and blue cheese crumbles.
Bake for 25 to 30 minutes.

Yield: 6 servings

PEPPER STEAK
6 to 8 - 8 to 10 oz. steaks
3 quarts beef stock

1/4 lb. bacon
1 cup carrots, diced
1 cup celery, diced
1 cup onions, diced
1/2 cup white wine
4 oz. butter
3/4 cup flour
3 3/4 quarts beef stock
1 large bay leaf
1 cup tomato purée
1/2 cup cognac
10 peppercorns

Marinate steaks overnight in brandy or cognac.

Make beef stock from bones.

In a sauté pan cook bacon, carrots, celery and onions until soft. Drain off fat and deglaze the pan with wine.

Make a roux with butter and flour in a large pot. Put vegetables and pan juices into pot with 2 1/4 quarts beef stock and bay leaf. Boil briskly 4 to 5 minutes, reduce heat and simmer 2 1/2 hours.

Strain and put stock back in pot and add the additional stock and tomato purée. Simmer 1 hour.

Add cognac and peppercorns and simmer 10 minutes.

Press steaks into pan of cracked pepper and broil. Cover with sauce and serve.

This is the place to come if you're interested in a restaurant with a view. The extra large windows run the length of this very long building.

Sit back and watch the tugs, freighters, pleasure boats going up and down the Columbia River.

The building that houses the Pier 11 Feed Store Restaurant was originally a freight depot for river cargo. It was back in the 1880's that the first paddlewheelers unloaded their goods at this site. Then in 1922 a fire swept through most of Astoria. The depot wasn't damaged, but it was converted into a feed mill and store. Most of what you will see here is the original structure, but the mill machinery was removed to make way for the last remodeling.

This is Cecil, and he is a wooden sea serpent, the product of a creative craftsman. He is located in the lounge so children may come in to see Cecil, and to touch him, but children are served their meals in the dining room. Adults could sit and have their drinks by the table across Cecil's back.

The menu stays pretty much the same - just as has been offered for years.

Lunch & dinner every day
Closed Thanksgiving & Christmas Day

225

MOULES MARINIÈRES

butter for frying
4 shallots, peeled and
 chopped
1 clove garlic, crushed with
 1/2 t. salt
1/2 pint dry white wine
1 bouquet garni*
freshly ground black pepper
4 dozen mussels (or steamer
 clams) scrubbed
2 T. parsley, chopped

Melt cube of butter in a large pan. Add shallots and garlic, fry for 5 minutes until golden.
Stir in wine, bouquet garni, pepper and mussels (or clams). Cover with tightly fitting lid and cook for 10 minutes or until shells open.
Remove top shells and place mussels in individual bowls.
Taste sauce for seasoning and pour over mussels.
Sprinkle parsley over and serve.

*Bouquet garni is a combination of fresh herbs. If you are unable to obtain you may substitute. If using fresh, use 3 bay leaves and a sprig of thyme, tied in a cheese cloth. If dried, use 1/2 t. thyme and 1/2 t. bay leaf tied in a cheese cloth.

WHITE CHILI

1 lb. small white beans
3 T. olive oil
1 large onion, minced
3 cloves garlic, minced
2 4 oz. cans chopped green
 chiles
1 T. ground cumin
1 T. dried oregano
2 t. cinnamon
1 pinch cayenne
8 to 10 cups canned
 chicken broth
4 cups cooked turkey, cut
 in 1 inch cubes
salt and ground pepper to
 taste
3/4 lb. shredded Monterey
 Jack cheese

GARNISH
salsa
sour cream
cilantro

Soak beans overnight, drain the next day.
Sauté onions in oil until tender.
Stir in garlic, chiles and spices. Sauté 3 minutes.
Add chicken broth and beans. Bring to a boil. Lower heat and simmer 2 to 3 hours.
Add turkey, season with salt and pepper. Add 1 1/2 cups cheese just before serving until melted.

Garnish with the salsa, sour cream and cilantro

Owners Jill and Fenton Stokeld have built a reputation in Astoria for a quarter of a century.

They are transplanted here from England. No one can prepare fish and chips like the English! I ordered fish and chips in Salisbury, took them to a park and unwrapped the newspaper to taste batter-dipped filets that were tender and not greasy.

That is how they're prepared at the Ship Inn. Mmm! They told me that the fish is double dipped. The chips are made from thick potato slices, and the potatoes don't seem oily either.

A couple of other English menu items are Cornish Pasties and a treacle tart.

The Ship Inn is located just at water's edge. Watch the ships go by - lots of activity. The Columbia River is quite wide here. The Stokelds call this a "family pub" and the bar next to the restaurant is usually very busy.

A nice feature: many items on the menu may be ordered as a lunch, à la carte or as full dinner.

Lunch & dinner every day

REDFISH PALERMO

I 6 to 8 oz. portion red snapper
   or other rock fish
1/3 cup Feta cheese, crumbled
I T. slivered sundried tomatoes
I T. slivered artichoke hearts
I t. slivered Kalamata olives
fresh oregano and fennel fronds
   (liberal amounts)
I T. Sambuca Romano liquor
   (Licorice Liqueur)

Preheat oven to 450⁰
Layer ingredients in the exact order given on a sheet of parchment paper, sprinkling the herbs over all and then the liqueur. Fold the edges to make a packet.
Bake for 20 minutes.

Serve with lemon polenta.

LEMON POLENTA

3 cups milk
2 T. butter
I t. salt
I t. pepper
grated peel of 2 lemons
I cup polenta
1/2 cup grated Parmesan

Heat milk, butter, salt and pepper and lemon peel slowly until steaming. Slowly add the polenta stirring constantly until thickened. Add Parmesan.
Pour into serving containers and refrigerate 2 hours. Rebake portions at 450⁰ for 15 minutes.

Note: I add some mascarpone and a little pesto on the top before baking.

This makes a big batch, but will keep in the refrigerator.

The Blue Sky Cafe sits back from the street aways, but this sign is easily identifiable.

Julia Barker, owner/chef states "At a time when we are seeking balance and meaning in our busy lives, it is essential to acknowledge art as an important role in expressing ourselves. The "zen" of the Blue Sky is food prepared with passion and significance, an atmosphere warm and relaxed, hopefully inspiring culinary consciousness."

And after having a little time with Julia before she left for her art class, I stayed and had an excellent dinner. Yes, the menu is truly inspired. My appetizer of Smoked Duck Rice Balls was smoked duck breast rolled in sushi rice, served with nori threads, pickled ginger, wasabi and daikon salad. Great flavors together.

My meat entree: Red snapper, baked with cilantro-olive tapenade over Mexican green rice with orange crema, toasted cumin seed and salsa.

You'll find Japanese, Thai, Mexican, French, lots of seafood, filet mignon, cajun.

Julia is sharing her recipe for "Redfish Palermo"- see opposite page. This is one of the first dishes she prepared after she started cooking dinners here, and it is very popular with the customers. (I am looking forward to try it - after the book's done!)

Dinner Wednesday - Sunday

229

DOOGER'S CLAM CHOWDER

51 oz. can chopped sea clams
5 oz. Idahoan diced potatoes,
  cooked
1 T. clam base
1/2 t. Season All
1/4 t. white pepper
1/8 t. ground thyme
1 quart half-&-half
1 cup whipping cream

Mix all ingredients except half-&-half and cream together, let sit overnight. Add half-&-half and whipping cream.
Heat and serve.

Yield: 6 servings.

MARIONBERRY COBBLER

2 1/4 cups water
2 T. butter or margarine
26 oz. berries
1 1/2 cup sugar
3 T. cornstarch

Preheat oven to 350⁰
Heat water to boiling, add berries and butter. Let come to bubbly stage. Mix cornstarch and sugar together. Stir into berries.

CAKE

3 oz. butter or margarine
3/4 cup sugar
1 1/3 cups milk
2 cups flour
2 1/2 T. baking powder
1/4 t. salt

Cake: Cream butter and sugar. Add milk. Sift together; flour, baking powder and salt. Stir dry ingredients into creamed mixture. Pour cake in bottom of pan, spoon berries on top. Bake for approximately 50 minutes.

SOUR HONEY DRESSING

2 cups mayonnaise
1/2 cup yellow prepared
  mustard
1/2 cup pure vegetable salad
  oil
1/2 cup honey
small pinch red pepper
1/4 t. onion salt
1/4 cup apple cider vinegar

Blend all ingredients until smooth. Refrigerate.
Note: This will keep in the refrigerator for 21 days.
Discard when the oil starts to separate.

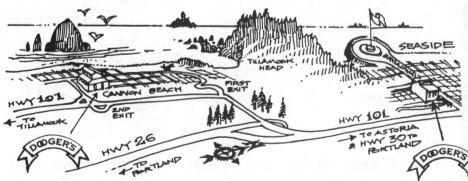

There were two Dooger's (both in Oregon). Now a third Dooger's - in Washington, located in Long Beach.

Years ago Dooger's was a totally non-smoking establishment - including the bar... long before it became the popular thing to do!

← This restaurant is in Seaside. I have included both places because of their good reputation. The homemade chowder is a real treat. Seafood is a specialty here - I ordered salmon that evening... cooked to perfection. Owner Doug Wiese told me "I strive for fast friendly service... and if something isn't on the menu - ask". The recipe given here for Sour Honey Dressing is good... but for myself, I made ½ of the amounts. Their good reputation has been written about in Bon Appetit, Best Places and in the Mobil Guide as well as newspaper articles.

← This Dooger's is located in Cannon Beach - southern end of downtown. Ample parking.

The desserts are worth saving room for ... if you can.

Seaside: Lunch & dinner every day
Cannon Beach: Breakfast, lunch & dinner every day

231

SWEET AND SOUR PORK MEDALLIONS

4 - 3 to 4 oz. slices of boneless
  pork loin, pounded flat
1/4 cup flour
1/4 cup bread crumbs
2 eggs
1 1/2 cups purchased sweet &
  sour sauce with pineapple
  chunks
2 T. toasted sesame seed
3 T. olive oil

Heat olive oil in skillet over medium high heat. Dust pork in flour. Beat eggs in dish. Dip pork in egg then roll in bread crumbs. Cook 4 minutes on each side, checking for doneness. Remove to plate.

Heat sweet & sour sauce and pour over top. Sprinkle with toasted sesame seeds. Salt and pepper to taste.

Yield: 2 servings.

SAUTÉED CHICKEN WITH SHERRY CREAM SAUCE

4 boneless chicken breasts,
  (skinless) pounded
1/2 cup cream sherry
1/4 t. basil
1/4 t. thyme
1/4 t. oregano
1/4 t. parsley
2 cloves garlic, chopped
1/4 cup flour
1 1/2 cups heavy cream
salt and pepper to taste
1/3 cup clarified butter
1 small onion, julienned
1/3 lb. mushrooms, sliced

Heat skillet and clarified butter on medium high heat. Dust chicken in flour and add to pan. Cook 3 to 4 minutes on each side, making sure chicken is cooked through. Add onion, mushrooms, garlic and herbs. Deglaze with cream sherry. Reduce liquid to 1/3 and then add the heavy cream. Reduce again and add salt and pepper to taste.

Yield: 4 servings

Chef Kenny Graves

The most dominant feature of the Camp 18 Restaurant is the 85 foot ridge pole in the huge main room - largest known in the United States! Weighing approx. 25 tons when cut, it has 5,600 board feet in it. The fireplaces have 50 tons of rocks.
You've got to see it!

Camp 18 is located 22 miles south of Seaside. It is owner Gordon Smith's dream. He began with a few pieces of equipment. Donated, loaned or purchased items led to the building of this very big log cabin (cabin may not be the best word).

Maurie Clark joined Smith in the early days of construction and was made "riggin' Boss". They found several pieces of old equipment. This collection grew until the present. It's like a museum - inside and outside. The most frequently asked question is "When will it be finished?" The answer is "Never". Old pieces of equipment keep turning up. To open the two main doors, grab an embedded ax handle. (It won't come loose.)

In 1986 an 80 foot addition was needed to house a larger kitchen.

Breakfast, lunch & dinner every day

233

COCONUT TOPPED OATMEAL CAKE

Cake:

2 1/2 cups boiling water
2 cups quick rolled oats
3 cups flour
1 t. soda
7 t. baking powder
1 t. salt
2 t. cinnamon
1 cup butter
2 cups granulated sugar
2 cups brown sugar
4 eggs

Topping:

1/2 cup butter
1/2 cup heavy cream
2 t. vanilla
1 cup brown sugar
2 2/3 cups coconut

Preheat oven to 350⁰

Cake: Pour boiling water over oats and allow to stand. Sift flour, soda, baking powder, salt and cinnamon. Cream butter and sugars until light and fluffy. Beat in eggs. Alternate flour mixture and cooled oats, mixing well. Pour into greased and floured cake pan. Bake until cake springs back and toothpick comes out clean.

Topping: Place all ingredients in a heavy saucepan and heat, stirring, to boiling, Pour evenly over cake and broil until toasted.

ALMOND ROCA COOKIE BARS

Shortbread:

2 cups butter
1 cup brown sugar
1 cup white sugar
2 egg yolks, beaten
2 t. vanilla

2 cups semi-sweet chocolate
  chips

Preheat oven to 350⁰

Mix shortbread ingredients in order. Pat into greased cookie sheet and bake for 20 minutes or until browned on top.

Remove from oven and pour semi-sweet chocolate chips over hot shortbread. When chips begin to melt spread evenly over shortbread.

Top with chopped walnuts and pat down.

Cool slightly and cut into bars.

The former owners are now living in Mexico, but left the Midtown Cafe in the good hands of owner Katie Trees, who has lived on the Oregon coast since 1984. She loves this work and the contact with the customers.

Katie and her mother spent many hours cooking and baking (her mother died in 1984.) A lot of her recipes are used here. Katie makes her own catsup! Jars of home-made jams and marmalades are for sale — my jar of Katie's orange-carrot marmalade is almost empty! Loaded with the oranges and carrots, but not too sweet. Fabulous on full grain toast. Also makes marion-berry jam from local berries. My Hungarian vegetable soup with sausage, and served with Italian sour dough bread couldn't have been any better! The ginger-bread scone following was to eat as I drove. (No wonder I put on pounds every time I do a book!) Did I mention the cran-berry date bar "to go"?

The crew working here is good — and has been here a long time.

Breakfast & lunch Wednesday - Saturday
Closed month of January

Brunch Sunday

CRUSTLESS SPINACH QUICHE

1 pkg. (10 oz.) frozen,
   chopped spinach (thawed
   and well-drained)
1 cup cottage cheese
1/2 cup sour cream
1/2 t. salt
1/4 t. pepper
1/4 t. seasoning salt
1 cup Tillamook medium
   Cheddar, grated
1 cup mushrooms, chopped
1/4 t. thyme
6 eggs beaten
1/4 cup Parmesan cheese

Preheat oven to 325⁰.
Combine all ingredients, except Parmesan cheese, in order given. Bake uncovered 45 minutes.
Sprinkle with Parmesan cheese. Let stand 10 minutes.
Cut into squares

Variations: Use Tillamook Monterey Jack cheese instead of Cheddar.

Yield: 6 servings.

PUFFY CHEDDAR OMELET

1 cup Tillamook medium
   Cheddar, grated
2 T. butter
3 egg whites
3 T. water
1/2 t. salt
few grains white pepper
3 egg yolks

Preheat oven to 350⁰.
Set out a heavy 10" skillet. Grate Cheddar and set aside. Heat skillet until just hot enough to sizzle a drop of water. Heat butter in the skillet.
Meanwhile, beat egg whites until frothy. Add water, salt and white pepper to egg whites. Continue beating until rounded peaks are formed.
Beat the egg yolks and spread over the egg whites and gently fold together. Turn egg mixture into skillet. Level surface gently.
Cook 1/2 minute on top of range; lower heat and cook slowly about 10 minutes or until lightly browned on bottom and puffy but still moist on top. Do not stir at any time. Place skillet with omelet in the oven for about 5 minutes. Remove and sprinkle all the grated cheese over top. Return to oven and continue baking until cheese is melted.
To serve, loosen edges with spatula, make a quick, shallow cut through center, and fold one side over. Gently slip omelet onto a warm serving platter, or omit the shallow cut and folding. Using two forks, tear the omelet gently into wedges. On warm serving dish, browned side is on top.

Yield: 3 servings.

It was a cold winter day and the first thing on my mind was to pull into the parking lot at the Tillamook Cheese Company. 10:30 a.m. Would the clerk think me strange if I ordered a double decker ice cream cone for my breakfast?

No need to worry as there were over 8 people in line with the same idea!

At the present time Tillamook has 45 flavors, and I test-tasted 4 before choosing one scoop of pistachio pecan and one caramel butter pecan. Here are some of their flavors: banana split, black cherry, lemon angel food, espresso latte, brown cow, black walnut, Oregon blueberry cobbler, Heath bar and 35 more. Testing is ongoing to find ever more flavors.

The dining room serves breakfasts and lunches... not fancy but just good stuff.

This is a time to stretch, take a tour of the cheese factory, see the whole operation.

The gift shop has cook books (including Coasting and Cooking), all kinds of food and wines, lots of gift ideas, and more.

P.S. They now carry sugar-free vanilla ice cream, and two fat-free ice creams.

Breakfast, lunch & dinner every day

♿

GINGERBREAD PANCAKES

3 cups flour
1 t. baking soda
2 t. ginger
1 t. cinnamon
1/4 t. cloves
3/4 cup molasses
2 eggs
2 T. melted butter
2 cups buttermilk

Combine flour, baking soda, ginger, cinnamon and cloves. In a separate bowl combine molasses, eggs, butter and buttermilk.
Add the wet ingredients to the dry ingredients. Do not overmix. Cook as you would regular pancakes. We serve the pancakes topped with toasted pecans and with a side of fresh fruit and warm maple syrup.

CHEESE NUT LOAF

4 cups Cheddar cheese, grated
2 cups onion, chopped
2 cloves garlic, minced
2 cups walnuts, chopped
2 cups mushrooms, chopped
1 cup cooked brown rice
3 eggs
1 cup parsley, minced

Preheat oven to 350⁰.
Combine all ingredients into a bowl. Press into a loaf pan and bake 60 to 70 minutes or until very brown and firm.
Cool before slicing

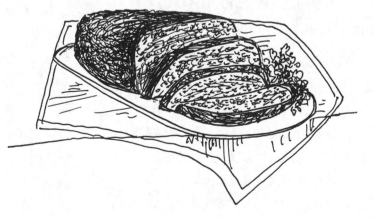

Grateful Bread and grateful customers... in this small town of Pacific City. Lots of tables outside for nice days.

Really extra special: Gingerbread pancakes, served with fresh fruit, pecans and pure maple syrup. I asked if they would share this recipe — see opposite page.

They did!

The soups offered are home made and include "Corn and Tillamook cheese chowder", and "Red Onion" soup with tomatoes and thyme. An unusual soup made without milk or cream, but with lots of garlic is the "Garlic Potato Soup".

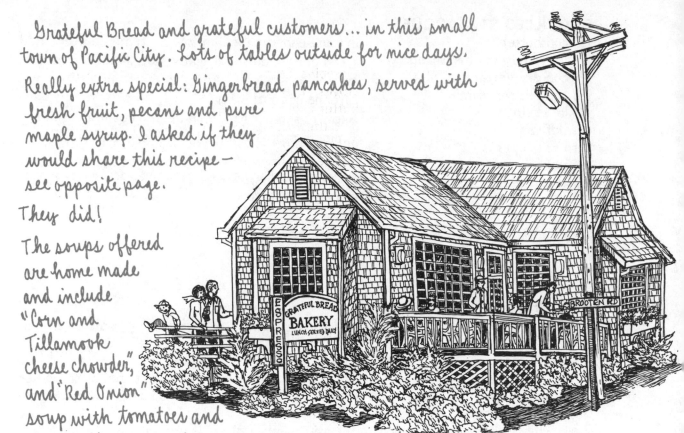

In the sandwich department are lots of the regulars, but how about "Cheese and Nut loaf", with, of course, nuts and cheese, but includes rice, mushrooms and onions.

Laura and Gary are from New York, so they serve up the pizzas on thin crusts with four delicious 14" choices: Greek, traditional, Hawaiian or "Bakery Special".

I ordered their garlic spinach bread to go, as I planned to be home much later that night. Oh, what a wonderful aroma all of the way home!

Breakfast, lunch & early dinner every day July & August
Breakfast, lunch & early dinner Thursday - Tuesday, September - June

COQUILLES ST. JACQUES

1/4 cup butter
1/4 fresh mushrooms, sliced
1/8 cup dry Vermouth
1/8 cup heavy cream
1/4 lb. scallops
dash of salt
dash of pepper
dash of cayenne
Parmesan cheese

In sauté pan, on medium-low heat, melt butter. Add sliced mushrooms and lightly sauté. Add Vermouth, cream and scallops. Add a dash of salt, pepper and cayenne in equal parts.
Allow to simmer for 1 minute, turn over and simmer 1 minute more. Pour off into individual ramekins.

Sprinkle with Parmesan cheese and place under broiler and lightly brown.

Yield: 1 serving.

RUM CHOCOLATE MOUSSE
RUM-SUGAR SYRUP
1/4 cup white rum*
1/4 cup sugar

1/4 lb semi-sweet chocolate
3 T. heavy cream
2 egg whites
1 pint whipping cream

In a saucepan over low heat (until just dissolved) stir rum* and sugar.

In a double boiler, melt semi-sweet chocolate. When melted, stir in heavy cream and rum-sugar syrup until smooth.
Set aside and cool to room temperature. When mixture is cool, fold into 2 stiffly beaten egg whites.

In a separate bowl, whip cream until stiff. Gently fold chocolate mixture into whipped cream.

Fill individual stemmed glasses and chill at least 1 hour to set.
Serve topped with whipped cream and sprinkle with nutmeg or chocolate.

Yield: 6 servings.

*or any liqueur to suit your taste, such as Kahlua, Amaretto, etc.

The saying "A river runs through it" was appropriate this past spring when the river flooded, and this sketch shows the piano atop a group of chairs. The water was 18" high inside the building, just about one inch under the piano.

I recently met a couple who said they use my book when they travel. Arriving here, the husband stated that the building was rustic, and located at river's edge. Seeing his hesitation, his wife said "But Barbara has it in her book!" Now it's their favorite spot whenever they are nearby.

Steven likes to surprise diners expecting basic food. Expect the unexpected. You'll be pleased. His recipe for salad dressings is so popular that he's been bottling and selling them several years!

Lunch & dinner every day

241

SEARED SALMON WITH HAZELNUT CRUST ON ROASTED BUTTERNUT SQUASH PURÉE

4 ea. 6 oz. fresh salmon filets
1 cup Oregon hazelnuts, chopped
3 T. olive oil

SQUASH PURÉE

1 butternut squash
1 cup melted butter
1/2 cup brown sugar
1 T. olive oil
2 T. onion, chopped
1 t. garlic, minced
2 1/2 cups chicken stock
1 T. ground coriander seed
1 lime
1/2 t. salt

Preheat oven to 375⁰

Cut off stem of squash. Cut squash lengthwise and quarter. Scrape seeds out with a spoon. Pour melted butter over squash and sprinkle with brown sugar. Roast on a sheet pan for 10 to 15 minutes until tender. Let cool. Remove skins from squash and set aside.

In a sauce pan, heat olive oil, add onion and garlic, stir 1 to 2 minutes. Add squash, chicken stock and coriander. Bring to boil and simmer 10 to 15 minutes. Remove and let cool 10 minutes. Ladle into blender and purée until smooth. Pour back into pan, return to stove. Squeeze juice of 1 lime and season with salt. Keep warm.

Preheat oven to 400⁰. Press each filet (bone side only) into hazelnuts, and season with salt and black pepper. Heat oil in sauté pan, when hot, place salmon in pan with nut side down and sear about 2 minutes or until nuts are lightly browned. Turn over and transfer to sheet pan to finish in oven for 5 to 6 more minutes, or until desired doneness.

Ladle 4 oz. sauce onto each plate. Serve with wilted greens and roasted potatoes. Place salmon on top.

PAN FRIED ALASKAN RAZOR CLAMS WITH SWEET PEPPER REMOULADE

SWEET PEPPER REMOULADE

1 roasted red bell pepper
2 large egg yolks
1 T. capers
2 anchovy fillets
1 T. chopped cilantro
pinch ground black pepper
1 1/2 cups olive oil

Yield: 2 cups.

CLAMS

1 lb. fresh razor clams
1 1/2 cup seasoned all-purpose flour
4 large eggs
1 cup olive oil

Remoulade: Roast pepper by placing on gas stove burner or under broiler. Rotate frequently until skin is blackened or blistered, about 5 minutes, place in bowl, cover with plastic wrap and steam for 3 to 4 minutes. Place strainer in sink and under cold running water peel skin from pepper. Pull stem from pepper and clean the seeds from the inside. In a food processor place all of the ingredients, except the oil. Purée for 1 to 2 minutes, then scrap down the bowl with a rubber spatula. Turn on processor and slowly stream in olive oil. Turn off processor and check seasoning. Place in squeeze bottle and chill.

Razor Clams: Lay out clams on cutting board and tenderize with meat hammer by pounding the neck on both sides. Do not pound the body. Place flour in an 8 x 10 inch cake pan and season with salt, black pepper and cayenne. In mixing bowl crack eggs and beat thoroughly. Place 4 T. of oil in large sauté pan and put on stove. Heat pan. Lightly dredge clams in flour and set on tray or plate. When oil starts to smoke, dip clams in beaten eggs one at a time and place in hot pan. Cook for 30 seconds or when edges become golden, turn over and cook other side for 30 seconds. Remove and place on 4 plates. Then squeeze remoulade over top and garnish with sprig of cilantro or Italian parsley.

The Bay House is just far enough out of Lincoln City to have a separate jewel-like setting, with a fabulous view of Siletz Bay and breath-taking sunsets! Their menu states "Relaxed dining on Siletz Bay" and that's the only way to fully enjoy the Bay House. The minute you walk in, there is a huge beautiful fireplace with a fire going (when the weather is right), rich wood cabinets displaying an excellent wine collection. Looking westward past the tables with white crisp tablecloths, you usually will see at least one or two blue herons. I quote now from a verse on their special Holiday menu – I couldn't say it better.

Cool crisp days; long cozy evenings;
candlelit dinners and warm conversations.
Fresh local oysters; hazelnut-crusted salmon,
sweet Dungeness crab; roasted duckling,
juicy steaks and heartier "red wine" fare,
These are a few of my favorite things.

Chef Greg Meixner gave me a tour of the entire place –(even the restrooms are beautiful!). Acknowledgements and awards for their inspired fare are many.

Dinner every day May - October
Dinner Wednesday - Sunday November - April

♿

243

KYLLO'S BLACK BEAN SOUP

1 lb. dry black beans
1 large onion, diced
5 oz. garlic, minced
2 T. dry oregano
salt to taste
1 gallon water
diced onion
low cal sour cream

Cover beans with cold water, bring to a boil. Turn heat to medium. Cover and simmer for about 1 1/2 hours, or until tender. Add more water if necessary. Add onion and garlic. When onion and garlic are tender, add oregano and salt to taste.
Garnish with fresh diced onion and low cal sour cream.

Yield: 12 servings.

KYLLO'S CLAM CHOWDER

17 or 18 oz. can chopped
  clams (set juice aside)
1/4 lb. green bell pepper
1/4 lb. leeks
1/4 lb. celery
1/4 cup clam base
1/4 cup vegetable oil
1/3 cup all-purpose flour
1/2 t. dry thyme
1/2 t. white pepper
5 1/4 cups half-&-half
1/3 lb. diced cooked potato

Heat oil. When hot, slowly add flour. Cook for about 6 minutes or until lightly browned. Add celery and cook for about one minute. Add onion, peppers and leeks, cook about one more minute. Add seasoning and clams. Bring clam juice to a boil. Add clam base, mix well.
Add clam juice and base mixture to the vegetable mixture, stirring constantly to avoid burning. Cook for about 15 minutes or until boiling.
Add half-&-half and boil, then add cooked potatoes.

Kyllo's has been a family business since 1984, with Craig Kyllo the owner. He said that at high tide the waves flow under the building, and just to the side of the restaurant is the "D" River (smallest river in the United States.)

I had an ideal table by one of the many windows looking out at the crashing waves. Prediction was 60 mile an hour winds and gusting to 90! My coffee arrived and I almost choked from laughing! I couldn't believe what I was seeing ... seagulls were coming in for a landing, then a gust of wind would push them into landing on the sand in reverse! Very comical.

The main dining room is huge, its high ceiling creates the effect of being part of the beach and the Pacific ocean.

It was breakfast time and I ordered the shrimp omelette. A good choice. All kinds of seafood offered here – for any meal. The hashbrowns were dark golden brown, almost crunchy (my favorite way).

Breakfast, lunch & dinner every day
Closed Thanksgiving & Christmas day

CHOCOLATE MINT MOUSSE PIE

CRUST

2 1/2 cups chocolate cookie
  crumbs
3 T. sugar
1/2 to 3/4 cup melted
  butter

MOUSSE

20 oz. semisweet chocolate
2 cups whipping cream, stiff,
  slightly sweetened
6 eggs, room temperature
  separated
1 1/2 envelopes Knox
  gelatin
water to cover
1/4 to 1/2 cup sugar
3/4 to 1 t. mint extract

1 1/2 cups whipping cream

Preheat oven to 350⁰.

Mix crust and press into bottom and up the sides of a 12" spring-form pan, bake 5 to 8 minutes.

Mousse: Melt chocolate and set aside to cool slightly.

Whip the whipping cream stiff and refrigerate.

Separate the eggs. Prepare bloom with just enough water to cover the gelatin. Set a pan of water on the stove for melting.

Whip the egg whites until stiff, gradually adding 1/4 cup sugar when they are frothy. Don't overbeat. Set aside.

Whip egg yolks until light, gradually adding 1/4 to 1/2 cup sugar. When yolks are light in color place mixture in a large bowl.

Melt the gelatin, stir to keep smooth and quickly and thoroughly fold into the egg yolks. Also, fold in mint extract.

Alternately fold in the melted chocolate and egg whites.

Fold in half the whipped cream and pour some of this mixture into the shell. Fold remaining whipped cream and fill the rest of the shell with it.

Whip remaining cream and decorate top of mousse with it.

Chill in refrigerator for a few hours before serving.

You can also decorate with chocolate curls or a dusting of cocoa just before serving.

Mousses of any kind are made by having a base - puréed and strained fruit, puréed vegetables or fish, or perhaps a custard or dessert cheese. The gelatin, brought to a "bloom" and melted is folded into the base, next meringued egg whites, then stiffly beaten whipping cream to lighten the texture. From there you can pipe the mousse through a pastry tube if you want to have a free form on a plate or want to use the mousse as layers between something crisp. Or, you can pipe the mousse into clear glass dishes and use as an appetizer or dessert, i.e. mousses of spring asparagus and smoked trout. The possibilities are endless once you learn a few techniques.   To use the gelatin, start with a soup bowl size (preferably metal.) Cover the quantity of gelatin you are using with enough water to dissolve it. Then go about assembling the rest of the ingredients. The gelatin will "bloom", or expand and make a solid blob that you will later melt, when all the other stages are ready, and fold into the base.

To melt the "bloomed gelatin", if using a metal bowl, place the gelatin in the bowl into a pan of hot water and stir as it melts. Use a sauté or frying pan with a couple of inches of water on medium heat. The gelatin will melt very quickly and then is ready to use. Don't do this step too soon or the gelatin will form a skin and be more difficult to fold in. If it seems too sticky you can add a few more tablespoons of water and mix it smooth.

If this mousse is your own creation and you're not sure you have enough gelatin, test the base by putting a small spoonful on a saucer and place in your freezer for a few minutes to set the gelatin but not to freeze. If the mixture does not set up, stop and "bloom" a little more gelatin, dissolve over heat and add to the base by folding it in and then continue to fold in the egg whites and cream. Fruit mixtures can vary according to ripeness and pectin content. Sometimes a fruit purée will need very little gelatin.

When adding the gelatin to the base, the base should be warm (at least room temp.) so that the gelatin doesn't immediately form into shreds of set-up gelatin. This mixture is chilled and stirred until just about set. Fold in the egg whites and whipping cream. Be sure the base is just getting set-up or you will have a runny mousse. If the base sets up too much, quickly hold your bowl over a little heat and give a few folds. As the mixture loosens a little take it off the heat and continue folding in the whites or cream. You may chill the base before folding the lighteners by placing the bowl in a bowl of ice and stirring gently. Just before it is set, quickly remove and continue to stir for a minute before adding anything. You can chill (or heat and chill) to gain the control you need.

Owner - chef Barbara Lowry trained in Seattle with classical French and American chefs, then spent nine years at the Bay House in Lincoln City. Subsequent years saw a television seafood series and she was also developing a catering business. Barbara has developed the idea of "Good food for people on the go", but of course there is a dining room here. Interesting to look at the good choices in the display case. She told me that catering now includes corporate dinners, business Open Houses, meetings, weddings and much more.... she's even open to ideas (in case someone craves something that's different) - she has lots of ingredients.

I asked if omelettes could be ordered for dinner? With a "yes" answer, I then narrowed my choice to #1: "the Paesano" with home-made sage-garlic sausage, roasted bell peppers, tomatoes, spinach and cheddar cheese or #2: "the Greek" with shrimp, tomatoes, spinach, Greek olives and Feta cheese. My choice was the Greek — very good.

Too full for dessert, but ordered a piece of Mike's Peanut butter pie (very rich) with layers of fudge and nuts with chocolate cookie crust. (Nibbled on it several hours later.)

Breakfast & lunch every day   **Dinner Wednesday - Sunday**   ♿

SEARED PANCETTA-WRAPPED SEA SCALLOPS

5 sea scallops, large, muscle
   removed
5 slices pancetta, paper thin
3 shallots, toasted
3 oz. Ancine de Pepe pasta,
   al dente
3 oz. seasonal wild mush-
   rooms, chanterelles,
   morels
1 oz. Riesling wine
1 oz. Reggiano Parmesan
   cheese, grated
1 pinch basil, fresh
1 pinch garlic, minced
2 oz. pale ale
2 oz. chicken stock
2 oz. whole butter
1 butternut squash,
   blanched, small dice

Wrap scallops with pancetta and pan sear until well browned. Remove to warming oven.

Deglaze pan with ale and reduce.

Add chicken stock and reduce by one third.

Thicken with butter and finish with chopped herbs.

In a separate pan, sauté the wild mushrooms with the garlic. Deglaze with Riesling and finish with Parmesan cheese. Then fold together with pasta.

To serve: Pack mushroom pasta into a ring mold in the middle of a plate and stack the scallops on top. Place shallots around the outside of the plate and drizzle with sauce. Finish with brunoise of butternut squash.

BOWTIE PASTA WITH CHICKEN AND LEMON-BASIL CREAM

4 oz. chicken breast
3 t. red peppers, roasted
   and peeled
5 oz. bowtie pasta
1 oz. chicken stock
4 oz. lemon-basil cream
salt and pepper to taste
Parmesan
scallions

Sear chicken breast pieces in olive oil. Add peppers and deglaze with chicken stock. Add lemon-basil cream and incorporate mixture until smooth. Add heated bowtie pasta and season to taste.

Serve in large bowl with vegetable of the day and garnish with Parmesan and scallions.

Major renovations... a mult-million dollar job for the Salishan Lodge is happening. It began in March 1997. Salishan Lodge is a beautiful 205-room golf resort set on the rugged Oregon Coast. The lobby, 2 restaurants and the renowned wine cellar were re-designed and are being expanded.

The sleeping rooms offer fireplaces, new 25" television sets, along with many other amenities, plus a spectacular view of Siletz Bay and the Oregon countryside. Recently Conde Nast Traveler said "One of the 15 best resorts in the U.S". This rustic resort offers much... indoor and outdoor tennis courts, swimming pool, saunas, a network of jogging and walking trails which link towering pines and the rugged beaches of the Pacific ocean.

The dining room at the Lodge is being expanded for both a la carte and Conference dining. The wine cellar, also being expanded, will feature the most complete selection of Northwest vintages on the Pacific coast.

I've mentioned more about the lodging than I usually do, but it's so integral and just dining here won't be enough. Stay and play..... as soon as this book has been printed, I intend to do just that!

Breakfast, lunch & dinner every day

CAPELLINI DE ANGELA
WITH FRESH TOMATO AND BASIL CONCASSE TOPPED WITH SCALLOPS

CONCASSE
2 medium ripe tomatoes, peeled, seeded
   and diced in 1/2" chunks
3 shallots, finely chopped
2 bunches fresh basil, finely chopped
4 oz. unsalted butter
2 oz. white wine
1 oz. olive oil
1/2 t. salt
1/2 t. black pepper

SCALLOPS
24 medium sea scallops
1 cup flour
1 oz. olive oil

CAPELLINI
2 lbs. angel hair pasta
2 gallons salted boiling water

Concasse: Combine tomatoes, shallots, basil, salt and pepper in bowl, mix. Heat oil in 12" sauté pan on medium heat, add tomato mixture and butter. Cook until heated through. Add white wine and reduce until thickened.

Scallops: Lightly dust scallops in flour and sauté in oil until cooked.

Capellini: Cook pasta for 1 to 2 minutes until al dente. Drain and place on plate. Spoon concasse over pasta and top with 6 scallops each plate. Garnish with fresh basil sprig.

MARINATED GRILLED SWORDFISH
6   8 oz. center cut swordfish steaks
1 cup orange juice
1/2 cup water
1/2 cup pineapple juice
2 oz. soy sauce
1 T. black pepper

SALSA
1 medium slightly ripened tomato, seeded
   and diced in 1/2" chunks
2 shallots, finely chopped
1 oz. unsalted butter
1 mango, peeled, seeded and diced in 1/2"
   chunks
1 papaya, peeled, seeded and diced in 1/2"
   chunks
1/2 bunch cilantro, finely chopped
1/2 cup black turtle beans, cleaned and
   cooked
1 oz. Liebframilch wine (or any fruity white
   wine)
1 small jalapeño, finely chopped

Swordfish: combine marinade ingredients in bowl and whip until incorporated. Place swordfish in shallow pan and pour marinade over fish. Marinate for at least 30 minutes but no longer than 4 hours. Broil on grill or bake in oven, cook until firm.

Salsa: In 10 or 12 inch sauté pan, melt butter on low-medium heat. Add shallots and tomato and cook until just heated. Add papaya, mango, jalapeño and black beans, toss well. Add wine and reduce. Pull from heat, put in bowl, add cilantro and mix well. Hold at room temperature.
Place swordfish on plate and top with salsa diagonally.
Serving suggestions: Roasted baby red potatoes with garlic, broccoli with cheese sauce.

Yield: 6 servings

I always look forward to my stop at Gracie's Sea Hag. The driving force here, Gracie Strom, is a pleasure to talk to... as busy as she is, she will stop for a few words with one of her customers... or if you request it, she'll grab her drumsticks, put a coin in the juke box and will proceed to accompany the music with an assortment of slide whistles, an old washboard, cowbells and a huge variety of old bottles... everyone enjoys her mini-recitals.

The motto at Gracie's is "Seafood so fresh the ocean hasn't missed it yet!"

The menu is loaded with offerings from the ocean. The seafood Hors D'Oeuvres, a selection of fresh fried and smoked seafoods and cheeses enticed me, and was my dinner. (I really eat at odd times so I am able to tell you about as much as I can.)

Sometimes I might neglect telling you of other entrees... the Pasta corner is worthy of note.. Fettuccine Primavera - vegetarian, another one is the chicken and scallop Fettuccine (not a usual combination) but popular. Steaks and chicken are on the menu. **Friday evenings: an "All you can eat" Seafood Buffet. Rated annually as one of the top 500 independent restaurants in the U.S.A. Early opening for fishermen.

Breakfast, lunch & dinner every day
Closed Christmas Day

OYSTER SPINACH BISQUE

1/3 cup butter
1 cup onion, chopped
2 cloves garlic, minced
1/2 t. lemon zest, minced
3/4 cup all-purpose flour
1/4 t. ground fennel seed
1/4 t. ground coriander
1/4 t. black pepper
4 cups fish stock or broth
1 quart clam juice
2/3 cup oysters, cleaned, cooked
  and chopped
1 bunch fresh spinach, chopped or
  1 10 oz. pkg. frozen spinach,
  thawed and drained
1 1/4 cups whipping cream
salt to taste
1/4 t. dillweed

Melt butter in soup pot over medium heat. Sauté onion, garlic and lemon zest in butter until onion is semi-transparent. Stir in flour, dill, fennel, coriander and pepper. Cook for 1 minute. Slowly add fish stock and clam juice, stirring with a whip to blend soup until smooth. Bring soup to a simmer, reduce heat and continue cooking for 15 minutes.

Place oysters in pan with just enough water to cover, bring to a boil. Cook 3 to 5 minutes. Drain oysters and reserve juice. Stir oysters, spinach and oyster juice into soup. Simmer for 5 minutes. Stir in cream and add salt if desired. Serve immediately,

CRAB CAKES

1 lb. Dungeness crab meat, picked
  clean of shells and loosely shredded
1/4 cup 1000 island dressing
1 T. Dijon mustard
1/2 T. garlic, minced
1/2 t, freshly ground black pepper
1 egg, lightly beaten
3 1/2 cups Panko breadcrumbs
3/4 cup milk or half-n-half
2 green onions, thinly sliced
1/2 cup vegetable oil

Mix the crab, dressing, mustard, garlic, pepper, egg, 2 1/2 cups of breadcrumbs (reserve remainder for breading the cakes for frying), milk and green onions. Allow to set for at least 15 minutes. Form into cakes about 3 inches in diameter and about 3/4 inch thick.

Dredge the cakes in reserved crumbs and pan-fry in hot oil until nicely browned on both sides. Serve immediately.

A letter arrived stating that in my next book, Tidal Raves was a must! So I arrived on a glorious evening in time to see the sunset while I dined on fillet of salmon with a pecan-shrimp butter. It had been charbroiled and was served with Basmati pilaf. Perfect!

"Smaller Portion" meals are offered, and include Cioppino, veggie stir-fry, petite N.Y. steak, and more.

The 3 soups were Black Bean and Snapper, Pacific Oyster Stew and Smoked Salmon Chowder. The salmon chowder was my choice on my next visit.

There is a book on a table at Tidal Raves that is full of "raves".
I read some, and added a rave of my own.
This is one restaurant that you should call for a reservation...
always busy, even on a cold, rainy winter day (my 2nd visit).

As the sketch shows, the view is non-stop. Tables are on different levels to allow the best possible view. It actually is high above the ocean. Spectacular.

Lunch & dinner every day   Closed most of December

253

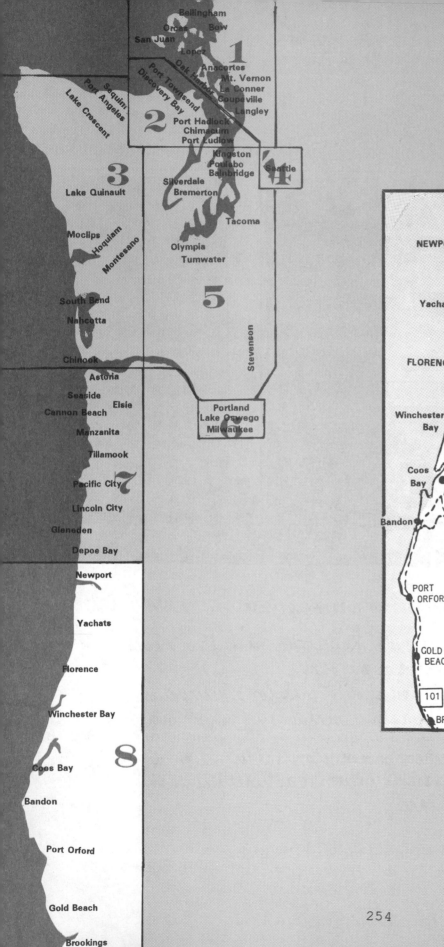

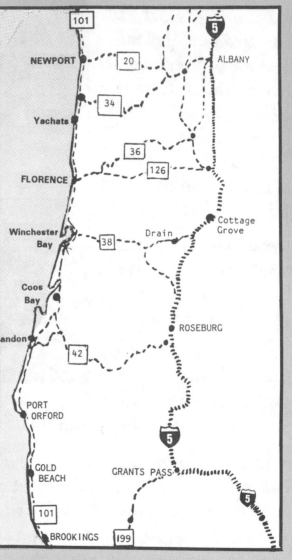

SECTION 8 OREGON

NEWPORT: Cosmos Cafe and Gallery, Gracie's at Smuggler's Cove, Whale's Tale

SOUTH OF NEWPORT: Yuzen Japanese Cuisine

YACHATS: La Serre

FLORENCE: Blue Hen Cafe, Bridgewater, Windward Inn

WINCHESTER BAY: Cafe Francais

COOS BAY: Blue Heron Bistro

BANDON: Christophe at Face Rock, Harp's, Lord Bennett's Restaurant

PORT ORFORD: Spaghetti West

GOLD BEACH: Nor'Wester, Tu Tu Tun

BROOKINGS: Rubio's, Sandy's

SEAFOOD BURRITO

tortillas
1 lb. any kind of fresh fish, diced
1/2 cup red peppers, diced
1 cup tomatoes, diced
1/2 cup black olives, sliced
1/2 cup any kind of salsa
1/4 cup lime juice
4 T. fresh cilantro, minced
4 cups Cheddar and/or
   PepperJack cheese, shredded
   (a combination of the 2 adds
   great flavor)
1/2 cup green onion, diced

In a large skillet, sauté diced fish 5 minutes. Add onions, peppers and black olives and sauté another 3 minutes. Add salsa, lime juice and tomatoes, cook until hot. Remove from heat.

On a grill, heat tortillas, flip and add 1/2 cup shredded cheese to each tortilla.

Remove and place on dinner plates. Put fish mixture on top of cheese. Divide minced cilantro, green onion and sour cream.

Serve either black beans or rice on the side, with a tossed green salad. A wonderful taste treat.

Note: In our restaurant we use our own homemade salsa, which has cilantro in it. The cilantro gives the fish a delightfully clean flavor. Our black beans are served on the side along with our Spanish rice. Any rice will enhance your meal.

GREEK FISH PITA

8 oz. any kind of fish, diced
1/4 cup onion, diced
1/2 cup zucchini, diced
2 T. black olives, sliced
1/4 cup mushrooms, sliced
1 bunch of spinach
1 medium tomato, diced
1 t. Greek seasonings
splash of balsamic vinegar
6 slices cucumber
3 T. crumbled Feta cheese
1 cup shredded lettuce
2 Greek-style pitas
mayonnaise

In a sauté pan, sauté fish and Greek seasonings for 3 minutes. Add tomato and splash of balsamic vinegar. Stir and add spinach, remove from heat and cover (this will wilt the spinach).

Grill pitas in a dry non-stick pan until warm and soft. Spread pitas with mayonnaise.

Divide mix into equal portions, place portion into center of pitas. Add 3 slices of cucumber to each one. Sprinkle with Feta cheese, top with shredded lettuce. Fold and serve.

The Greek pita is a thick pancake-like bread. It can be purchased at any Greek restaurant or deli. It can be used in a variety of ways and is great toasted.

The Cosmos Cafe and Gallery is now located in their new building just across from The Performing Arts Center in Newport. My last trip here was before this new place was ready to open. What fun!!! As you can tell from the sketch, this is a whimsical cafe, with the ceiling stippled in dark blue and many painted stars and the galaxies. What they say is "Find your place in the Cosmos."
There are six large display boards on the wall listing great selections of all kinds. I must have stood about 5 minutes trying to make the decision on what to have.

I finally chose Hot Szechuan Chicken over pasta — a warming choice on this chilly winter day.
There are six different Pitas, using home made Greek Pita. Another favorite of mine: eggplant sandwich, and they know how to make 'em! Garlic basted and baked eggplant, served with roasted red peppers, provolone cheese, plus the usual lettuce, tomatoes, red onions and mayo, mustard and served on sourdough bread.
Desserts galore.
This is self-serve.... line-up at the counter - order, then around the corner to get your silverware and drink. The order is brought to you, but please cart your dirty dishes. A casual spot.

Breakfast, lunch & dinner Monday - Saturday

SZECHUAN SALMON

6 oz. boneless salmon fillet
green onions, chopped
sweet red bell pepper, julienned

SZECHUAN SAUCE/MARINADE

1 1/2 cups dry sherry
1 cup rice wine vinegar
2 T. garlic, finely minced
1 T. ginger root, finely minced
1/2 T. red pepper, crushed
1/8 cup fermented Chinese black
  beans
1/2 oz. Szechuan peppercorn oil

Place fillet in an 8 oz. rarebit casserole dish.
Pour Szechuan sauce/marinade over salmon to
cover. Top with onions and pepper.
Steam 7 to 8 minutes or until salmon is done.

Szechuan sauce/marinade: Combine all ingredients in a non-reactive container and refrigerate for 24 hours. Makes enough marinade for
3 to 4 servings.

BOUILLABAISSE

3 quarts fish stock
3 cups tomatoes, chopped
1 cup dry sherry
1/4 cup garlic, minced
1 T. fresh basil, minced
1 T. lobster base (optional)
1 1/2 t. thyme
5 stalks celery, chopped
1 bunch leeks (white and pale green
  parts only), chopped
1 large yellow onion, chopped
1/2 t. saffron
18 steamer clams
8 oz. halibut, bite size pieces
8 oz. salmon, bite size pieces
8 prawns (21/25), peeled and
  deveined
8 sea scallops
2 cups baby cocktail shrimp
12 crab leg sections in shell
salt and pepper to taste

In a large pot combine fish stock, tomatoes,
sherry, garlic, basil, lobster base and thyme and
bring to a boil. Reduce heat to low, cover and
simmer 1 hour.
Add celery, leeks, onion and saffron and simmer 5 minutes. Add halibut, salmon, prawns
and scallops and simmer until fish is cooked,
about 10 minutes. Stir in baby cocktail shrimp
and crab leg sections and simmer until heated
through. Season with salt and pepper to taste.
Serve in large bowls.

Yield: 6 servings.

The history of Smuggler's Cove goes back over 100 years. In 1875 the property was granted to Samuel Case, the town's first subdivider, under a Public Sale Land Patent signed by Ulysses S. Grant, president of the United States.

The town's first doctor, James Bayley, and his wife, Elizabeth, built their home on this hill overlooking Yaquina bay. 18" thick foundation walls were laid in 1885, and the first concrete in Lincoln County was poured here.

In 1905 this property became the "Grand Pacific Hotel (rumored to be a bordello). A fire destroyed everything except the fireplace and the basement foundation. It had more interesting history after this, but fell into disrepair.

Howdy Eddleman, a local contractor, acquired the property in 1978 with plans to restore the mansion to its former elegance. Natural springs above were harnessed and piped to turn the 24' waterwheel that has become a local landmark. The lights on the wheel are a reference point to boats returning to the harbor at night.

Gracie Strom spearheaded remodeling, but two days before the planned opening in 1991, fire delayed the opening another 40 days. Everyone worked night and day to make this possible. Gracie is making her own history now. With her colorful personality and reputation for serving good food, this place is a "must" place.

Dinner every day   **Lunch every day July - October**

Off season lunch Saturday & Sunday in Lounge   **Closed Christmas Day**

GRILLED SALMON SALAD with BLACKBERRIES and HAZELNUTS

6 oz. mesclun mix salad greens

6 oz. salmon fillet

salt and pepper to taste

sprinkle of thyme leaves

4 oz. fresh Oregon blackberries

3 oz. toasted hazelnuts, coarsely
   chopped

1 scallion, sliced

Vinaigrette: Cook berries until tender, about 10 minutes. Purée in food processor and strain and discard seeds. To the approximately 1/2 cup of purée add raspberry vinegar, lemon juice, mustard, salt, pepper and garlic. Place ingredients in mixing bowl and using a wire whisk beat in the olive oil in a thin stream.

BLACKBERRY VINAIGRETTE

1 cup blackberries, fresh or frozen

1/4 cup water

1/4 cup sugar

1/4 cup raspberry vinegar

2 T. fresh lemon juice

1 t. Dijon mustard

1/2 t. salt

freshly ground black pepper to
   taste

2 cloves garlic, minced

1 cup olive oil

Arrange greens on 2 dinner plates. Drizzle with blackberry vinaigrette and scatter blackberries, hazelnuts and scallions over the salads.

Season salmon and rub with vegetable oil. Grill or sauté until just opaque and separate into large chunks.

Arrange warm salmon over salad and serve immediately.

Yield: 2 servings

Recipe by Chef Celeste Mathews

In May 1976 this opened as a small delicatessen, and the Whale's Tale has been an important part of the Newport community now for 21 years.

The interior is finished with native woods, inlaid wood tables and art on the walls by local artists. Dick Schwartz began as a hobby cook turned restaurateur, and is now recognized in both national and regional publications.

An excellent (and unusual) choice on the breakfast menu is "Eden's Garden": pancakes topped with seasonal fruit, Nancy's honey yogurt, coconut and almonds!

The mainstays are hearty Cioppino, German black bread, Catch of the day fresh fish, and a variety of ethnic dishes. Most of the breads and desserts are baked at the Whale's Tale... always a varying assortment of their delectable dessert recipes. The emphasis on the local seafood from "home port" fishing boats.... with seasonal specialties including salmon, halibut, mussels and oysters.

It is located on the Bayfront in Newport... on the old waterfront... when you enter, it's reminiscent of a Steinbeck novel set in Monterey.

Breakfast, lunch & dinner every day
Closed Wednesday in Winter

CABBAGE WRAPPED SALMON IN HOT MUSTARD SAUCE

2 T. dry mustard
1 T. sugar
2 t. dillweed
1/2 cup grapefruit juice
6 T. vegetable oil
1 t. mustard seeds
1/2 t. garlic
1 t. vegetable oil
8 oz. fillet of salmon
leaves of a green cabbage
red peppers, diced
cucumbers, diced
scallions
1 t. grated ginger

Place filet in a baking dish lined in the outer leaves of a green cabbage. Top salmon with cucumbers, red peppers, scallions and ginger. Fold leaves over and steam for 10 to 12 minutes.

Sauce: Mix the dry mustard, sugar and dillweed. Whisk in the grapefruit juice and vegetable oil. Toast the mustard seeds, garlic in oil. Combine ingredients and whisk.

Spoon sauce over cabbage wrapped salmon.

CIOPPINO

1/4 cup olive oil
1/2 green bell pepper, julienned
1 yellow onion, julienned
1 bunch green onions, sliced
2 T. garlic
1 tomato, diced
1 cup red wine
4 cups clam juice
2 cups tomato puree
2 bay leaves

2 T. salt
1/2 T. black pepper
1/2 cup chopped fresh parsley
1 T. oregano
2 T. basil
2 t. jalapeños
1 1/2 lb. steamer clams, scrubbed
1/4 lb ling cod, skin and fine bones removed and cut into serving pieces

1 1/2 lbs. mussels, cleaned and debearded
12 large shrimp, peeled and deveined
1 cooked Dungeness crab, cleaned, cracked and divided into serving size pieces
12 oysters, shucked
6 oz. bay shrimp

Heat oil in a large pot. Add green bell pepper, onions and garlic and sauté over medium heat until tender and lightly browned (about 5 minutes.) Add tomato, wine and clam juice and bring to a boil. Add tomato puree, bay leaves, salt and pepper, lower heat. Cover pot and simmer for 10 minutes. Add parsley, oregano, basil and jalapeños and continue simmering for an additional 45 minutes or until sauce is thick. Add the clams, ling cod, mussels and shrimp. Cover and cook over medium heat for 5 minutes. Then gently stir in the crab, oysters and bay shrimp. Continue simmering until the clams and mussels have opened and the remaining seafood is cooked through, about 10 minutes longer. (If some of the seafood is cooked before the rest, remove it and set aside, covered to keep warm.) When ready, divide the seafood evenly into individual bowls and pour the sauce over it. Sprinkle each serving with parsley and serve.

Yield: 8 servings.

If this is your first time in Yachats, everyone will know it if you pronounce it as it looks. Instead say "Ya-hots". This picturesque town is commonly known as the "Gem of the Oregon coast."

When this sketch was shown to owner Joanne Lambert, she said "Oh, I'm not sure our chef, Renee Greenspan, will like it." (Look behind the counter, above the painting, and you'll see glasses and a relaxed chef's hat above the glasses... that's Renee! I replied "I think she likes it, because she grinned when she saw it." She and her staff are turning out great food... daily fresh seafood specials, delightful pastas, creative vegetarian dishes. Steaks grilled to perfection plus many superb entrées.

So it's O.K. if you only see the top of her head, Renee's on the move!

The active "Bistro" has a full service bar... a fine selection of Oregon and California wines, plus selected French regional wines. I have always liked the spacious dining area. It suggests a charming country garden atmosphere, where the aromas of the open kitchen are not far away.   Reservations are a good idea.

Dinner Wednesday - Monday   **Breakfast only Sunday**   ♿

CHOCOLATE PEANUT BUTTER PIE   Yield: 10 servings

Crust:
1 1/2 cups flour
2/3 cup sugar
2/3 cup cocoa
2/3 cup cold butter
2 t. vanilla
4 t. ice water

Filling:
16 oz. cream cheese
2 cups peanut butter
1 3/4 cup sugar
1 T. vanilla
1/2 cup butter, softened
1 1/2 pints heavy whipping
   cream, whipped

Options:
chocolate curls
grated chocolate
chocolate chips
peanuts

Crust: Combine in food processor flour, sugar and cocoa, cut in cold butter until mixture is in fine crumbs. Add vanilla and approximately 4 t. ice water, drop by drop, just enough to bind ingredients together. Roll dough into ball, flatten and refrigerate 1/2 hour. Roll out to fit pie plate, prick bottom and side all over gently. Bake for 13 minutes or until set. Cool to room temperature and refrigerate a while.
OR: You may use pie crust for Limon Cheesecake, using chocolate filled cookies such as Oreos.
Filling: In largest mixing bowl blend softened cream cheese (not soft or whipped cream cheese) with peanut butter. Add sugar, vanilla and butter, blend until smooth and creamy, about 5 minutes on medium speed. Gently fold in whipped cream. Gently spoon into crust.
Decorate with chocolate curls, grated chocolate or chocolate and peanuts. To make curls or grated chocolate, use sharp potato peeler on semi-sweet or milk chocolate squares at room temperature.
Refrigerate.

LIMON CHEESE CAKE   Yield: 12 to 16 servings.

Crust:
3 cups crushed vanilla
   filled cookies
2/3 cup melted butter

Filling:
1 1/2 Lbs. cream cheese
1 cup granulated sugar
2 cups sour cream
4 eggs
1/2 cup fresh squeezed
   lime juice
1/2 cup fresh squeezed
   lemon juice
1 package Knox gelatin

Topping:
1/3 cup granulated sugar
1 1/2 cups sour cream
1 T. vanilla

Preheat oven to 350⁰.
Crust: Mix crumbs and butter together, press mixture firmly into 10 inch well greased and floured spring form pan. Bake for 10 minutes, remove from oven and cool to room temperature.
Filling: In a large bowl, cream together in mixer (with flat beater if available) cream cheese and sugar for 2 minutes. Add 2 cups of sour cream, beat 1 minute. Add eggs, beat 3 minutes. In a small bowl sprinkle gelatin onto juice mixture and stir until well blended and dissolved. Add remaining ingredients immediately and blend for an additional 3 minutes on medium high speed. Add 2 or 3 drops of green food coloring (optional). Pour into cooled crust and bake for 15 minutes, turn oven down to 325⁰ and continue baking for 45 more minutes. Top will be firm. Cool on rack while mixing topping.
Topping: Mix together sugar, sour cream and vanilla, beat for about 2 minutes. Spoon very carefully on top of cake, return to 350⁰ oven for 7 minutes. Remove cheese cake and cool on rack for 3 hours or until room temperature. Refrigerate until chilled and set (about 4 additional hours). Remove carefully from pan. Garnish with whipped cream if desired.

The aroma of cooking chicken traveled on the wind to the Blue Hen parking lot, and I knew I was hooked the minute that I opened the door of my car!

You will see chickens every-where... on shelves, walls, counters, and on the menu. But the best is "on the plate"! Here is the story of a couple who decided to go into the restaurant business with no background. Renting a little house, they remodeled it into a 16-seat cafe. Opened in 1988 – not a single customer came through the door! Persevering through fires, dishonest employees, equipment failures, this

couple can now look back and smile. The parking lot is usually filled; the restaurant is many times larger.

What a big choice of vegetarian lunches – 12! (and this a chicken place). Vegetarian includes "Pasta Mazithra (Mazithra is cheese) with garlic butter sauce, sautéed onions, mushrooms, and smothered with cheese.

The sage walnut stuffing that's served with some chicken dinners is very good. Lots of desserts, if you have room.

Breakfast, lunch & dinner every day   ♿

265

SNAPPER DIABLO

6 - 8 oz. red snapper (rock cod) fillet
1/2 cup tomato salsa
1/4 cup Monterey Jack cheese, grated
1/3 cup white wine
2 T. butter, melted
1 t. garlic, chopped
1 green onion, diced (scallion)

Preheat oven to 350⁰
Place fillet in shallow pie pan with wine, melted butter and garlic. Bake until snapper is flakey (about 10 - 15 minutes). Remove from oven and top with salsa and Jack cheese. Broil in oven until cheese is golden brown.
Garnish with green onions (scallions).

Serve with rice.

Yield: 1 serving.

Scallion: 1 of any 3 varieties of onion : shallot, leek or green onion.

SAUTÉED SCALLOPS AND MUSHROOMS

8 to 10 oz. bay scallops (fresh or thawed)
3/4 cup sliced mushrooms
1/4 cup white wine
1 1/2 t. garlic, chopped
1/2 t. shallots, minced
2 T. cold butter
1 T. lemon juice
2 t. fresh basil, chopped

In a non-stick sauté pan, combine scallops, white wine, garlic, shallots, lemon juice and basil. Sauté until wine and lemon juice have reduced by 2/3, stirring frequently. Add mushrooms and cook for an additional 60 seconds. Remove from heat, add cold butter and stir until butter has melted.

Serve over rice.

Yield: 1 serving.

In book number 3, I mentioned the feeling of Rick's Cafe in the movie "Casablanca", so this time while I was at the Bridgewater, I did this sketch with the poster from the movie. This old building is open, high ceiling, and has many beautiful huge plants scattered around. It is located in historic old town of Florence.

I arrived too early for dinner, but returned an hour later for the following buffet feast: fresh cracked crab, seafood fettuccine, fresh local yearling oysters, steamer clams, fresh Chinook salmon, blackened red fish, calamari, crab and shrimp enchiladas and a super seafood jambalaya! Just reading this list is enough to bring a smile to any seafood lover. This bountiful feast also includes clam chowder or a crisp green salad.   Of course, if seafood isn't "your cup of tea"... not to worry.

There are many other very good selections.

It was a cold rainy evening when I arrived, but a fire was burning in the dining room.

A warm fire, a wonderful meal. What more can you ask? If I were a cat, I would be purring.

Lunch & dinner every day

267

GRATINÉED ONION SOUP

12 medium sweet onions, thinly
  sliced (about 1 1/2 lbs.)
1/4 cup oil
2 T. butter
1/2 t. sugar
3 T. flour
2 qts. stock or bouillon
1/2 cup dry sherry
1/3 t. Dijon mustard
salt and pepper to taste
French bread slices 1" thick
butter grated Swiss cheese
3 T. brandy or cognac

In large pan melt butter with oil and add onions and sugar. Simmer slowly for at least one hour, stirring as needed. Onions should be rich golden brown. Sprinkle flour over onions and blend well. Turn off the heat, blend in the boiling stock or bouillon (this can be beef or half chicken and half beef), then the sherry and mustard. Cover partially and simmer again on low heat for approximately 30 to 40 minutes. Season with pepper and salt to taste. Thin soup as necessary with additional stock.

Stir the brandy into the soup. Butter the french bread. Toast under the broiler. Ladle soup into heat-proof bowls, float the bread crouton on top and top that with grated Swiss cheese. Run under the broiler until bubbly.

SEVEN GRAIN BREAD

Served daily as a hot demi-loaf

3/4 cup millet seeds
3/4 cup sunflower seeds
1/2 cup sesame seeds
1/4 cup poppy seeds
1 t. salt
1/2 cup vegetable oil
1/2 cup molasses
10 1/2 cups white bread flour
5 1/2 cups whole wheat flour
3 pkgs. dry yeast
5 cups water

Preheat oven to 375°.

Soften yeast in 1 cup of warm water, (110°). Combine water, molasses, oil and salt. Stir in whole wheat flour, seeds and part of white bread flour beating well. Stir in softened yeast. Add enough of remaining flour to make a moderately stiff dough. Turn out on lightly floured surface and knead until smooth and satiny (10 to 12 minutes). Shape into ball and place in lightly greased bowl. Cover and let rise in warm place until double in size. Punch down and divide into portions, shape and cover. Let rise again. Bake until done. Time will vary according to size of loaf.

LEMON/BASIL BEARNAISE BASE

1 cup shallots, minced
1 cup lemon juice, fresh
1/8 lb. fresh basil, minced
  (substitute 3 T. whole dry
  basil in an emergency)

Combine all ingredients in stainless steel saucepan. Slowly bring to a simmer. Simmer stirring occasionally until reduced to a thick, chunk syrup. Do not completely evaporate liquid or it will scorch. Store in stainless steel container.

Add 1 T. to each cup of hollandaise in processor to blend well.

The Windward Inn and Courtyard Lounge offers a coffee shop, a formal hall with French doors and a grand piano, a library-like room and a courtyard setting in the lounge. Magnificent warm woods, tall Ficus trees and cathedral ceiling in the lounge. This all helps create the perfect surroundings for relaxing while you dine.

Owner David Haskill takes pride in offering fresh seafood and features at least a dozen or more seafood entrées on the menu: oysters grilled with Pernod, local chinook salmon, mussels au gratin, baked or sautéed Tiger prawns and more!

For breakfast: what better way to start the day than with baked Oregon apple with Crème Fraîche – or maybe Belgian waffles with a fruit topping.

It's located on the north end of Florence, west side of Highway 101.

Almost in time for this book, but not open as this is being made ready for printing: David is putting the finishing touches on the Bay Street Grill in "Old Town" Florence.

Breakfast, lunch & dinner every day
Closed Christmas Day

YUZEN ROLL

1 sheet of Nori (seaweed)
2 boiled Ebi (prawns)
Some avocado, cucumber,
   and Unagi (eel)
Some Tobiko (flying fish roe)

SUSHI RICE

2 1/2 cups short grain rice
2 3/4 cups cold water
5 T. rice vinegar
2 T. sugar
2 t. salt

Spread and press sushi rice evenly onto a sheet of Nori, covering the entire sheet. Spread a layer of Tobiko over the rice. Turn the seaweed over. Into the center of seaweed sheet, place thinly sliced cucumber, avocado and Unagi. Place prawns so that the tails extend past the edge of the seaweed and meet at the center. Roll up pressing firmly, being careful not to puncture seaweed.
Cut into 4 pieces

Serve with Wasabi and Gari (pickled ginger).

BEEF SUKIYAKI

1 lb. lean boneless beef
beef suet
8 oz. Udon noodles
10 oz. tofu
3 Shitake mushrooms
1 large carrot
1 zucchini
1 large leek
some spinach leaves

SUKIYAKI SAUCE

1/2 cup Soy sauce
1/4 cup Sake
1/4 cup Mirin
3 T. sugar
1 cup water

Cut beef into thin strips. Cut tofu into 1 inch cubes. Remove mushroom stems. Cut leek diagonally into 1/2 inch slices. Cut spinach leaves crosswise in halves. Cut carrot diagonally into large thin ovals. Cut zucchini into long wedges.

Arrange beef and vegetables on a large platter.

Make Sukiyaki Sauce.

Heat skillet on medium-high heat. Add beef suet and melt. Add beef and cook until lightly browned. Add sauce, add noodles. Carefully arrange vegetables around the skillet attractively and keep covering with sauce until desired tenderness.

Serve very hot in skillet with a bowl of rice on the side.

Enjoy!

First week of Dec. '96: Oregon coast. Winds of 50 miles with gusts to 80! But it didn't matter, Yuzen's was busy serving lunch. The restaurant has been in the town of Seal Rock for 7 years and I heard of some "regular" customers driving 2 or 3 hours to get here.... also a big local following. (I'd be here more frequently if I lived closer.)

Just come and sit at the Sushi Bar, and watch the Chef while he prepares his fresh seafood "works of art" and then enjoy!

Many appetizers to try, like the Shitake mushroom and spinach sauté. Excellent!

Owner Takaya Hanamoto serves up a salad with an incredible dressing (but he said it's secret!) There's a large selection of delicious dinners, and as I watched the waitress delivering four to a table nearby, I could see that each was beautifully prepared.

There are a few large tables in the Sushi room for big parties. The waitress suggested that it is wise to call for reservations all year long.

Many different kinds of Japanese beers, sake, Oregon wines and cocktails are available.

Lunch & dinner Tuesday - Sunday

271

SAFFRON PRAWNS

Prawns, 16/20, butterfly
1/2 shallot, minced
1 t. butter
1/4 cup dry white wine
1 T. cognac
dash of saffron
salt and pepper to taste
1/8 cup cream

In pan, melt butter, add shallot and heat until almost transparent. Throw in prawns and cook about 1 minute. Remove and place prawns on serving tray.

In pan on medium heat, add wine, saffron, salt, pepper and cognac, heat until reduced, about 5 minutes when sauce is a nice consistency.

Pour sauce over prawns and serve.

PORK LOIN WITH CHANTERELLES AND PORT REDUCTION

pork loin or tenderloin, fat
   removed, sliced 1/4" thick
mushrooms

1/4 cup Port wine
1/4 cup cream
salt and pepper to taste
mushrooms

Sauté pork on high heat 2 minutes on each side. Remove to serving plate. Heat mushrooms and remove to serving plate.

In same pan heat the wine, cream and salt and pepper. Reduce until gravy-like consistency. Pour over pork and mushrooms.

Chef/owner Francois Pere looked a long time for the right place for his first restaurant. He took this building, knocked out walls, added a kitchen that would be open, and would let diners watch the meal preparations. In June of 1995 the doors opened to the first customers.

Francois shops in the nearby area for poultry, seafood and fresh organic vegetables. His soups, sauces and his own crusty Old Style French bread are prepared daily.... it's a pleasure to see that he serves no deep-fried food! I don't know why, but ordering my dinner I said "Surprise me". I leave the choices to the chef, and here is what was served.

After an appetizer of stuffed mushrooms the entrée was the pork loin with a port reduction sauce. I praised him for a meal not only beautifully presented, but truly memorable! So when he was willing to share the recipe, I knew I'd be trying it soon. After listening to some of his ideas, it is obvious that he loves what he is doing and takes pleasure in making his customers' meals extra special.

Dinner Wednesday - Sunday

CHICKEN SATÉ
Boneless chicken meat

Peanut Sauce:
5 cups creamy peanut butter
I can coconut milk
6 cups water
1/2 cup soy sauce
1/4 cup Sambal Oelek
1/3 cup chopped garlic
I cup sugar
1/4 cup curry powder
1/3 cup powdered ginger
I T. salt
I T. white pepper
I t. ground cloves
I t. nutmeg

Marinate overnight in a smoky BBQ sauce, thinned about half-and-half with water, as much boneless chicken meat as you think you may need. I prefer thigh meat for moisture, but follow your preferences. Drain chicken and save marinade. Thread chicken onto bamboo skewers, cook on grill or in a large fry pan with a bit of peanut oil. Turn once and brush with marinade if chicken seems to become dry.

Sauce: With a whip, mix together in a mixing bowl the ingredients for the sauce.

Chicken can be cooked on an outdoor BBQ. However unless you're an expert, pre-cook the chicken, and then finish on the BBQ. This assures you that the chicken is completely done without becoming bone dry.

NASI-GORENG (Indonesian Fried Rice)
I quart white rice
2 quarts water

1/2 lb. sliced bacon, chopped
1/4 cup peanut oil
3 yellow onions, coarsely
   chopped
I green bell pepper
I red bell pepper
I bunch green onions

Spice Mixture:
6 T. soy sauce
2 T. sugar
I T. curry
I T. ginger
2 T. tomato ketchup
2 T. chopped garlic
I T. Sambal Oelek, **flat**

3 scrambled eggs
I lb. thinly sliced ham

Preferably the day before, steam rice. While separating the grains, rinse with cold water, drain and let cool uncovered, so it won't be sticky.
In a large frying pan, fry bacon. When bacon is nearly done, add peanut oil and onions, cook until onions are transparent. Add peppers and green onions.
Add rice to the mixture; then stir in spices.

Fry scrambled eggs in a separate fry pan. Chop and add to rice when done. Chop ham and add to mixture. Heat, while stirring thoroughly. Do not over-cook.

Nasi-goreng can make a meal by itself. If no meat is served with it, people in Holland like to top it with a fried egg.

Note: Sambal Oelek is a very hot Indonesian red pepper sauce. If you can't find it in your local store, try a Vietnamese or Thai red pepper sauce, which are generally less hot.

The place in Coos Bay is Wim de Vriend's Blue Heron Bistro — true international dining. On my last visit I ordered one of his German dinners: a large bratwurst, made by a local German Wurstmeister from pork and veal (with no nitrites). Delicious! — as were the hot potato salad, red cabbage, and sauerkraut cooked with apples and caraway... like my grandmother used to make. They also have a great German garlic-roasted pork.

There's also a good selection of Italian dishes, plus Cajun and Tex-Mex specialties, many involving seafood.

The home-made, fresh avocado-tomatillo salsa is a bit spicy, but not extremely so. It's served with some of the grilled fish dinners, the burrito & shrimp Quesadilla "Mazatlan". There are several excellent vegetarian entrees as well.

Last year, Wim and his wife rescued an old, battered mahogany bar and restored it to its former glory. It's now a stylish frame for the 18 spigots (that's eighteen!) dispensing the Northwest's micro-brews, hard cider→ and several imported draft beers.

**Lunch & dinner every day Summer
Closed Sundays Winter, Spring & Fall**

275

PEPPER STEAK

4 pieces filet mignon
cracked black pepper
1 cup demiglace
green and/or pink peppercorns
butter
cream

Press cracked pepper into steaks. Heat 2 T. oil in pan until VERY hot. Place steaks in the hot oil and let sit for about 2 minutes, turn steaks over and repeat.
Remove steaks from pan when cooked to your desire. Drain oil from pan and add demiglace and peppercorns. Turn heat down, add about 1/4 cup of cream and allow to reduce. After reduced well, add some butter and let it melt while stirring sauce. Allow to reduce just a little more and serve.

Yield: 4 servings

SALMON WITH RASPBERRY BEURRE BLANC

4 pieces fresh salmon
3/4 cup dry white wine
1/4 cup lemon juice
1 to 1 1/2 sticks butter
1/4 cup shallots
1/2 cup fresh raspberries
salt and pepper to taste

Poach salmon in lemon juice and white wine on low heat in a covered pan. Allow to reduce to about 1/4 of liquid that it was before. Remove salmon from pan.
Add shallots and raspberries to white wine and lemon juice. Reduce for another couple of minutes. Start to slowly add the butter into the sauce, stirring constantly until desired consistency occurs.

Yield: 4 servings

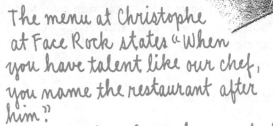

The menu at Christophe at Face Rock states "When you have talent like our chef, you name the restaurant after him."

I ordered the salmon burger, but is much more than a "burger"! (Can't think of another name.) A tender moist piece of salmon, placed on puff pastry and topped with their own tartar that included capers. It melts in your mouth. With this came a beautiful salad that had a number of garden greens, carrot, avocado and more...

enhanced by the herb, oil and vinegar dressing.

Not usually seen on a menu: Roasted rabbit, tender, and comes with a mustard sauce. An unusual pairing: an entrée of duck breast and fresh Oregon oysters with a delicate chardonnay sauce.

The sketch gives part of the scene – it seems to go on forever!

Breakfast, lunch & dinner every day May 1st - Nov. 1st
Inquire for Winter hours

277

PASTA A LA HARP

5 or 6 large shrimp
1 1/2 T. olive oil
1 T. butter
1 clove garlic, minced
crushed red pepper

Sauté shrimp in olive oil. Add butter. Add garlic and red pepper. Simmer until shrimp are done.
Serve over fresh pasta.
Garnish with sliced lemons and parsley.

Yield: 1 serving.

GAME HEN WITH A BLUSH

1 whole game hen (18 oz.)
flour
pepper
celery salt
whole berry cranberry sauce

Preheat oven to 350°.
Rinse hen and pat dry. Coat with the flour, pepper and celery salt.
Place hen breast up in a roasting pan and cover with cranberry sauce. Cover pan and roast for 40 minutes. Remove cover and baste. Roast for 10 more minutes.

Very pretty and very tasty!

Harp's 480 First Street, S.W., Bandon

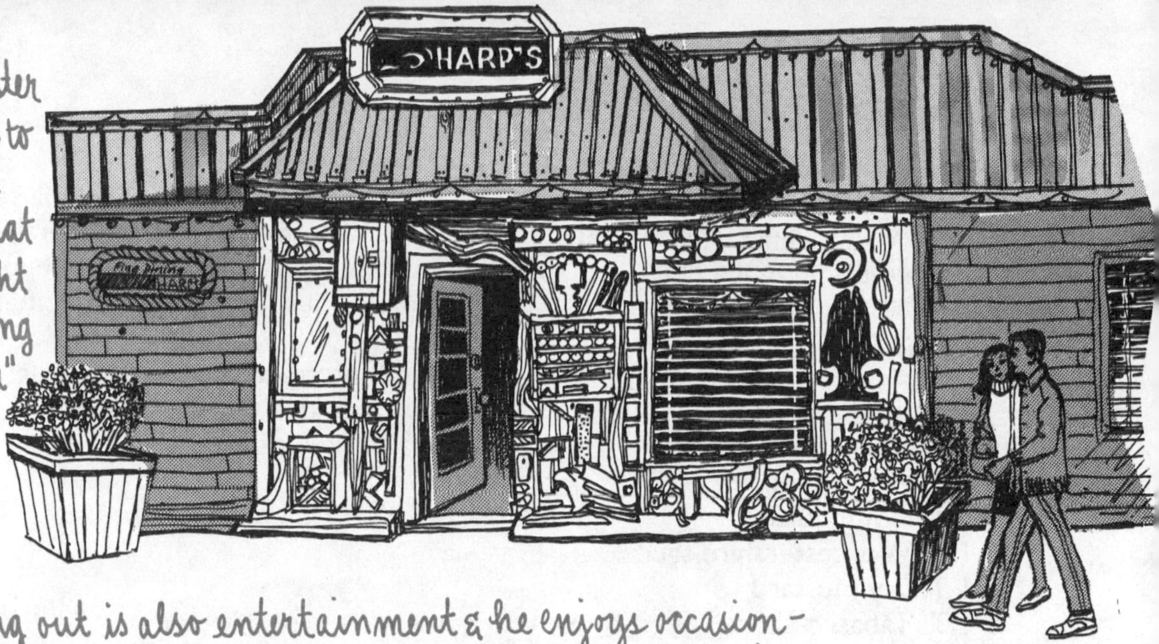

Michael Harpster is a pleasure to talk with. I discovered that he was taught "Home cooking with a flair" – by his mother. Michael believes that eating out is also entertainment & he enjoys occasionally sitting and visiting with customers when possible. The restaurant was named after his Dad. Soon to be: the new restaurant shown below. Harp's always uses local products abundantly when available... definitely an Oregon dining experience - at its best.

I had some of their "Scallop Seviche", scallops marinated in the juice of lemon, orange and lime with added cilantro. Try it! A big favorite here: Scampi Montezuma. It's Scampi sautéed with green chilis, garlic and olive oil, smothered with Romano cheese and served over a bed of fresh pasta.

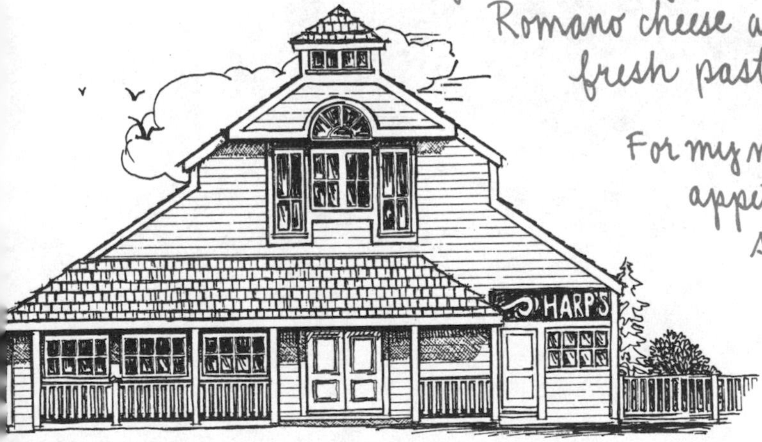

For my next visit – Can't wait to order the appetizer: Smoked Game Hen that's smoked & basted with Kahlua & honey. Served with almonds and cheese.

Lunch & dinner every day
Closed Christmas Day & New Year's Day

DUNGENESS CRAB CAKES with SHERRY AIOLI

3/4 lb. Dungeness crab meat
1 3/4 cup bread crumbs
1 1/2 stalks celery, chopped fine
3 scallions, chopped fine
3/4 carrot, chopped fine
1 T. parsley
3 eggs
3/8 cup mayonnaise
3 T. sour cream
1 T. garlic, chopped
1 T. lemon juice
1 T. Worcestershire sauce
1 T. dry mustard
1 T. Tabasco sauce
1 T. black pepper

Aioli
1 cup mayonnaise
1/4 cup sherry
2 T. chopped garlic

Combine bread crumbs, celery, scallions, carrot, parsley and eggs. Add mayonnaise, sour cream, garlic, lemon juice, Worcestershire sauce, dry mustard, Tabasco sauce and pepper so mixture is moist, but not runny. Combine with the crab meat.
Form into patties and grill or pan fry in butter. Mix together the ingredients for the Aioli and top cooked cakes.

Yield: 12 - 3 oz. portions.

Lord Bennett's Restaurant opened in the summer of '89. Why this name? George Bennett founded Bandon, coming here from Bandon, Ireland. The nickname "Lord" was given to him. Rich Iverson, a graduate of the Culinary Institute, is the guiding force. The setting, the food, the view — everything is "just right." (See the cover of this book — it's Lord Bennett's.)

For lunch the day of my visit I chose a salad that was presented so beautifully that I took a picture of it! The base: red cabbage leaves, spinach, several varieties of lettuce and greens. Next: red, yellow bell pepper, cucumbers. Topped with shrimp, Chinese pea pods sautéed in toasted sesame oil and soy. The waitress recommended raspberry vinagrette dressing. A winner!

The menu listed many hot items, 5 great salads, plus fish, steak, fish sandwiches (and hamburgers.)

Checking the dinner menu: House specialties included "Noisettes of lamb, pan-fried small loin steaks, served with mint, garlic and red wine sauce". Can be served blackened too. A veggie plate and a veggie fettuccine also. Reserve wine list from $40 to $70.

**Lunch & dinner Monday - Saturday
Lunch/Brunch & dinner Sunday**

SEAFOOD MEATBALLS

2 cups fresh salmon
2 cups fresh halibut
1 cup fresh tiger prawns, peeled
garlic, to taste
salt and pepper to taste
white wine

Grind all the ingredients, except the wine, until they stick together well. Roll into meatballs and poach in the wine for about 5 minutes on medium heat or until done in the center.
Wonderful when served with angel hair pasta and cream sauce.

CHICKEN GORGONZOLA AND ALMONDS

1 whole chicken
salt and pepper to taste
garlic to taste
1 cup Gorgonzola (blue) cheese
1/2 cup roasted sliced almonds
1/2 cup cream
1/4 cup butter
2 servings fresh fettuccine,
   cooked

Cut the chicken into pieces and bake in oven with salt, pepper and garlic.

Sauce: Place cream and 1/2 of the butter in a saucepan. Cook on medium heat until it starts to simmer. Slowly add the butter, then the Gorgonzola cheese in large chunks. Remove from heat (sauce should still have some chunks of Gorgonzola).

Place cooked fettuccine in sauce and mix in well. Place fettucine and sauce on 4 plates and lay a few pieces of chicken on each. Garnish with roasted almonds.

Yield: 4 servings.

What a transformation! Walls were knocked out, arched openings were created, new paneling over the old flooring..... too much to describe! On the right (behind that arch) there was a small set back and it was creatively painted with cattle walking behind the fence. See sketch below. You've got to see it. And while you're there, sit down and have a lunch or dinner. Good pasta dishes — or Barbecued and grilled meat. Famous for their baby back ribs. For an unusual but great combination, try the grilled chicken in Gorgonzola sauce with toasted almonds and green apples. For vegetarians there are meatless pasta dishes. Different recipes for the lasagnes... changing frequently. Nice Oregon, California and Washington wines. Desserts are creative.

Lunch & dinner every day July 1st - September 30th
Lunch & dinner Thursday - Monday October 1st - June 30th

BAJA BBQ COD

3 lbs. fresh ling cod
1 red onion
2 tomatoes
1 red bell pepper
1 yellow bell pepper
4 garlic cloves
2 T. olive oil
1/4 t. ground black pepper
1 T. fresh oregano
1 T. fresh cilantro
1 t. fresh thyme
1/2 t. salt
1/4 t. cumin
1 T. butter

Cut fresh ling cod into 8 individual servings (2 x 3 inches). Finely julienne the onion and peppers. Peel and chop the tomatoes into 1 inch cubes. (To peel tomatoes: blanch them in boiling water for 1/2 minute.)
Finely chop garlic and herbs.
Sauté all the vegetables in olive oil, season with herbs and spices.
Arrange cod on buttered baking sheet. Lay vegetables on top of cod.

To grill: When coals or mesquite become grey, bank coals to the side of kettle. Place apple branches on coals. Place baking pan on grill. Cover BBQ kettle and cook until tender, approximately 25 to 30 minutes.

LEMON CRAISIN POPOVERS WITH LEMON HONEY BUTTER

1 1/2 cups all-purpose white flour, sifted
3/4 t. salt
1 1/2 T. melted shortening
1 1/2 cups milk
3 eggs
2 t. lemon rind, finely grated
1/3 cup craisins (dried cranberries)

Preheat oven to 400°.
Sift dry ingredients together in a large mixing bowl. Mix with remaining ingredients. Beat on low speed for 1 minute, then beat on medium speed for another minute. Batter will be slightly lumpy.
Grease heavy cast iron popover pans (12 six ounce). Heat the greased pans for 15 minutes. Fill 2/3 full with batter. Bake for 10 minutes, then reduce oven temperature to 350°. Bake for another 30 minutes or until browned.

LEMON HONEY BUTTER

1/2 cup butter, room temp.
2 T. honey
2 t. lemon juice
2 T. finely grated lemon rind

Lemon Honey Butter: Beat butter until smooth. Whip in honey, lemon juice and rind. Serve at room temperature.
Refrigerate, tightly covered for up to 4 days.

TuTu Tun takes its name from Indian words meaning "People close to river". This is very close to the Rogue River. In fact in the summer Madrone wood bonfires burn on the terrace that overlooks the Rogue.

The lodge was built 7 miles from the Pacific Ocean in 1970 by the Van Zantes. Dirk and Laurie Van Zante bought the lodge from his father in 1980. In 1991 it was totally refurbished. It reflects the open-beamed, heavy timbered style of the Northwest. A beautiful job! This is a 4★ lodge with warm hospitality. While dining, you might see a family of deer grazing in the orchard. Also there are 2 resident bald eagles nearby.

If you are staying here some of the activities are fishing, whitewater rafting trips, hiking, lawn games, with a game room in the lodge. Gourmet 4-course dinners are so good that many publications give them very high ratings. If you aren't registered, call for reservations (not always available, but very possible). And not to forget the bountiful Northwest breakfast. I have talked to Laurie and it is evident that she is very involved in seeing that the best-possible recipes and best ingredients are used.

Lunch for registered guests only
Breakfast & dinner every day May 1st - November 1st
Breakfast only November 1st - May 1st
Reservations required for non-registered guests

MARINATED MUSHROOMS

5 lbs. fresh mushrooms
1 1/2 cups white onion, minced
4 cloves garlic, minced
3/4 cup fresh parsley, chopped
5 bay leaves
1 1/2 t. salt
1/2 t. ground pepper
1 t. tarragon
2 1/2 cups dry white wine
1 1/4 cups white wine vinegar
3/4 cup salad oil
juice of one lemon

Lightly towel rub mushrooms to clean. Set aside. Combine remaining ingredients in a large stainless steel pot. Bring to a boil and simmer for 15 minutes. Add mushrooms and continue to simmer 5 minutes. Cool, cover and refrigerate at least 4 hours.

CRANAPPLE NUT CAKE WITH BOURBON SAUCE

2 eggs
2 cups sugar
1 t. vanilla
2 cups flour
2 t. baking soda
1 cup canned apples
1/2 cup cranberries
1/2 cup walnuts, chopped

BOURBON SAUCE:

1 cup butter, softened
2 cups sugar
1/2 cup water
2 eggs, beaten
2/3 cup bourbon
1 t. vanilla
1 t. lemon juice

Preheat oven to 350°
Grease and flour bundt pan.
Beat eggs, sugar and vanilla until sugar is dissolved. Beat in flour and baking soda. Fold in fruit and walnuts. Pour batter into pan.
Bake 45 to 50 minutes.
Remove from oven and let set 10 minutes.
Turn out onto cake rack to cool.
Serve with bourbon sauce.
Add whipped cream if desired.

Bourbon sauce: Melt butter in medium saucepan. Add sugar and water, stir constantly for 2 minutes. Slowly add butter mixture to egg, beating until smooth. Drizzle and stir in bourbon, vanilla and lemon juice. Cool. Refrigerate.

The picture on the back wall is of Patrick Bernard Harold, grandfather of owner Colleen Harold-Combs. This picture had been rolled for years... painted on thin metal sheeting, it became dented and was almost discarded.

I arrived on a cold winter evening to find a crackling fire – very inviting. The Nor'Wester overlooks the Boat Basin at the Port of Gold Beach. Siskiyou Chicken, a breast of chicken broiled with orange sauce and served with cranberry-apple relish was my order. My spinach salad had crumbled bacon and chopped eggs + a great salad dressing.

Dinners include both a salad and New England clam chowder. Most places say "either". If you have a smaller appetite, "or" is available with fish, chicken or top sirloin entrees.

Seafood galore! Available in many different ways and combinations.

Oregon Magazine, Northwest Best Places, Frommer's Dollarwise Guide have all recommended Nor'Wester and so do I !

Dinner every day

287

PORK CHILI VERDE

1 t. vegetable oil
2 1/2 lbs. pork roast
1 (8 oz.) can Ortega whole, peeled chiles
1 white onion
1 cup tomato sauce
2 t. salt
2 t. garlic
1 t. black pepper
1/2 bunch cilantro, finely chopped

Cut pork roast into cubes and brown in oil over medium heat. Tear the chiles into strips and cut the onion into strips. Put chiles and onion in with pork. Add tomato sauce, salt, garlic, pepper and chopped cilantro. Add enough water just to cover mixture. Bring mixture to a boil, lower heat to simmer and cover. Cook 45 minutes or until pork is tender. Serve with rice and tortillas.

Yield: 6 to 8 servings.

RUBIO'S SPICY BEAN DIP

1 cup refried beans
1/4 onion, diced
1/4 tomato, diced
1 oz. Monterey Jack cheese, shredded
1/4 cup Salsa Rubio, mild or macho*

Combine all ingredients in bowl and microwave for 2 minutes or until heated through.
Serve sprinkled with Jack cheese.
Yumito!

If unable to find Salsa Rubio, substitute another brand of salsa.

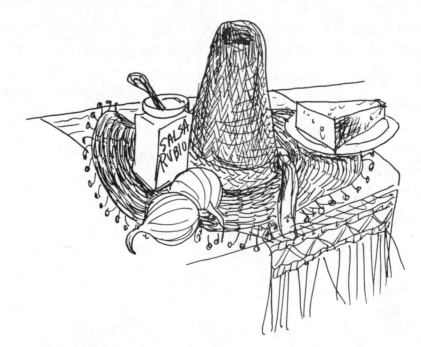

Since 7-7-77 Rubio's has been owned and operated by the same family—ready to celebrate 20 years this summer! This bright yellow, red and green restaurant is on the north end of Brookings, on east side of the highway..... a "must stop" place. Rubio's, often jammed, also has a drive-thru window.

All of the expected items are on the menu, but there are some family favorites, too. "Chito Rubio" is a choice of shredded beef or chicken, mixed with chorizo and baked in a flour tortilla, then smothered in a mild red sauce, cheese and sour cream. Yumito!

On the soup list is Menudo—something I had never tasted before. I love it.

It is served with cilantro, onions, oregano and a side of corn tortillas. (Wish I had the recipe for this.) Maybe for Coasting and Cooking #5?

If someone in your group isn't fond of Mexican food, I feel sorry for them, however there is a "Menu Americano" with 9 different burgers, 6 sandwiches, hot dogs, and fish and chips. There's the usual french fries, but also Mexi-fries.

Owners John Doering and Eilene Gordon do a great job and Rubio's has been noted in numerous publications: "Highways", "Good Sam", "Oregon Coast", and 5 years in "Northwest Best Places."

Lunch & dinner Tuesday - Saturday

289

BLACK BEAN SOUP

1 lb. dried black beans
2 cups chicken broth
1 t. coriander
1 t. cumin
1 t. garlic
1/4 cup sherry
1 orange, rind grated and meat cut
  up in chunks
2 cups carrots, grated
1 onion, chopped medium
2 cups celery, chopped medium

Cook beans in chicken broth or stock for 2 to 3 hours. Add carrots, onion, celery, orange and orange rind. Add water as necessary while cooking.
During final hour add sherry to the beans. Add cayenne pepper to taste.

Serve with a spoon of sour cream on top of each bowl.

PUMPKIN DESSERT

1 8 oz. pkg. cream cheese
3/4 cup sugar
1 16 oz. can pumpkin pie filling
3 T. brandy
1 t. pumpkin pie spice
1 8 oz. carton Cool Whip
1 cup nuts

Combine the cream cheese and sugar until blended. Add the pumpkin pie filling, brandy, spice, Cool Whip and nuts.
Prepare a graham cracker crust and press into a 13 x 9 inch baking pan. Add the filling. Serve.

FROZEN MANDARIN SALAD

60 Ritz crackers, crushed
1/4 lb. margarine, melted
1/4 cup sugar
6 oz. frozen orange juice
  concentrate
1 can sweetened condensed
  milk
1 8 oz. carton Cool Whip
2 cans mandarin oranges,
  drained

Mix the crackers, margarine and sugar in a bowl to form a crust.
Thoroughly combine the orange juice concentrate and sweetened condensed milk. Fold in the Cool Whip and then fold in the mandarin oranges.
Press crust into pan and put the filling on top.
Freeze.

When I placed my order for the Chicken Omelette, I said to the waitress "This should be named "Which came first Omelette" because it had both eggs and tender chunks of chicken, guacamole, green peppers and sour cream.

Sandy's father was superintendent of the Brookings Harbor Plywood Sawmill, and she's lived here since she was 13 years old. She learned to cook as she was growing up, because her mother was very ill. Her father said he "put up with having tapioca every day."

The building is loaded with antiques – the sign on the door stated "Closed tomorrow for Spring House Cleaning". Everything taken off the walls and shelves, dusted, then returned to the right spots. The antique horses are not for sale, but there's a room full of stuff next door that is.   An interesting note: all of the waitresses, except one, have been here since the restaurant opened over 12 years ago.

Upon checking the menu, I found good choices throughout the day... including many Italian specialties, veal served 1. Parmegiana, 2. Piccata, 3. Marsala. (My choice for my next visit: Pork tenderloin roll, stuffed with red bell pepper, pesto, fresh spinach and mushrooms and served with Pasta Marinara.)

Breakfast & lunch every day   **Dinner Monday - Saturday**   ♿
Closed Christmas Day

INDEX

BISQUES, STEWS & GUMBO

SALADS

DRESSINGS, SAUCES, PATES, SALSAS, MARINADES, RELISHES, CHUTNEYS, BUTTERS

PASTA

DUCK, QUAIL & ALLIGATOR

CHICKEN & TURKEY

SALMON

FISH

PIES, CAKES, CHEESECAKE & MOUSSE

The recipes in *Coasting and Cooking* have been proofed 3 times, but have not been tested by the author. The chefs from each restaurant chose the recipes that he or she wished to share. In some instances there are duplications, but upon checking, the ingredients differed, so try both yourself and find your personal preference.

Bon Appetit!

My home, snuggled just below a natural preserved park in Port Townsend has a wonderful kitchen facing both south and west, with Mt. Rainier in the distance, 2 islands, the Cascade Mts. to the west... a never-ending parade of boats, ships, tugs pulling their loads, and the ferries to and fro to Whidbey Island. It is a joy working in my kitchen.

The recipe below is one first used during World War II when there was rationing, but still a favorite. There are no eggs or shortening (the mayo takes care of that). A rich moist cake.

Barbara

MAYONNAISE CAKE

3/4 cup mayonnaise
1 cup sugar
3 T. ground chocolate
1 t. cinnamon
1 t. vanilla
1/2 t. salt
2 cups flour
1 cup raisins
1 cup nuts
1 cup boiling water
1 t. baking soda

Preheat oven to 350°.
Grease and flour cake pan.
Dissolve soda in boiling water, then pour water over raisins and nuts and let stand 5 to 10 minutes.
Sift sugar, cinnamon and chocolate and mix with mayonnaise.
Add water, nuts and raisins and blend well.
Sift four and salt together and add to mayonnaise mixture.
Add vanilla, blend well.
Bake approximately 50 minutes.

GLOSSARY

BRUNOISE: Diced vegetables slowly cooked in butter and used to flavor soups.

BRUSCETTA: Toasted bread rubbed with garlic, drizzled with olive oil, then served warm.

CARPACCIO: Thin shavings of raw beef, usually drizzled with olive oil and capers and served as a first course.

CONFIT: Meat salted and cooked slowly in its own fat, then packed into a jar and preserved. It is usually goose or duck.

COULIS: A thick purée or sauce, often of tomatoes or perhaps raspberries, on which the main dish is placed.

COUSCOUS: Arab dish made of crushed grain, usually steamed, often added to with raisins, pine nuts and herbs. Served with poached chicken or lamb.

CRÈME FRAÎCHE: This is a mature cream with a nutty, slightly sour tang.

CROSTINI: Crisply toasted little rounds of bread, sometimes smeared with oil and garlic.

GALETTE: Round flat cake or tart, known specially in France, often topped with fruit, jam or nuts.

GARAM MASALA: Mix of Indian spices used in curry.

GREMOLATA: A garnish made from lemon peel, garlic and chopped parsley.

JULIENNE: Something cut into thin strips (i.e. julienned carrots).

MASA HARINA: Flour made from corn kernels, used in Mexican food.

MASCARPONE: A creamy cheese from Lombardy in northern Italy, can be blended with anchovies, mustard and spices.

MIREPOIX: Diced onions, carrots, celery and herbs sautéed in butter, often a base for braising meat or fish.

MIRIN: Japanese sweet golden wine made from rice.

ORZO: A tiny oval-shaped Italian pasta.

OSSO BUCO: Classic Italian dish of braised lamb or veal shanks with herbs and wine, tomatoes and garlic.

PANCETTA: Italian bacon, cured with spices, not smoked.

PATE BRISEE SUCRE: Sweet flaky dough used for pies and tarts.

POLENTA: An Italian favorite: cornmeal mush, often used under a stew like osso buco.

PROSCIUTTO: A spicy Italian ham, cured by drying and served in very thin slices.

PUTTANESCA: Spicy pasta sauce, very "in" at the moment, made of red peppers, tomatoes, garlic and herbs.

RAMOULADE: French sauce based on mayonnaise with mustard, pickles, anchovies, herbs and capers. Served cold with cold meats and fish.

ROULADE: A piece of meat rolled round a stuffing, often of minced veal with herbs.

SLURRY: A thin watery mixture.

SPATZLE: A German pasta or dumpling, steamed, served with creamed veal.

TAMARIND: A tropical fruit used in beverages in India. Also used in chutneys and curries.

ZEST: The outermost, colored part of citrus fruit. It is freshly peeled or grated from the fruit.

Has anyone ever seen Barbara Williams sit still ... absolutely still? If she's not whizzing down the Pacific Coast in search of great restaurants she's handling a fork with great aplomb, testing out the chef's wonders. Or she's wielding that camera or that pencil or both, capturing the essence of the place she has discovered and loved.

Or.. or. She is popping up and down England, Wales, Scotland and Ireland, on and off the local buses, chatting up the locals in the country pubs, searching, searching, for the essence of the place. And then -- and this is her special delight -- she is on her next overseas visit guiding and encouraging a group of American travellers, introducing them to a Britain they would likely never _ever_ find on one of the usual mass tourism packages.

Barbara has worked for five years now with a Port Townsend travel agent, stirring interest in tours of Britain, lining up folk who see travel as she sees it. Enthusiasm never ebbs. "Would you believe it?" she bubbled over a recent artichokes and cold turkey lunch, "that I have found the most wonderful narrow-boat canal journeys, a firm based in Wales, and they'll let my group hire the entire 2 boats, take us anywhere the canals lead us, for however long a time we like to be afloat. Now how about _that_!"

It goes without saying -- but let's say it anyhow -- that travellers on Barbara's team eat well. She susses out just which country pubs do the best roast beef and Yorkshire pudding, which hotels give you a smashing British breakfast with grilled tomatoes, sautéed mushrooms, eggs as you like them, the lot.

Food matters deeply to this California-born graphic artist who, after a fine career in art, publishing and teaching in the Monterey area, picked up stakes and moved to Port Townsend a dozen years ago. There she and her son Gene gaze out over the Strait of Juan de Fuca from the curiously octagonal-shaped house Barbara herself designed, with its windows at every turn, its fascinating collection of old Americana bric-a-brac, its shelves upon shelves of cookbooks and art books.

She entertains at a long oak table looking out at snowtipped Olympics on one side, at brilliant blue sea on the other, and between meals this becomes a good work table for drawing, proofreading, assembling pages for the book. This book has a life far beyond the reading of it: people write to Barbara from all over America saying they take it in their car when they head west, that they plan entire coastal trips by what time they can reach a certain restaurant that Barbara has featured. They stop off faithfully, as migrating birds dip down to ponds on their way to Baja.

You're holding right now the fourth edition of this guide, and coincidentally this next trip escorting travellers to Britain will be Barbara's fourth. "We move fourward" she can't resist saying with a grin.

In this ten years of sampling and judging the good foods of the west, what has changed? "Extremes. The mundane factory-line food gets more and more mundane so that you can predict every mouthful. But the creative chefs, those who care deeply about natural ingredients, organic produce, exciting flavors, these have become even more numerous -- and even more imaginative!"

Serena Lesley

Dear Mrs. Williams,

Whenever my husband is on a business trip or we're together on a vacation, his "job" is to get me regional cook books. He does not take this lightly as he is so afraid he's going to miss the "best chocolate recipe" in the world. So he scours the books like a little computer and always makes good choices. My favorite books have become the story ones such as yours. I almost always add that author to my list of friends.

Arden Faulkner
Los Angeles, California

The first thing I did when we moved here was to join Friends of Sequim Library ... Barbara Williams, who writes cookbooks about local restaurants, was a speaker at one of our meetings. My husband and I use her cookbook to figure out where we want to eat when we drive around. "We drove over to the Skagit River to see the eagles and explore along the way. We drove out to Neah Bay to see the eagles and explore. We have been to Hurricane Ridge. We have been to watch the starlings at sunset at the Union Wharf in Port Townsend -- an awe-inspiring sight. We're having a wonderful time, very inexpensively."

Anonymous
from Peninsula Daily News, 1996

I originally picked up your "Coasting & Cooking" #3 as a thank you gift for my dad and his wife for letting me stay at their beach house in Glen Eden. Despite my good intentions, I fell in love with your book and wanted to keep it myself ... Could you please let me know how to order not only a copy of Coasting & Cooking #3, but also any other books you have written? I use it as a tour guide and cookbook and absolutely love it!

Roxanne Hubbling
Forest Falls, California

Sorry — no other books.

After getting Barbara's first cookbook from my friend, I decided to take it along on a trip to Washington and Oregon. Actually, my husband made great fun of the whole thing until he realized how well we were eating as well as having great fun looking up the out of the way places.

But actually the River House in Pacific City was the real test. We pulled up to the little unassuming sort of cabin looking place and he said "Are you sure??"

Sure enough - the food was wonderful and the atmosphere great - Nestucco River right outside the windows. The food was just the freshest (of course we ate fish) and very well prepared. We were back again this year - three years straight.

Riverton Building Supply
Riverton, Kansas

Dear Barbara,
Thank you for sending your cookbook so promptly. Do you have any copies of book 1 or 2? We would like to buy either or both of them also.

Books 1 and 2 are both sold out.

Barbara Williams:

We have and are enjoying your "Coasting & Cooking" book you mailed us! We have been looking for a "Chicken Angelo" recipe for quite a while.

Don & Betty Aumiller
Port Orchard, Washington

Dear Barbara
... Congratulations on your third edition of Coasting and Cooking, etc. the best recipe book I've ever seen, and the artwork makes it all the more interesting. I'm happy to know another edition is in the making.
God Bless,
Hazel Cosgrove
Bandon, Oregon

Before Christmas I called you and left a message asking to have your Coasting & Cooking book sent to me. You did so and I was very grateful.
Jo Anne Laz
Seattle, Washington

Book III is great, have used it and read it from cover to cover.
Josefa Hojem
Olympia, Washington